England's Railway Heritage
from the Air

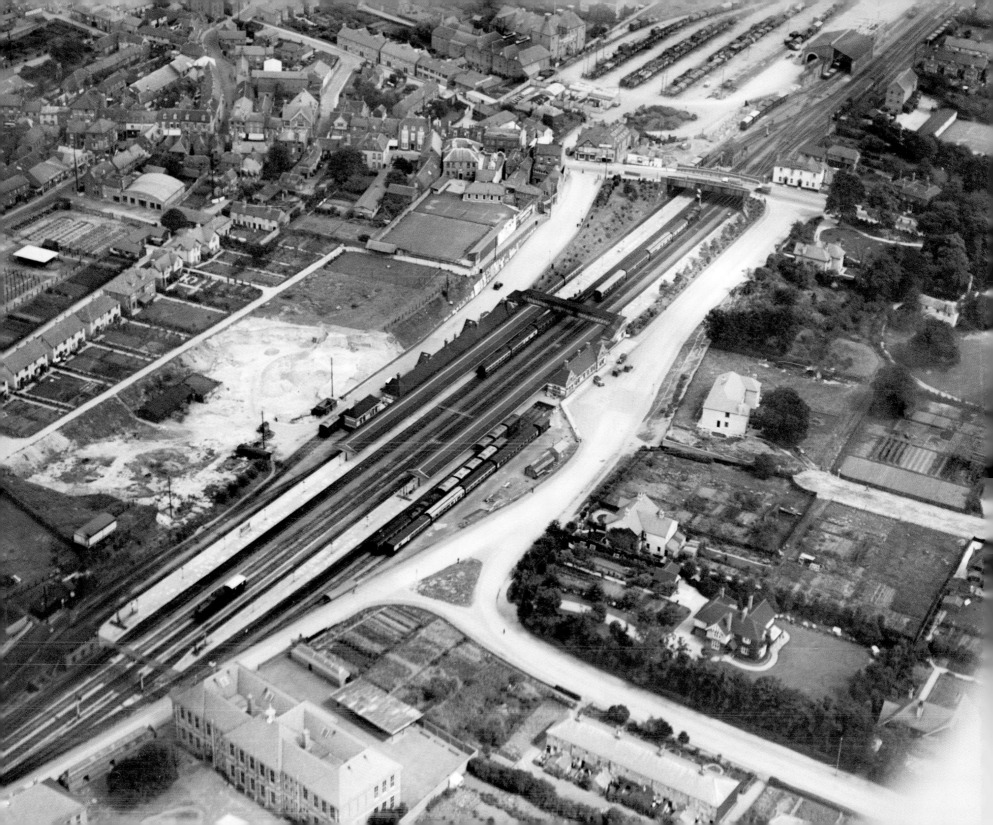

England's Railway Heritage from the Air

Peter Waller

Historic England

Published by Historic England, The Engine House, Fire Fly Avenue, Swindon SN2 2EH
www.HistoricEngland.org.uk

Historic England is a Government service championing England's heritage and giving expert, constructive advice, and the English Heritage Trust is a charity caring for the National Heritage Collection of more than 400 historic properties and their collections.

The views expressed in this book are those of the author and not necessarily those of Historic England.

Images © Historic England Archive, Aerofilms Collection. The Aerofilms Collection was acquired by English England (previously English Heritage) in 2007 and has been digitised and made available on the *Britain from Above* website at www.britainfromabove.org.uk.

First published 2018

ISBN 978-1-84802-4762

British Library Cataloguing in Publication data
A CIP catalogue record for this book is available from the British Library.

Historic England holds an unparalleled archive of 12 million photographs, drawings, reports and publications on England's places. It is one of the largest archives in the UK, the biggest dedicated to the historic environment, and a priceless resource for anyone interested in England's buildings, archaeology, landscape and social history. Viewed collectively, its photographic collections document the changing face of England from the 1850s to the present day. It is a treasure trove that helps us understand and interpret the past, informs the present and assists with future management and appreciation of the historic environment. For more information about images from the Archive, contact Archives Services Team, Historic England, The Engine House, Fire Fly Avenue, Swindon SN2 2EH; telephone (01793) 414600.

Brought to publication by Victoria Trainor, Publishing, Historic England.

Typeset in Source Sans Pro 9/12pt

Edited by Kathryn Glendenning
Page layout by Hybert Design
Proof read by Kim Bishop
Printed in Czech Republic via Akcent Media Limited.

Frontispiece: EPW022626 Newbury

Contents

Preface

I have been in the fortunate position to have worked with the Aerofilms Collection for a quarter of a century. Originally, this was while I was with Ian Allan Publishing and the archive was still owned by the Hunting Group and its immediate successors. More recently, a chance conversation with Robin Taylor, then of English Heritage, resulted in a renewed contact with the collection, which was by then based with English Heritage (now Historic England) at Swindon.

The first fruits of this relationship came with the publication of *England's Maritime Heritage from the Air* in 2017. This was a project I had tried to get off the ground while with Ian Allan Publishing, but changed circumstances prevented its development. This volume, *England's Railway Heritage from the Air*, is a companion to the earlier book and is designed to complement four volumes that I compiled (anonymously) while at Ian Allan Publishing – *Britain's Railways from the Air: Then and Now*, *From the Air Britain's Railways Then and Now*, *Railway Stations from the Air* and *London's Railways from the Air*. These were the result of the close working relationship that existed at the time between Ian Allan Publishing and the staff at Aerofilms. Although one or two locations are common between these volumes and this new book – it would be impossible to exclude such vitally important buildings as London Euston, for example – every effort has been made to ensure that in most cases, when this happens, images supplement each other. It has always been a privilege to work with the Aerofilms Collection and I am delighted that the images are now in the safe custody of Historic England (plus the equivalent bodies in Scotland and Wales) to ensure that this unique material is preserved for future generations.

Introduction

During the 19th century, Britain experienced perhaps its most significant period of change. It became the world's dominant industrial and military power, with a global empire on which, famously, the sun never set. Britain's economic influence stretched well beyond the empire into countries such as Argentina, where British capital played a crucial role in the development of local economies.

This dramatic growth, which saw Britain emerge as the 'Workshop of the World', was made possible due to a number of factors: these included population growth, urbanisation, more efficient farming, a strong and supportive banking system, inventiveness and a government that pursued, generally, a laissez-faire policy domestically while offering some protection to trade internationally. Central to this success was, however, the revolution in transport that occurred from the mid-18th century onwards. If the country had been forced to rely on its inadequate road system, there would have been no great economic boom as it would have been impossible to feed the growing urban population, let alone move the vast quantities of raw materials and finished goods that were the concomitants of the period commonly known as the Industrial Revolution.

Initially, water was the key: it could provide the power needed by the early mills and factories, while navigable rivers could be used for the movement of raw materials and goods. The river network was expanded by the massive investment in canals during the 18th and early 19th centuries. But transport by water posed its own problems – it was slow and lacking in capacity.

A better and more robust type of transport was required and this was what the railway provided. Although from around the 18th century onwards there had been simple wagonways and plateways, often linking mines and quarries to canal or river wharfs, it was from the early 19th century that the railway age truly dawned. The opening of the Stockton & Darlington Railway in 1825 and the success of Stephenson's *Rocket* at the Rainhill Trials for the Liverpool & Manchester Railway five years later are events that are ingrained in popular knowledge.

From these small beginnings came the first era of massive investment in the railway industry, at the end of the 1830s and during the first half of the 1840s. As is so often the case, however, boom led to bust. In 1846, at the height of the 'Railway Mania', no fewer than 272 Acts of Parliament for railway schemes were passed. Many were speculative and others probably fraudulent but all sought funding – with the result that many failed. Entrepreneurs such as George Hudson, the 'Railway King', were beneficiaries of the initial boom but, by the end of the decade, were disgraced through fraud. While the government's laissez-faire attitude to domestic policy had undoubtedly benefited the wider economy, in terms of the development of the railway network, it was, perhaps, not so advantageous. Elsewhere in Europe, railway networks were often developed in whole or in part by the state identifying strategic needs and undertaking construction to achieve those aims. In Britain it was down to individual – often local – entrepreneurs to identify a need and to act upon it. As a result, the British railway network grew piecemeal, with companies often competing against each other to access lucrative markets.

This often resulted in duplicate routes, which was not necessarily a major issue while the railway offered the only viable means of bulk transport for people and goods but was to become problematic once an alternative means of transport – powered by the internal combustion engine – was developed.

Almost from the dawn of the railway age the new companies employed engineers and architects; the former were essential to the construction of the lines. Tunnels, viaducts and bridges were required and the early railway engineers were often working at the extremes of known skills. The difficulty that the Liverpool & Manchester faced in crossing the boggy Chat Moss was an early example of the major challenges that the early railway engineers faced but this was by no means unique. Challenges could be financial as well as technical. Isambard Kingdom Brunel's decision to construct part-wooden viaducts through Cornwall demonstrates his response to both pressures. Earlier, his adoption of the atmospheric system for the South Devon Railway between Exeter and Plymouth, and his choice of route, had been determined by his concern that an inland route, with the necessary gradients, would have been impossible for contemporary steam locomotives to handle.

Sometimes the railway's engineers also acted as architects but, recognising that an attractively designed station was a good advert for the railway, many companies employed well-known architects to design stations and other buildings. William Tite, for example, who was president of the Royal Institute of British Architects between 1816 and 1863, was a highly influential architect of railway stations for a number of railway companies, including the London & Southampton Railway and the Eastern Counties Railway. He worked throughout much of the country, with Carlisle Citadel, Lancaster Castle and Perth stations being examples of his work during the late 1840s. By the second half of the 19th century some of the railway companies had become large enough to be able to employ company architects. The Midland Railway, for example, achieved a definable style through the work of in-house architects such as John Holloway Sanders and his successor Charles Trubshaw.

By the end of the 19th century, with the completion of the Great Central main line from Nottingham to London Marylebone, the country's railway network was at its apogee. Most cities had at least one grand station and many had several: Liverpool, for example, could claim Central, Exchange and Lime Street, while Manchester had Central, Exchange, London Road and Victoria, as well as the additional platform accommodation that Mayfield offered to relieve London Road. Stations were often supported by railway-owned hotels – Bradford, for example, possessed the Great Northern-owned Victoria and the Midland-owned Midland – that were among the most prestigious facilities on offer. Even humble warehouses and goods sheds were built on a grand scale. The railway industry had a swagger and self-confidence that was reflected in the architectural styles of its buildings.

As with so many aspects of history, World War I was a watershed for the railway industry. The rise of the private car, better local public transport (provided initially by the electric tram and then by the bus) and the growth of the road haulage industry all represented competitive threats to the railways. Line closures, a rarity in the late 19th century, became more prevalent from the late 1920s onwards, as a result of competition from these alternative forms of transport and also the economic downturn following the Wall Street Crash. Earlier in the decade, the first attempt at rationalising the railway industry came with the Grouping in 1923. This resulted in most of the myriad railway companies that had been developed in the 19th century being combined into the so-called 'Big Four' – the Great Western, the London, Midland & Scottish, the London & North Eastern and Southern railways – although a number of smaller and joint lines retained their separate existence beyond that date. During this period the railway companies were still constructing new buildings – such as the impressive hotels in Leeds and Morecambe and the rebuilding work undertaken by both Great Western Railway and Southern Railway – but elsewhere there was evidence of a lack of investment. The strain imposed on the industry by World War II compounded the problem of underinvestment and the British Transport Commission (BTC) inherited a largely Victorian business at nationalisation in 1948.

Line closures continued in the early 1950s as, for the first time, there was some rationalisation of competing lines. This process was accelerated from the late 1950s onwards with the reorganisation of the regions, as rail traffic continued its inexorable decline. The great hope for the future that was enshrined in the Modernisation Plan of 1955 was undermined by the ongoing deterioration of the industry's finances. This process culminated in the appointment of Dr (later Lord) Richard Beeching to the BTC and to the British Railways Board. This is not the place to argue about the strengths and weaknesses of Beeching's report – *The Reshaping of British Railways* – published in March 1963, as those arguments have been well aired elsewhere. Suffice to note here that the implementation of the closures advocated – both by the Macmillan and Wilson governments – resulted in the reduction of the railway network by some 6,500km. Not all the lines that Beeching recommended for closure were lost while, conversely, a number that he recommended retaining actually disappeared.

The gradual decline in the size of the railway industry meant that many of its buildings were now too large for operational needs or were altogether surplus to requirements. The challenge the industry faced was what to do with the redundant buildings. During the 1950s and 1960s appreciation of Victorian architecture was probably at its lowest ebb and the closure of so many railway lines resulted in the demolition of many significant examples of railway architecture and threatened demolition to many others. The demolition of Euston station in the early 1960s, and in particular its great arch (strictly a propylaeum), acted as a rallying cry to those who sought to champion the great Victorian architecture that the railways had bequeathed to Britain; this resulted in the survival of stations like St Pancras. Looking back 50 years, it seems inconceivable now that great stations like Huddersfield and Liverpool Street were ever under threat, but the loss of such stations as Birmingham Snow Hill, Birkenhead Woodside and Bradford Exchange in the decade after the demolition of Euston demonstrates how real that threat was.

That books such as Gordon Biddle's seminal *Britain's Historic Railway Buildings* need to list over 50 gems as 'important losses' in that disastrous 20-year period from the mid-1950s to the mid-1970s when demolition was often the norm is a testament to the damage done to our national heritage.

Today, there is a greater appreciation of the architectural value of the railway industry; bodies such as the Railway Heritage Trust are investing millions of pounds in ensuring the survival and restoration of key buildings. There is, and remains, however, a fundamental issue: for any historic building to have a long-term future it needs a use. That might be an ongoing use for operational purposes – the signal box at Stourbridge Junction, for example, survives because Chiltern Railways found a use for it – or some sort of alternative use. The listed structures, such as signal boxes, that have no operational use but are deemed worthy of preservation pose a challenge for the future, particularly as the railways undergo significant modernisation and electrification.

For almost a century, the photographers employed by the Aerofilms company recorded the changing face of Britain's railways. Sometimes the images they created focused on the railway itself; sometimes the railway content is almost accidental. There is, however, one common feature: the aerial views offer a unique perspective on how the railways could dominate the landscape and how significant was the industry's ownership of land in urban areas. Even in historic cities like Exeter and York, stations, goods yards, sidings and other infrastructure could and did occupy swathes of land. Other towns – such as Crewe, Swindon and Wolverton – were almost entirely creations of the railway age. The photographs selected for this book, some 150 in all, are designed to reflect various aspects of England's railway heritage.

Acknowledgements

This is the second book that I have compiled for Historic England following a chance conversation with Robin Taylor at the launch of Steven Brindle's excellent account of the history of Paddington station. I am grateful to him for first introducing me to the Historic England team.

At Historic England, I would like to thank John Hudson, Head of Publishing, for allowing me a further opportunity of looking through the files of the Aerofilms company; it brought back many memories of delving through the archives at Gate Studios and Potters Bar. The project was excellently managed through the Historic England process by Victoria Trainor. Kathryn Glendenning did a superb job on the copy-editing and in drawing my attention to a number of areas where amplification was required; often working closely with the images it is easy to spot what you know is there but less straightforward trying to explain it. Kim Bishop as proof-reader also made a number of useful suggestions. I would like to thank Katia Wickens at Hybert Design for the layout. Claire Blick again controlled the marketing for the book whilst the PR was managed by Ruth Killick; my thanks go to both for their excellent work.

I would also like to thank my good friend Gavin Watson for reading through the proofs and making pertinent comments upon them. Another good friend, John Glover, was also of assistance in trying to resolve some queries regarding locations in the Greater London area.

A book of this nature draws upon a wide range of publications; the majority of the books and journals used are cited in the bibliography. Three websites – www.engineering-timelines.com; www.gracesguide. co.uk; and historicengland.org.uk/listing/the-list/ – proved invaluable in trying to resolve dates and the listed status of the buildings recorded. In researching the book, it became evident that contradictory dates and information could and did exist. I hope that I've exercised due care in trying to reconcile these inconsistencies; if there are errors, please write to me c/o the publishers. Needless to say, in the event of any mistakes, these are entirely my responsibility.

Photographed from the north-west, this view of the Great Western Railway's station in Birmingham records the approaches from the Wolverhampton direction. This was the third station on this site and it dated to a major rebuilding completed just before the outbreak of World War I. When recorded in 1937, the GWR was developing plans for the major rebuilding of the main frontage. These plans were thwarted by World War II and not progressed after the end of hostilities.

The first – temporary – station on this site opened with the line to Banbury on 1 October 1852. It was initially known simply as 'Birmingham' but carried various suffixes before becoming 'Birmingham Snow Hill' in February 1858. The hotel providing the frontage on Colmore Row was not constructed by the railway but by a private company. The building, designed by Julius Chatwin (1830–1907), opened in January 1868, three years before the completion of the second station on the site. The hotel had a relatively short life: it was acquired by the GWR and converted into offices in 1906, then became a restaurant in 1909, as the actual station lacked one.

The construction of the third station, authorised by an Act of Parliament of 1 August 1899, commenced in 1909. The work was supervised by Walter Young Armstrong (c 1853–1934), the GWR's New Works Manager, and the resident engineer was C E Shackle. The building work was undertaken by Henry Lovatt & Co Ltd. The new station, as shown in the view, had a substantial ridge-and-furrow roof over the platforms; this extended some 152.5m and covered an area of some 10,000sq m. The steelwork for this and the other roofing sections, including the single-span arch over the booking hall, was supplied by the Darlaston-based company E C & J Kray. As the station continued to operate throughout the rebuilding work, it was never formally reopened, but work was completed on the expansion in late 1912.

Snow Hill station suffered a slow fall from grace. The completion of the West Coast electrification scheme resulted in the withdrawal of through services to London in early March 1967. Also diverted were services to and from the Stourbridge direction, which were transferred to Birmingham New Street, although a shuttle service to Langley Green was retained so that passengers from the Worcester direction could still reach Snow Hill. British Rail sought permission to close the line from Moor Street to Wolverhampton in late 1967 but the then Minister of Transport, Barbara Castle, refused this, although she permitted the closure of the line south of the station through Snow Hill Tunnel. This took place on 4 March 1968 and on 6 May 1968 the remaining services to Wolverhampton and Langley Green were reduced to peak hours only. In mid-1969 work started, despite opposition, on the demolition of the 1868 frontage of the station and the track was progressively rationalised. On 31 March 1971 BR announced the final closure of the station and surviving lines; this was finally completed on 4 March 1972. The station, used primarily as a car park thereafter, was demolished, with work commencing on 19 May 1977. Once the demolition work was completed, only minor fragments of the original station, including an original entrance on Livery Street, survived. Certain features were retained and used subsequently in the refurbishment of Birmingham Moor Street station.

This was not to be the end of the Snow Hill story: from the early 1980s plans were developed for its reopening and services through Snow Hill Tunnel to a new station were introduced on 28 September 1987. These were extended north to Stourbridge and Worcester on 24 September 1995. Between 31 May 1999 and 24 October 2015, Snow Hill also accommodated services operated by Midland Metro; these were diverted away from the station as part of the project to provide a link across to New Street station.

EPW053096

The first railway to reach Bradford was the Leeds & Bradford. This was authorised by an Act of Parliament of 4 July 1844 to construct a 22km route from Leeds, via the River Aire valley, to Shipley and then to run parallel to the Bradford Canal through to Bradford. Passenger services were introduced on 1 July 1846 to a station located at the end of Market Street. Initially, this was known simply as Bradford; it was not until the opening of the Lancashire & Yorkshire Railway's station at Drake Street (later Exchange) in 1850 that some sort of differentiation was required. There is some uncertainty as to the actual sequence of suffixes used: 'Midland', 'Market Street' and 'Forster Square' were all used at various times, although from 1924 onwards the station was known solely as 'Bradford Forster Square'.

The Leeds & Bradford Railway constructed a neoclassical station for its new services. However, following the takeover by the Midland Railway, authorised by an Act of Parliament of 24 July 1851, the new owners constructed a larger station in 1853. By the 1880s that station was proving insufficient, with North Eastern Railway also now serving the station (courtesy of the Otley & Ilkley Joint Railway and running powers over the MR route from Milner Wood Junction to Bradford). A new station, including a hotel, was completed in 1890. This was designed by Charles Trubshaw (1840–1917) and this is the structure illustrated in this 1937 view from the south-east. Visible are the hotel, the station with its six platforms and overall roof, the goods offices (with the main MR Valley Road goods shed beyond) and the screen arcade, forming the porte cochère between the hotel and goods offices. Bradford, as home to the wool trade, possessed a number of significant freight yards, but Valley Road was the last to survive.

Under the *Reshaping* report of 1963, most of the passenger services from Forster Square were listed for closure. These included all of the local services from Bradford to Leeds, to Skipton (via Keighley and via Ilkley) and to Harrogate (via Otley). While the Leeds-to-Bradford and Harrogate-to-Bradford services were withdrawn – although subsequent electrification saw the former reinstated in the 1990s – local authority support resulted in the retention of the local services to Ilkley and to Skipton via Keighley. Forster Square station also underwent rebuilding in the 1960s. The overall roof was removed and replaced with concrete platform awning, while the concourse area was also rebuilt in concrete. Part of this was to handle parcels traffic – Bradford was home to a number of the country's largest mail-order businesses and much of this traffic was carried by rail. As a result, from the mid-1960s Forster Square was perceived primarily as a parcels concentration depot. However, this traffic declined and had largely ceased by the early 1980s.

Today, there are only limited survivals of Trubshaw's rebuilding work. The most significant is the Midland Hotel, which is now Grade II listed and, after some years of disrepair, recently underwent a restoration. Also surviving is part of the screen arcade that linked the hotel and goods offices. This is, however, now devoid of the roof and extends only about half the distance that it once did. The railway station itself underwent a further rebuilding in 1990 when it was reduced in size and relocated slightly further from the city centre. The site of the original station is now occupied by an office development. Electric services to the rebuilt Forster Square commenced in 1994. Following closure of the Valley Road goods yard, the site was cleared and redeveloped as a retail park.

EPW054317

Bristol Temple Meads
May 1975

Authorised by an Act of Parliament of 31 August 1835 to connect Bristol with London, the Great Western Railway's terminus in Bristol opened on 31 August 1840, when the line extended as far as Bath. The terminus was designed by Isambard Kingdom Brunel (1806–59) and finally completed in 1841. The station included a three-storey Bath-stone frontage in a neo-Tudor style with two supporting gatehouses (only the southern one now survives). The platform area was accommodated under a 60m-long train shed. Between this and the frontage was a second – 47m-long – roof under which locomotives were housed. The station was used by the Bristol & Exeter Railway (from 14 June 1841), with its trains reversing into and out of the platforms, and the Bristol & Gloucester Railway (from 8 July 1844; this railway was taken over by the Midland Railway on 1 July 1845 and subsequently converted to mixed and then standard gauge).

The Bristol & Exeter constructed its own station at right angles to the existing station; this included a through platform on a curve. The new facility opened in late 1845 (the exact date is unrecorded). Although the actual station was somewhat basic, the railway constructed an impressive headquarters between 1852 and 1854 in a neo-Jacobean style to a design completed by Samuel Charles Fripp (1812–82). This structure is still extant and is now Grade II* listed.

As the number of services increased, so the original Brunel and the later Bristol & Exeter stations proved inadequate. Following agreement between the Bristol & Exeter, Great Western Railway and Midland Railway, powers were obtained through an Act of Parliament of 6 July 1865 for the construction of a new joint station in Bristol. However, delays in agreeing its funding meant it was not until 1871 that construction started. Although the design work is sometimes attributed to Sir Matthew

Digby Wyatt (1820–77), who had been Brunel's assistant, all the evidence suggests that the bulk of the work was actually undertaken by the Bristol & Exeter's engineer, Francis (later Sir Francis) Fox (1844–1927).

Fox's work included the eastern extension of the original train shed by 194m and a three-platform through station under a curved wrought-iron train shed. This was 150m in length and 38m in width. The Bristol & Exeter station, which had been known locally as 'The Cowshed', was demolished and its site used for a carriage shed. The new station was provided with a new entrance block in a French Gothic style; this was the work of Wyatt and included a new booking hall. The new station was finally completed in 1878.

While the new station was under construction, the process of converting the Bristol & Exeter and GWR lines to mixed gauge was also progressing. However, it was not until the final abolition of the broad gauge on 21 May 1892 that the station was exclusively served by standard gauge trains. The removal of the broad gauge track permitted the realignment of the through platforms to create two additional platform faces.

By the interwar years, with the station now controlled by the GWR and the London, Midland & Scottish Railway, a further enlargement was undertaken. This work took place between 1930 and 1935 to the art deco designs of the GWR's then chief architect, Percy Emerson Culverhouse (1871–1953). It included the construction of additional through platforms on the eastern side, the alteration of the existing through lines under the train shed to permit the widening and lengthening of the main Up and Down platforms, and the extension of the platforms southwards. The approach lines to the station were also quadrupled.

With the reduction in services post-war, use of the original Brunel terminus ceased. The new Bristol power

signal box was constructed in 1970 and this resulted in the demolition of much of the Wyatt extension to the earlier station. The 1970s box replaced a number of earlier boxes that were the result of a resignalling scheme in the late 1930s.

Bristol Temple Meads station (viewed here from the west) is now Grade I listed. Over recent years it has benefited from a significant amount of investment to ensure that its historic fabric is preserved for future generations, as well as to prepare it for the electrification of the ex-GWR main line towards Paddington.

EAC297008

Carlisle
12 September 1977

The grand station at Carlisle (known as 'Carlisle Citadel' for much of its history) played host to no fewer than seven pre-Grouping companies. It was originally designed for the Lancaster & Carlisle Railway, authorised by an Act of Parliament of 6 June 1844, with the support of the Caledonian Railway, authorised by an Act of Parliament of 31 July 1845. However, the latter's failure to provide funding caused the station's completion to be delayed, with construction work suspended for a period in the autumn of 1847. Initially it was planned that the Newcastle & Carlisle and Maryport & Carlisle railways would also be involved with the project but this did not happen and it was only after the station was completed that these two lines eventually transferred their services to it.

The site for the station was identified in 1845 and powers for its construction were obtained in 1846. The Lancaster & Carlisle employed William (later Sir William) Tite (1798–1873) to design the building. The actual construction was handled by Thomas Brassey (1805–70), William Mackenzie (1794–1851) and John Stephenson (1794–1848). Although incomplete at the time, the new station opened on 10 September 1847; it was not until 1850 that the building was substantially completed and it was only in 1853 that the clock was ordered. The main station building was designed by Tite in a grand neo-Tudor style. Built in grey sandstone, the 143.3m-long structure includes a five-bay arcade (which incorporates the royal coat of arms plus those of the Caledonian and Lancaster & Carlisle railways), as well as an octagonal clock tower. The original station included a train shed supported on iron columns.

During the 1850s there were modifications but the next significant change followed the Carlisle Citadel Station Act of 21 July 1861. This formally enshrined the Carlisle Citadel Station Agreement of 10 May 1857,

which organised the joint management of the station as additional railways started to operate into it. As a result, additional platforms were added in the early 1860s.

It was the imminent arrival of the Midland Railway, via the Settle and Carlisle line (which opened in 1876), that led to the final major development of the station. From the early 1870s planning for the further expansion of the station was undertaken following an agreement between the railway companies and the passing of Carlisle Citadel Station Act of 21 July 1873. The contract for the new work was let in July 1878 to the Glasgow-based Morrison & Mason, with work completed during the summer of 1881. The work included the widening of the station, the provision of a new island platform with two-storey buildings, thus increasing the number of through platforms to three with five bays, and the construction of new screen walls, 313.6m in length, to accommodate the new overall roof. The latter was designed by the Edinburgh-based engineers Blyth & Cunningham (Benjamin Hall Blyth, 1849–1917, and George Miller Cunningham, 1829–1897) and spanned some 85m, with a total area of some 2.6 hectares. The ridge-and-furrow roof was completed by a timber-and-glass end screen at both the north and south ends of the station, completed in a neo-Gothic style.

At Grouping, five of the companies that operated into Citadel passed to the London, Midland & Scottish Railway; the two exceptions – the North British and the North Eastern railways – passed to the London & North Eastern Railway.

Towards the end of the 1950s, concern was growing over the condition of the end screens and the roof. Lack of maintenance had led to their deterioration and, during 1956 and 1957, the western half of the roof was removed completely, while the eastern half was cut back at both ends and new end screens provided for the

reduced – 14-bay – section. New platform canopies were provided to replace the overall roof on those platforms now exposed to the elements.

Although the ex-North British routes – to Edinburgh and Silloth – closed in the 1960s, Carlisle station (viewed here from the north) remains an important junction station and is now Grade II* listed. The detached screen wall on the southern side, orginally used for the now-demolished section of roof, is also listed.

EAW343755

Derby
25 June 1989

From the early 1830s Derby was the focus for three major railway schemes and from late 1835 the idea of a single station serving the trio first emerged. The first of the new railways to open was the Midland Counties. This had been authorised by an Act of Parliament of 21 June 1836 and services commenced between Derby and Nottingham on 4 June 1839. The next arrival was the Birmingham & Derby Junction Railway. This had been authorised on 19 May 1836 to construct a line from Derby southwards to connect with the London & Birmingham Railway at Hampton-in-Arden and its 62km line opened formally on 5 August 1839. The third company was the North Midland. Authorised on 4 July 1836, the railway opened from Derby to Rotherham on 11 May 1840. These three railways merged on 10 May 1844 to become the Midland Railway.

The first station to serve Derby was designed by Francis Thompson (1808–95), who was appointed by the North Midland in February 1839 to design the structure, with construction work handled by Thomas Jackson of Pimlico. The building included a 320m-long facade that incorporated a prominent central block along with a three-bay train shed over the platforms and running lines. Adjacent to the station were two hotels – the Midland for first-class passengers and the Brunswick for second class. Again designed by Thompson and built by Jackson, the former, which opened in 1842 and was acquired by the MR in 1862, is still extant. Extended in 1874 and now Grade II listed, it is the oldest surviving station hotel in Britain.

By the mid-1850s the existing station was no longer adequate. During the decade, the station facade was modified by the construction of a two-storey office block containing the shareholders' room, additional office accommodation at the southern end, a porte cochère and a new island platform. The new work was designed by the MR's then chief architect, John Holloway Sanders (1825–84). Two decades on, Sanders was again called upon to increase the station's capacity with additional platforms added, along with new waiting and refreshment rooms; this work was completed in 1881. In 1891 the porte cochère constructed in the 1850s was demolished and a new facade, along with a new porte cochère, was constructed in front of Thompson's surviving original structure. This was completed to the designs of Charles Trubshaw (1840–1917), who had been appointed to the post of chief architect following Sanders' death.

The station remained intact until World War II. On 15 January 1941, the structure – and in particular the train shed – suffered severe damage, although the main building survived. Following nationalisation, the station was renamed Derby Midland on 25 September 1950 – it lost the 'Midland' suffix on 6 May 1968. Two years later, a two-year project costing £200,000 was undertaken to replace the platform canopies with new structures constructed in reinforced concrete. This work was completed in 1974.

The station, as illustrated in this 1989 view from the south-east, has undergone a significant transformation. In 1985 the bulk of the Victorian facade was demolished and replaced with a more modern structure. The Victorian entrance clock and its surrounding brickwork with stone detailing were, however, relocated and can now be found at the north end of the car park. Since the date of the photograph, the concrete platform canopies have also been replaced; these were discovered to be in a poor condition during work to replace the footbridge. As a result, the canopies constructed in the early 1950s were demolished and replacements installed between 2007 and 2009.

Of the Victorian station, some of the two- and three-storey red-brick office blocks constructed at the southern end between 1853 and 1857 are still extant, albeit unlisted. Two office blocks, designed by Sanders on Nelson Street and dating to the early 1870s, for use by the MR accounts department and the goods manager, also survive; these are Grade II listed. Some of the original railway housing, designed by Thompson and dating to 1841, is also extant; recently restored, this is Grade II listed. One part of Trubshaw's work from the 1890s to survive is the former Midland Railway Institute. This two-storey block, constructed in brick with terracotta detailing, is unlisted and now in commercial use, albeit still emblazoned with 'Midland Railway Institute' above the main entrance.

EAC570936

Doncaster

18 August 1981

Incorporating two earlier projects – the London & York and the Direct Northern railways – the Great Northern Railway was authorised by an Act of Parliament of 26 June 1846 to construct a main line from London to York through Peterborough, Retford and Doncaster, along with a second route between Peterborough and Bawtry via Boston and Lincoln. The first part of the GNR to be completed was the short section north of Arksey that opened on 5 June 1848 in connection with the L&YR Knottingley branch. The first railway passengers from Doncaster were those, therefore, that were conveyed by coach to the station at Arksey.

The initial station at Doncaster was a temporary structure that opened with the line from Stockbridge (to the north) on 7 September 1848. This was replaced by a new facility located 400m to the south in September 1850. The section from Retford to Doncaster opened on 4 September 1849. The importance of Doncaster as a railway centre grew following the decision of the GNR to base its main workshops in the town in 1851. The first phase of the works opened in June 1853 and by 1900 the works complex covered around 80 hectares and employed some 4,500 men. Of the buildings constructed for the works, a number of structures are now listed. These include the erecting, boiler and spring shops of 1853, the tender shop of 1866 and the red-brick office block (c 1900), which are all now Grade II listed.

The station itself underwent expansion between 1873 and 1877, when the two main island platforms were established and new buildings erected. The basic arrangement of the station is largely unchanged in this view of 1981, taken from the west, although the original platform canopies had been replaced (except on the westernmost platform where some ex-GNR ironwork is still extant). The most significant change after the expansion of the station in the 1870s was the replacement of the main station building. This work was completed in 1933 and resulted in a restrained red-brick structure with ashlar stone detailing.

Since the photograph was taken, the major change to affect Doncaster station has been the arrival of 25kV electric services. The catenary from Peterborough to Leeds was energised in 1988 and that from Doncaster to York the following year. More recently, in a project started in May 2015 and opened on 12 December 2016, a new platform 0 has been constructed on the site of the former cattle dock (adjacent to the Frenchgate Centre). This new platform is designed for trains to Beverley, Bridlington, Scarborough and York, so that these services can be handled without conflicting with those on the East Coast Main Line. The platform is linked to the station by a footbridge. Elsewhere the station remains very much as it appeared in 1981, although the old Royal Mail sorting office was demolished in 2016 (to facilitate the construction of a replacement car park). The station's then owners, Virgin Trains East Coast, had, at the time of writing, announced plans for a further upgrade to the station's facilities. The new work includes the addition of a glass canopy along the existing 1933 facade. Doncaster Council gave formal approval for the design of the new structure in November 2017.

EAC414476

Exeter Central
7 August 1973

With Exeter St David's in the background, this view from the south-west records the ex-Southern Railway Central station. The original St David's station dated to 1 May 1844 and the opening of the Bristol & Exeter Railway, and was designed by Isambard Kingdom Brunel (1806–59). In the 1860s it was replaced by a new station with an impressive facade, designed by the Bristol-based architect Henry Lloyd (1812–87) in conjunction with the Bristol & Exeter's engineer Francis (later Sir Francis) Fox (1844–1927).

The London & South Western Railway line from Yeovil Junction to Exeter, authorised by an Act of Parliament of 21 July 1856, opened on 19 July 1860. The new line's engineer was John Edward Errington (1806–62), with William Robert Galbraith (1829–1914) as resident engineer; the contractor for the work was the Exeter-based James Taylor. A new station – called Queen Street – was provided with a single platform and two tracks over which there was a train shed. The line was originally single track, but the section from Broad Clyst to Exeter was doubled on 11 April 1864. In addition to services towards Salisbury, Queen Street was also the terminus for branch line services to Exmouth from 1 May 1861; the steeply graded connection through to St David's was opened on 1 February 1862. This gave the LSWR access to its previously isolated network of lines to the north and west of Exeter. With increased traffic, a further platform with a second train shed was added in 1874, with two through, non-platform, tracks also added.

In 1923 Exeter Queen Street, along with the rest of the LSWR, passed to the newly formed Southern Railway. Two years later the new owners lengthened the eastbound platform from 180m to 370m; this took the platform beyond the New North Road overbridge. A further two years later, on 3 June 1927, a fire damaged the wooden buildings on the western platform and the decision was taken to rebuild the station. Plans for the new station were drawn up by the SR's then chief architect, James Robb Scott (1882–1965), in 1931, but these were deemed too expensive and a cheaper solution was sought. However, intervention by the council resulted in the board's approving a more ambitious scheme in May 1931, although it is uncertain who was the architect of the final station that emerged. Work started on the new station in late 1931, with construction undertaken by A N Coles Ltd, and it was formally opened by the then Lord Mayor on 1 July 1933. The station was renamed 'Central' from the same date. The new station included a three-storey main building designed in a neo-baroque style in brick with stone detailing flanked by a curved arcade of two-storey shops. At platform level, the train sheds had been replaced by canopies constructed in concrete while, adjacent to New North Road, a concrete footbridge, installed on 17 April 1932, resulted in a new entrance onto New North Road.

At nationalisation, Exeter Central passed to British Railways (Southern Region) but control was to be transferred to Western Region following a revision of the regional boundaries. This, combined with the gradual elimination of the services handled by the station, resulted in the gradual reduction in the station's facilities. The New North Road entrance closed in 1966 (it was, however, reopened on 2 July 1984). The eastbound through line was taken out of use on 9 November 1969, followed by the westbound on 13 October 1984. Although general freight traffic to Central ceased on 4 December 1967, cement traffic continued to be handled until January 1980.

The view taken in 1973 shows the station during the years of rationalisation. Today, the station, currently unlisted, largely retains its 1930s look, with the track layout now rationalised to the two platform lines plus a single bay at the eastern end of the westbound platform. The once extensive goods yard to the north of the station has been redeveloped, as have the sidings that once existed between the station and St David's Tunnel.

EAW269118

Hull Paragon
22 October 1997

Powers to construct a new terminus in Hull were obtained by the Manchester & Leeds and York & North Midland railways via the York & North Midland (Hull Station) Act of 1847. The station opened the following year – on 8 May – although the station buildings, designed by George Townsend Andrews (1804–55) in an Italian Renaissance style, were incomplete. The new station included a main facade on Anlaby Road that had a stone-built, two-storey central booking hall with two 11-bay, single-storey wings, with three-bay, two-storey buildings at either end. These two structures provided accommodation for the stationmaster and a parcels office. Access to the booking hall was via a small porte cochère – which by the late 1880s had been infilled using matching stone and windows – while the platform area was covered by a three-span train shed. At the eastern end of the station Andrews designed the Station Hotel, again constructed in stone in an Italianate style. The hotel was formally opened on 6 November 1851.

Over the next two decades the number of services handled by Hull Paragon increased, with the result that minor expansion of the platform facilities was undertaken in the mid-1870s and again in the late 1880s. However, by the 1890s even these improved facilities were inadequate and, in 1897, the board of the North Eastern Railway gave approval for the expansion of the station. The new station, with its five-span train shed, was designed by William Bell (1844–1919), whose initial plans envisaged the replacement of Andrews' original structure. Fortunately, this did not happen when construction of the enlarged station commenced in 1902. The completed station opened on 12 December 1904. In addition to the 121.9m train shed, the new structure also included a transverse, two-span roof over the concourse area. Platform canopies were also provided for a short distance beyond the main train shed, while the 1887-built roof over the bay platforms on the southern side was also retained.

The hotel, which is now Grade II* listed, underwent expansion during 1931 and 1932. It was seriously damaged internally by fire in 1990, although its ground-floor interiors were restored to the original designs prior to its reopening in 1992. Following privatisation, the hotel is now known as the Britannia Royal Hotel.

The new station had nine platform faces under the four southern spans of the train shed. The northernmost – fifth – span accommodated special traffic, including fish, and was screened off from the rest of the station. Additional platform accommodation was provided by the reuse of the bay platforms on the southern side, with their surviving late 19th-century canopies. The station was resignalled at the same time as it was enlarged. This equipment was itself replaced in 1938 by a new box constructed for the London & North Eastern Railway (the 1938 box is still extant to the west of the Park Street road overbridge). In 1962, following the demolition of the glass-and-iron porte cochère designed by Bell, a new office block – Paragon House – was constructed. As a result of the reduction in services to and from Hull Paragon from the mid-1960s onwards, the track serving the station was rationalised and, as shown in this 1997 photograph, the platforms that served the northern two spans were removed, providing space for car parking.

Since the photograph was taken (from the south-west) in 1997, Hull Paragon has received a considerable amount of investment to improve its facilities. Paragon House was demolished in 2006 and replaced with a new canopy that once more reveals to good effect Bell's facade of 1904. This work was in connection with a scheme for an integrated bus and railway station (known as Hull Paragon Interchange), formally opened by Queen Elizabeth II on 5 March 2009. This now utilises the northern two spans of the train shed and the land immediately to the north of the station to provide accommodation for bus services. The station itself, now Grade II* listed, retains its train shed as well as the section of the 1887 canopies visible in 1997.

EAC672570

Leeds City
1 April 1964

A number of stations have undergone dramatic changes on several occasions. Few, however, have had as many radical changes over the years as Leeds City. Indeed, at the time of writing, a further major redevelopment has been announced to accommodate the terminus of the HS2 project in Leeds.

The first terminus in Leeds, that of the Leeds & Selby Railway, opened at Marsh Lane on 22 September 1834. This was followed by the North Midland Railway (the Midland Railway from 1846), which opened a separate station at Hunslet Lane on 1 July 1840. It was the Leeds & Bradford Railway, authorised by an Act of Parliament of 4 July 1844, that started the development of the future City station when it opened a station on Wellington Street on 1 July 1846. A month later, on 26 August 1846, the Leeds & Bradford was leased by the MR and most MR services were extended from the station at Hunslet Lane to that at Wellington Street. A second station vied with Wellington to serve the centre; this was Leeds Central, which over the years was used by services operated by the Great Northern Railway, the Lancashire & Yorkshire Railway, the London & North Western Railway and the North Eastern Railway.

The joint Leeds New station, situated on the through line to the south of Wellington station, was authorised by an Act of Parliament of 5 July 1865 and opened on 1 April 1869. The station as illustrated in this view was the result of an enlargement undertaken following a further Act of Parliament of 16 July 1874, with the expanded station opening on 5 January 1879. New station was a joint LNWR/NER station and was situated on a short section of joint line. The LNWR access to the station was improved following the opening, on 1 March 1882, of the direct line (now disused following closure on 11 October 1987) from Canal Junction to North Junction.

In the mid-1930s, the LNER (joint owners of New station with the London, Midland & Scottish Railway) and the LMS (sole owner of Wellington) undertook a project to connect the two stations. The work was designed by the LMS's then chief architect, William Henry Hamlyn (1889–1968), and included a new hotel, on which William Curtis Green (1875–1960) was also involved, which replaced an earlier hotel dating to 1867.

The 1964 view, taken from the south-east, shows the station shortly after the completion of British Railways House. This office block, designed by the controversial 'architect' John Poulson (1910–93) and built by Taylor Woodrow, was completed in 1962. The building, unlike much of the station illustrated, remains, albeit having undergone refurbishment, and is now known as City House.

Since the photograph was taken, Leeds City has undergone two rebuilding projects. The first was completed in 1967 and was designed to facilitate the closure of Leeds Central (which occurred on 1 May 1967). This work resulted in the removal of the existing train shed and its replacement, track reconfiguration and the installation of new platforms. At the same time, the platforms of the former Wellington station were converted for use by parcels traffic. With the closure of Central, the suffix 'City' was dropped. The modernised station was planned at a time when a number of local routes – such as that to Ilkley – were under threat of closure. The reprieve of these services, along with track capacity problems on the two-track section west of the station, meant that the facilities soon became inadequate. Between 1999 and 2002 a further rebuilding project was undertaken; this saw the 1967 overall roof replaced and further platform accommodation provided, including the reuse of the former Wellington platforms.

Of the structure illustrated in 1964, two significant elements do, however, survive other than the 1962 office block. These are the reinforced concrete north concourse and the associated Queens Hotel. These both date to the rebuilding project of the late 1930s and are now both Grade II listed. The former had deteriorated significantly during its period in use as a parcels depot but was fully restored in 1999. The nine-storey hotel was privatised in 1984.

EAW124534

Liverpool Exchange
9 May 1969

Of the three great termini built to serve Liverpool, Exchange station was the second to open. Jointly promoted by the East Lancashire and Lancashire & Yorkshire railways, the station was designed to replace the two companies' existing – and inadequate – terminus at Great Howard Street. The new station, which opened on 13 May 1850, was designed by John (later Sir John) Hawkshaw (1811–91) and was known by the East Lancashire Railway as Liverpool Tithebarn Street and by the Lancashire & Yorkshire as Liverpool Exchange. Disagreements between the two companies went beyond the simple naming of the station and the former complained to the Railway Commissioners over the allocation of the station's facilities. The original station was elevated above the street level as its approaches had to pass over the Leeds & Liverpool Canal, and the main station building was a two-storey neo-Italianate structure. The East Lancashire Railway was absorbed by the L&YR on 13 May 1859.

As traffic into the station grew, so the facilities proved increasingly inadequate with the result that the L&YR obtained two Acts of Parliament – of 24 July 1882 and 2 August 1883 – to permit the widening of the lines into the station from the north and for a complete rebuilding of the original station. Following a competition to design the new station, the railway decided that none of the entries were suitable and it instead commissioned the local architect Henry Shelmerdine, aided by its own chief engineer, William Hunt (1843–97), to design the new station and associated Exchange Hotel. Construction work commenced in 1886 and the new structure opened on 2 July 1888. The hotel, with its impressive frontage on Tithebarn Street, opened on 13 August 1888. The new station had 10 platforms under the four sections of the long, iron train shed. The next development, in the early

20th century, was the third-rail electrification of the suburban service to Southport; work on this started on 8 March 1903 and the first non-steam services commenced on 22 March the following year.

Along with the rest of the L&YR, Exchange station passed to the London & North Western Railway as a result of the merger between the two railways on 1 January 1922 and thus to the London, Midland & Scottish Railway the following year. The station suffered severe damage during World War II as a result of the Luftwaffe's assault on the port of Liverpool; a viaduct to the north of the station was destroyed in December 1940 and services into the station were disrupted to some extent until fully restored on 18 August 1941. More significant, in May 1941 the station itself was hit, resulting in the demolition of part of the north-western section of the train shed. The loss of this structure is evident in this view of the station, looking towards the north-east, in 1969.

By this date the future of Exchange station was in some doubt. Although the station was the departure point of the last scheduled main line steam service on British Rail on 3 August 1968 (the official last main line steam service – the 'Fifteen Guinea' special of 11 August – departed from Lime Street), by this date many of the long-distance services had been diverted from Exchange to Lime Street. The last long-distance services from the station – to Glasgow – operated on 3 May 1970 and by that date three platforms had already been taken out of use. The period also witnessed the development of plans to divert the electric services underground as part of the Merseyrail project. In furtherance of this, three more platforms were closed on 6 May 1973 to permit the construction of the new Moorfields station and the underground line beneath Exchange station.

With work on the new alignment complete, Exchange station closed on 30 April 1977; the hotel had closed its doors for the last time six years earlier.

Following closure, the platform area and the land previously occupied by the approach lines became a car park. The train shed was demolished, while the hotel was redeveloped as an office block in the 1980s; its facade on Tithebarn Street was retained and incorporated into the new structure.

EAW192904

Liverpool Lime Street
22 March 1980

When the Liverpool & Manchester Railway first opened to the city in 1830, its original terminus was on Crown Street, Edge Hill, which was outside the city centre. Construction for a new central station commenced in October 1833. This initial station was designed by John Cunningham (1799–1873), Arthur Hill Holme (1814–57) and John Foster Jr (1786–1846). Access to the station from Edge Hill involved a tunnel and a steep gradient; this resulted in trains from Edge Hill descending by gravity, while those departing from the station were hauled up the gradient by rope powered by a stationary steam engine. This arrangement continued until 1870.

As traffic grew, so the original station proved inadequate and by the end of the 1830s work was in hand on its enlargement. The new station featured a single curved train shed roof, designed by William (later Sir William) Fairburn (1789–1874) and Richard Turner (1798–1881), with a station building designed by William (later Sir William) Tite (1798–1873). This work was completed by 1849. Two decades on, the station was again rebuilt; the northern train shed was completed in 1867, designed by William Baker (1817–1878), who was the London & North Western Railway's chief engineer until his death, and Francis Stevenson (1827–1902), who became chief engineer on Baker's death. This structure, which was the first in the world to be completed entirely in iron, had a span of 61m; at the time this was the largest in the world.

The next phase in the development of the station came with the construction of the North Western Hotel. This was designed by Alfred Waterhouse (1830–1905) and was completed in 1871. Built in stone with a slate roof, the hotel was completed in a Renaissance Revival style. Its construction required the demolition of the bulk of the station building designed by Tite. The hotel, although a landmark, closed in 1933, largely as a result of its outdated facilities, and was converted into the Lime Street Chambers. Now Grade II listed, it was converted by Liverpool John Moores University in 1994 into student accommodation.

In 1879 the train shed completed in 1849 was replaced by a new southern shed. This was again designed by Francis Stevenson, this time with the assistance of Edward William Ives (c 1851–1914). This structure had a span of slightly over 58m and included a glass screen as a facade. The structure, along with the group of four columns (attributed to Edward Woods, 1814–1903, and dating to the rebuild of the 1840s), was obscured in the early 1960s by the construction of an office block – Concourse House – and a row of small shops.

This was, therefore, the condition of the station when recorded from the west in 1980. Although not visible in this view, a new signal box had been commissioned on 28 January 1948. Internally the concourse had been modified in 1955, while 25kV electric services were introduced on 1 January 1962. Shortly after the photograph, during 1983 and 1984, the concourse area was further modified as part of an improvement of facilities for the Liverpool Garden Festival. Since the start of the new millennium, the station, now Grade II listed, has undergone a radical transformation spurred on by Liverpool's 800th anniversary in 2007 and by the city being the European Capital of Culture the following year. In all, some £35 million was spent on the Lime Street Gateway project. This included the demolition of Concourse House and its associated shops, a project completed in 2009, which has revealed the full extent of the colonnade completed in 1879 and has provided a dramatic new station entrance.

The station is, at the time of writing, undergoing a further remodelling; this will see two new platforms inserted between the existing platforms 7 and 8 in place of the cab road. This is designed to increase capacity and to permit the introduction of additional services from 2019.

EAC389835

London Charing Cross
30 May 1953

When the South Eastern Railway, authorised by an Act of Parliament of 21 June 1836 as the South Eastern & Dover Railway, finally opened to London in 1845 its initial terminus was at Bricklayers' Arms to the south of the river, and subsequently at London Bridge. The railway aspired, however, to extend further towards the city but was thwarted until the Charing Cross Railway was authorised on 8 August 1859. The Act of Parliament permitted the construction of a 3km line from London Bridge, across the River Thames (involving the demolition of a suspension bridge designed by Isambard Kingdom Brunel, which had opened in 1845) to the site of new Hungerford Market on the south side of the Strand. Although a market had been established here since the late 17th century, the building that was destined to be demolished for the railway was of relatively recent construction, having been built following an Act of Parliament of 1830.

The new station was designed by John (later Sir John) Hawkshaw (1811–91) and the six platforms were covered by a single-span wrought-iron train shed that extended to a length of 155m and a width of 50m. The first services into the new station operated on 11 January 1884. The associated Charing Cross Hotel, designed by Edward Middleton Barry (1830–80), opened on 15 May 1865. Such was the hotel's success that an annex, across Villiers Street and linked to the main hotel by a bridge, was added in 1878. In order to complete the station forecourt, Barry also designed a replica of the Eleanor Cross that had once stood on the site; the original cross had been first erected at Whitehall in 1291 but had been removed, on the orders of Parliament, in 1647.

The Charing Cross Railway was formally absorbed by the South Eastern on 1 September 1864. As traffic increased, so the railway undertook the widening of the railway bridge across the Thames; this project was completed in 1887. Tragedy struck the station on 5 December 1905 when a 21m section of the overall roof collapsed. Fortunately evidence of its imminent failure was noted and so trains and platforms were quickly evacuated, but six people were still killed. Following the collapse, it was decided to replace the Hawkshaw roof with the ridge-and-furrow design shown in this 1953 view from the north-west. Work was completed and the station reopened partially on 19 March 1906.

During World War II, Charing Cross station and hotel suffered severe damage; during the night of 16/17 April 1941, for example, the hotel was damaged by fire. This resulted in the upper storeys and mansard roof being rebuilt in 1951 and evidence of this replacement work, to a slightly different profile to Barry's original work, can be clearly seen in the photograph.

The hotel, now Grade II listed, is still extant today, as is the replica of the Eleanor Cross. However, the latter, Grade II* listed, had deteriorated to such an extent that it was placed on English Heritage's Buildings at Risk Register in 2008. A ten-month-long restoration project, completed in August 2010, has seen it fully repaired. Of the station itself, while the concourse is still covered by the replacement roof erected in 1906, the bulk of the ridge-and-furrow work visible in this view has been replaced. In 1986 work started on the construction of a new office block, known as Embankment Place and designed by Terry (later Sir Terry) Farrell (born 1938) and Partners. This structure was completed in 1991. More recently, completed in 2002, two new footbridges have been erected alongside Hungerford Bridge; these replaced the single – cramped – footbridge that had existed on the downstream side of the bridge.

EAW049765

London Euston
20 June 1957

Pictured from the south towards the end of its life prior to rebuilding, Euston station is perhaps the most significant architectural loss of all Britain's railway structures. The announcement in 1959 that British Railways intended to rebuild the station as part of its ambitious plans for the electrification of the West Coast Main Line sparked a massive campaign, involving such influential figures as John (later Sir John) Betjeman (1906–84), against the loss of the great Doric Arch (or propylaeum) and Great Hall in particular. The rejection of these pleas for preservation by the then Conservative government under Harold Macmillan and the commencement of demolition in November 1961 stimulated the growth in awareness of railway architecture. This undoubtedly aided campaigners such as the Victorian Society (established in 1957 with Betjeman as one of its founders) in their successful defence of other threatened buildings, most notably St Pancras (see p 27) and Liverpool Street stations.

The origins of Euston lay with the London & Birmingham Railway. This was authorised by an Act of Parliament of 6 May 1833 to construct a line north to Birmingham from a terminus planned at Camden Town. However, a second Act, dated 3 July 1835, permitted the extension southwards to Euston. The railway's engineer was Robert Stephenson (1803–59) and the line opened from Euston to Boxmoor on 20 July 1837. Initially services out of the station over the 1 in 68 gradient to Camden Town were cable hauled; this persisted until 1844.

The new station was designed by Philip Hardwick (1792–1870), who was employed as the London & Birmingham's architect, and included the famous arch. This was constructed in sandstone from the West Riding of Yorkshire, and was 21m in height, 13m in depth and with columns that were 2.59m in diameter. The arch was flanked by four small lodges, two on each side, and gave access to the two-platform station that was enclosed by a 61m train shed designed by the engineer Charles (later Sir Charles) Fox (1810–74). Each of the platforms, one for arrivals and one for departures, was 130m in length. The contractor for the construction of the station was William Cubitt (1791–1863). Inevitably, as traffic grew, so the original station became increasingly inadequate.

The first expansion occurred in 1846 when two new platforms were added on the west side of the existing station. The Great Hall, designed by Hardwick's son Philip Charles (1822–92) and opened on 27 May 1849, was constructed on the site of the original train shed and was set back from the Drummond Street frontage. Additional platforms were added, both to the east and the west, between 1863 and 1892, taking the total to 15 by the end of the 19th century. By the 1930s, the London, Midland & Scottish Railway was considering rebuilding the station. Limited work was undertaken towards the end of the decade but the outbreak of war resulted in the end of work.

The 1957 view illustrates to good effect the distance between Euston Road – seen in the foreground – and the actual station, which fronted onto Drummond Street. In the foreground are the two small lodges on Euston Road. These were designed by the London & North Western Railway's architect James B Stansby, and were the result of an Act of Parliament of 1869 that permitted the LNWR to purchase land from the then Lord Southampton to construct a road from the station through to Euston Road. The two lodges, one of which was used as a parcels office and the other for enquiries, were constructed in Portland stone and were completed in 1870. These structures, now Grade II listed, are still extant, having been converted into pubs. Between the lodges there was a statue of Robert Stephenson.

This was created by the sculptor Baron Carlo Marochetti (1805–67) and presented by the Institution of Civil Engineers. Now Grade II listed as well, the statue was relocated during the rebuilding of the station.

Following the demolition of the Victorian station, which started in November 1961, a new station, designed by William Robert Headley and Ray L Moorcroft, was formally opened by Queen Elizabeth II on 14 October 1968. The office blocks that are now a feature of the redeveloped Euston site were constructed from 1979 onwards and were designed by Richard Seifert (1910-2001) & Partners, an organisation that acted as consultants for the reconstruction of the station. With the development of HS2, Euston will again see further expansion, including – possibly – the restoration of the arch.

EAW067809

London King's Cross and St Pancras
8 October 1964

There is probably no greater contrast in railway architecture than that evinced by the flamboyant Gothic architecture of St Pancras and the more utilitarian style of King's Cross – and their close proximity, on the north side of Euston Road, emphasises this. (St Pancras is to the west and King's Cross to the east; the photograph is taken from the south.)

The Great Northern Railway (authorised by an Act of Parliament of 26 June 1846) opened to a temporary terminus at Maiden Lane on 7 August 1850. The site for the final terminus had been identified by the railway's engineer, George Turnbull (1809–89), who was responsible for the construction of the first 30km of the route northwards. The actual design of King's Cross station was undertaken by Lewis Cubitt (1799–1883). The completed station, which opened on 14 October 1852, included a 34m-high clock tower and two arched train sheds, each 32m in width, 244m in length and 22m in height. Initially the roof ribs were constructed in timber, but these were replaced by iron in 1866 (eastern roof) and 1886 (western). Cubitt was also responsible for the Great Northern Hotel, which opened alongside the station in 1854. Initially the station accommodated two platforms – those numbered 1 and 8 today – with several carriage sidings, but from 1862 onwards the number of platforms was increased, eventually to total the eight in operation today under the main twin train sheds. Further platform accommodation – now numbered 9 to 11 – was added in August 1875 when the separate suburban station to the north-west was added; this was extended, with a ridge-and-furrow roof, in 1895.

From 1 February 1858, King's Cross was also the terminus of Midland Railway services following the opening of the company's Bedford-to-Hitchin line. The MR was, however, ambitious for its own terminus in London and, following powers to construct a line south

from Bedford, a new station was erected to the west of the existing GNR terminus. The future St Pancras station was designed by William Henry Barlow (1812–1902) with the advice of Rowland Mason Ordish (1824–86) on the construction of the single-span train shed. The latter structure, constructed by the Butterley Iron Co of Derbyshire, had a length of 210m, a span of 74.3m and a maximum height of 32m. The station, completed in 1868, was constructed above an iron plate deck that was itself some 4.5m above street level. The space beneath the deck was used in part for the storage of beer from Burton-on-Trent, one of the MR's principal sources of freight traffic to London. For the station's facade, the MR held a competition, which was won by George (later Sir George) Gilbert Scott (1811–78). The Midland Hotel was formally opened on 5 May 1873, with work finally being completed three years later.

The hotel, despite its grandeur, had a relatively short life in that guise – considered outdated and closed in 1935, the building was converted into offices and became known as St Pancras Chambers. It is in this guise that the building is recorded here (at the southern end of the train shed). By the date of the photograph both the former hotel and Barlow's station were under considerable threat. However, campaigns led by figures such as John (later Sir John) Betjeman (1906–84) led to their retention and, in 1967, both were Grade I listed.

King's Cross station, also Grade I listed with the hotel Grade II listed, underwent modernisation in the 1970s, with the construction of a new concourse across Cubitt's facade. This was completed in 1972 as part of a project to improve interchange facilities with the new Victoria Underground line.

More than 50 years after the photograph was taken, the scene here is now radically different. The key buildings illustrated in 1964 remain – indeed have

undergone massive refurbishment (the former Midland Hotel has now been returned to its original purpose). However, the transfer of Eurostar services from Waterloo to St Pancras and the extension of the train shed to accommodate these and domestic services, as well as a £500-million project to renovate King's Cross (work that included the removal of the 1970s concourse), have transformed the location into an award-winning station and a superb point of entry for those arriving in Britain by train from France and beyond.

EAW143766

London Paddington
25 April 1950

When the Great Western Railway was first proposed in the early 1830s, it was planned that the new line would use the London & Birmingham Railway's new station at Euston via a junction at Kensal Green. However, the new company, authorised by an Act of Parliament of 31 August 1835, opted eventually to create its own terminus at Paddington. The first station, situated to the west of the future Bishop's Bridge Road bridge (on the site of the goods station in this view, taken from the south-east), opened with the line on 4 June 1838. This was only a temporary station as a grander edifice was planned.

The new Paddington station, designed by Isambard Kingdom Brunel (1806–59) and Matthew Digby Wyatt (1820–77), opened in two stages: the departure platforms on 16 January 1854 and the arrival platforms on 29 May 1854. The original station was completely closed on this latter date and became solely a goods depot. The new station had three train sheds – 21m, 31m and 21m in width with a length of 210m – that were linked by two transverse transepts. The view shows to good effect the facade of the Great Western Hotel (at the south-east of the station). This was constructed to a design of Philip Charles Hardwick (1822–92), son of the designer of the Euston Arch (see p 25), between 1851 and its opening on 9 June 1854. Originally, ownership of the hotel was by a private consortium; it was not formally taken over by the railway until 1896. The area between the hotel and the train shed – the Lawn – was originally left uncovered but a roof was subsequently added to create a concourse.

When constructed, the station was approached by double track; the section west to Westbourne Park was quadrupled on 30 October 1871 and the internal platform arrangements were modified in 1879 and again in 1885 to increase capacity. The fourth span,

on the north side of the station, was added as part of a further enlargement of the station completed in 1916; this had a span of 33m and was designed by the GWR's then chief engineer William Wylie Grierson (1863–1935). During the 1920s, Brunel's original roof was completely reconstructed, with steel columns – to the original design – replacing the earlier cast-iron ones. As traffic and the length of trains increased further, work was undertaken between 1930 and 1934 to extend platforms 2 to 11 beyond the Bishop's Bridge Road bridge. The station was further extended by the incorporation of the rebuilt Bishop's Road station at the same time; this added platforms 13 to 16 to the station. During World War II, the station suffered some damage but this had been repaired by the date of this photograph.

To the west of the Bishop's Bridge Road bridge, following the closure of the original GWR station, a goods depot was constructed in 1858. In 1906 new offices were constructed; these were sited on the west side of Bishop's Bridge Road. By the early 1920s, it was apparent that the existing facilities were inadequate and in 1925 the GWR decided to rebuild and enlarge the depot. This work was completed in the early 1930s. The depot was rationalised in 1969, when a number of sidings were taken out of service. Transferred to National Carriers in 1970, the depot remained rail served until it closed in December 1975. Empty for a decade, the building was finally demolished in March 1986 and the site has been subsequently redeveloped.

Today, Paddington station, now Grade I listed, and the hotel, Grade II listed, are still extant. For a period there was a threat to the fourth span, with Network Rail determined to replace it with an office block. Following pressure, however, this was rejected and this span – along with the earlier three – has now been fully

restored. The most significant alteration to the station has been the redesign of the Lawn; this was completed in 1999 to a design of Nicholas (later Sir Nicholas) Grimshaw (born 1939) and Partners.

EAW028804

London Victoria
14 March 1952

Viewed from the north, the scale of Victoria station is clearly demonstrated. It was originally two stations built alongside each other, that on the west belonging to the London, Brighton & South Coast Railway and that on the east to the London, Chatham & Dover Railway (plus the Great Western Railway, which operated trains into it until 1915 and owned it in part until 1932).

The origins of the station lay with the desire of the LBSCR and the East Kent Railway (as the LCDR was known until 1 August 1859), plus the GWR and the London & North Western Railway, to create a station on the north bank of the Thames, which would be more convenient for the West End than the existing termini on the south side of the river. The four railways jointly backed the Victoria Station & Pimlico Railway, which was authorised by an Act of Parliament of 23 July 1858 to extend the line from Stewarts Lane, over the river, to a new terminus to be constructed on the site of the disused Grosvenor Canal. However, while work was under way the partners fell out – largely as a result of the LBSCR's desire to take over the new line and station. A further agreement was required that saw the LBSCR permit the trains of its former partners within its station while an additional station, on the east side, was completed.

The first phase of the station opened on 1 October 1860. The LBSCR station was designed by Robert Jacomb-Hood (1822–1900), who had been the LBSCR's engineer since 1846. On the north-west corner of the new station was the Grosvenor Hotel; this was designed by James Thomas Knowles (1806–84) and was originally independent of the railway. The eastern half of the station – physically separate until after the Grouping in 1923 – opened on 25 August 1862, with GWR services being introduced the following year. Although the eastern half initially had a less prepossessing entrance

– constructed in wood on Wilton Street – it did provide the train shed roofs visible in this view, designed by John (later Sir John) Fowler (1817–98).

The LBSCR station underwent considerable modernisation in a project that commenced in 1898. While the original hotel was retained, the station itself was completely upgraded. In order to increase capacity – impossible to the east as a result of the LCDR station – the platforms were lengthened to stretch beyond the Elizabeth Bridge. Jacomb-Hood's original ridge-and-furrow roof was replaced and a new nine-storey facade was added to extend the hotel, which had been acquired by the railway in 1899, and to replace the original basic facade provided when the station opened in 1860. The architect for this new work was Charles (later Sir Charles) Langbridge Morgan (1855–1940), who had been appointed the LBSCR's chief engineer in 1896, with the work being completed in 1908.

In 1899 work started on the reconstruction of the facade of the eastern half of the station. The South Eastern & Chatham Railway (a joint committee formed from the LCDR and the Southern Eastern Railway that same year) employed Sir Alfred William Blomfield (1829–99) and William James Ancell (1852–1913) as architects to design its rebuilding. The resulting structure, which features carving by Henry Charles Fehr (1867–1940), is built in Portland stone in an elaborate neo-baroque style and was completed in 1908. In 1926 part of the forecourt was converted into a bus station. During the interwar years, the Southern Railway slightly amended Blomfield's facade, adding a rectangular pediment – with 'SOUTHERN RAILWAY' carved into it – over the massive segmental arch that acted as the station's entrance.

Although Victoria station was damaged during World War II, with a flying bomb causing damage on 27 June

1940 and an aircraft crashing onto the eastern part on 15 September 1940, the building was restored. Today, the bulk of the structure remains as illustrated in this 1952 view. The original Grosvenor Hotel is now Grade II* listed, with the remainder of the ex-SECR station Grade II listed. The only significant alteration to the basic structure has been the loss of the southern section of Morgan's roof, which was removed between 1981 and 1984 to permit the construction of the Victoria Plaza shopping centre.

EAW041939

London Waterloo
9 May 1946

Taken shortly after the end of World War II, this view of Waterloo station (seen from the south-west) shows to good effect the scale of the former London & South Western Railway terminus. When the London & Southampton Railway (later renamed the LSWR) first opened to London on 21 May 1838, its initial terminus was at Nine Elms. However, this was unsuitable for access to central London and in 1845 powers were obtained to extend the line to Waterloo Bridge, where a new station, designed by William (later Sir William) Tite (1798–1873), opened on 11 July 1848. This relatively modest station, called Waterloo Bridge, was designed as a through station because the LSWR planned to take the railway further towards the city. Through much of the 19th century the station grew in a fairly haphazard form. This included, in 1860, the platforms on the north side that served the Windsor lines and, five years later, the completion of a short link to connect to the South Eastern Railway's line from Charing Cross to London Bridge. The latter briefly carried a passenger service. This ceased in 1868, although the link itself was not removed until 1911 during the major rebuilding of the main station. The SER's Waterloo Junction station, with its four platforms, opened on 1 January 1869; it was renamed Waterloo on 7 July 1935 and Waterloo East on 2 May 1977.

The LSWR opened the Waterloo & City underground line on 8 August 1898, realising that it would not be able to extend its main surface line from Waterloo into central London. Powers were obtained in 1899 and 1900 for the massive expansion of the main Waterloo station into a significant terminus. The enlarged station required 2.5 hectares of land and involved the demolition of a significant number of dwellings and one church. Work started on the construction of the new station in 1903. The main station and its roof were designed by John Wykeham Jacomb-Hood (1858–1914), who was the LSWR's chief resident engineer from 1901 until his sudden death in March 1914. The work was completed by his successor, Alfred Weeks Szlumper (1858–1934), with the curved office block that forms the station's facade designed by James Robb Scott (1882–1965), the LSWR's chief architectural assistant and later chief architect to the Southern Railway. The new building, constructed in Portland stone in the so-called Imperial baroque style, included, as the main pedestrian entrance, the Victory Arch. This acts as the war memorial to the 585 employees of the LSWR killed during World War I and is now Grade II listed. The new station was formally opened by Queen Mary on 21 March 1922. During the long reconstruction of the station, the LSWR introduced electrified services to its suburban routes; the first service was that to Wimbledon via East Putney on 25 October 1915.

With the construction of the new signal box (commissioned on 18 October 1936), the top of which can be seen in the extreme foreground to the west of the station, this was how Waterloo was recorded in this view. Although the station had suffered some damage during World War II, this was relatively limited and by 1946 it had been repaired. The station remained largely unchanged until the late 1980s, when platforms 20 and 21 were taken out of use and demolished to enable construction of platforms for the new Eurostar services. The new Waterloo International, with its dramatic curved train shed designed by Nicholas (later Sir Nicholas) Grimshaw (born 1939) and Partners, opened on 14 November 1994. The new platforms also required the demolition of the 1930s signal box and the insertion of two new platform faces in place of the cab road at the centre of the station.

With the opening of St Pancras International, Waterloo International closed on 13 November 2007. For some time there was doubt as to the future use of these five platforms; however, it was eventually decided to incorporate them into the domestic station. The work, costing some £600 million, is expected to be completed by the end of 2018 and also sees the extension of platforms 1 to 8. Earlier work included the construction of a mezzanine floor over the existing concourse area in order to increase the number and range of retail outlets.

EAW000539

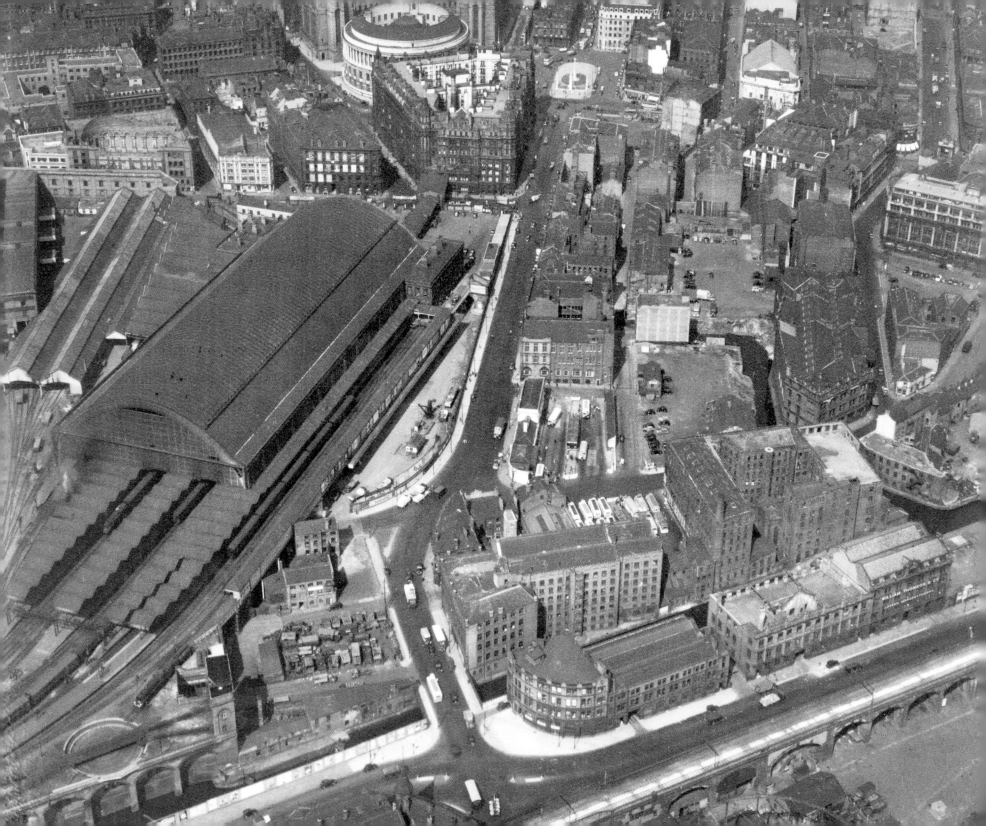

Manchester Central
19 May 1948

Taken in 1948, shortly after the nationalisation of the railways, this view portrays Manchester Central station seen from the south. The photograph illustrates to good effect the station's wrought-iron train shed; this had a length of 168m, a span of 64m and a maximum height of 27m and was supplied by the Derby-based iron founder Andrew Handysides & Co.

The genesis of Central station lay in 1865 with the creation of the Cheshire Lines Committee by the Great Northern Railway and the Manchester, Sheffield & Lincolnshire Railway in order to construct a number of lines in the Manchester-to-Liverpool corridor. The following year, the committee was joined by the Midland Railway. The CLC maintained an independent status – controlled by the London, Midland & Scottish Railway and the London & North Eastern Railway after 1923 – through to nationalisation in 1948. Historically, the three partners in the committee had been allowed access to the LNWR London Road (later Piccadilly) station (see p 37) but, with the growth of traffic and the opening of new routes, congestion arose. Thus on 27 June 1872 the CLC obtained powers to construct a short line from Throstle Nest Junction into central Manchester and to construct a new terminus. The new station was designed by John (later Sir John) Fowler (1817–98) of the MR and the project was engineered by Lewis Henry Moorsom (1835–1914), the CLC's resident engineer. Work on the station's construction started in 1875 and was undertaken by Robert Neill & Sons. The new station cost £124,778, with the building opening formally on 1 July 1880. Prior to its completion, a temporary station – known as Manchester Free Trade Hall – was in use from 9 September 1877; the site of this station was later used as Manchester Central goods yard and can be seen to the west of the main station in this view.

As well as accommodating services operated by the CLC, Central also operated as the Manchester terminus for MR services on the line across to Derby and southwards. The MR had also used London Road for these services, but it employed powers obtained in 1877 to construct a line from Throstle Nest Junction to Heaton Mersey to gain direct access to Central.

Initially, Central had a temporary wooden building to accommodate the ticket offices and waiting rooms. There were plans to construct a more permanent building but these were not progressed. When, in the late 19th century, the MR decided to construct the Midland Hotel, a new site – across from the station (and visible to the north of the station in this view) – was selected for this purpose. Construction of the Midland Hotel, designed by Charles Trubshaw (1840–1917) in the prevailing Edwardian baroque style, began in 1898 and the building opened on 5 September 1903. The hotel remains and is now Grade II* listed.

Although not specifically listed for closure under the Reshaping report of 1963, the rationalisation of the local network and the concentration of main line services at Piccadilly following the electrification of the West Coast Main Line rendered Central surplus. Passenger services were withdrawn on 5 May 1969; the goods yard had closed earlier – on 7 September 1964 – and was subsequently demolished and the site redeveloped. The train shed, however, survived, albeit in an increasingly derelict condition, in use initially as a car park. The building was purchased by Manchester City Council in 1978 and work started in 1982 to convert it to an exhibition hall. Listed as Grade II* the following year, the building finally reopened on 7 March 1986. Known initially as GMEX, it was renamed Manchester Central in 2007. Today the building continues to host exhibitions and concerts, while the former line south to Cornbrook Junction again plays host to railed vehicles – it has accommodated services operated by Manchester Metrolink since 1992.

EAW016003

Manchester Piccadilly
17 July 1972

When the Manchester & Birmingham Railway (authorised by an Act of Parliament of 30 June 1837) first opened to Manchester on 8 May 1842 it served a station, Store Street, on London Road. This small station – it possessed two platforms with offices – was shared by the Sheffield, Ashton-under-Lyne & Manchester Railway (authorised by an Act of Parliament of 5 May 1837) from the opening of its line to Woodhead on 8 August 1844. The station was renamed London Road in 1847. A third company – the Manchester, South Junction & Altrincham Railway (authorised by an Act of Parliament of 21 July 1845) – opened a station slightly to the south of the existing facility on 1 August 1849; this single platform ultimately formed the basis of the through platforms at Piccadilly.

As traffic increased, so the existing facilities at London Road became increasingly inadequate and relations between the two occupants of the station – by now the London & North Western Railway and the Manchester, Sheffield & Lincolnshire Railway – deteriorated. In 1862, it was decided to rebuild the station, with work being completed in 1866. The result was the construction of the first two – northernmost – spans of the train shed. The new station was designed by William Baker (1817–78) and Lewis Henry Moorsom (1835–1914) and the new train shed extended for 200m, with each span stretching for 29m. The MS&LR services operated from the northern section and the LNWR from the southern. The work also included each company constructing a goods shed to the north of the passenger station and the quadrupling of the approach tracks.

Two decades on and capacity was again an issue; this resulted in the construction of two new spans – each 21m wide – on the southern side, for use by LNWR services. This work was completed in 1883. As part of the same rebuilding, the MSJ&AR platform was replaced by the island platform and connected to the main station by a footbridge. This work was completed in May 1882.

This view, taken from the south-east in 1970, shows the effect of the rebuilding of Piccadilly station between 1958 and 1966 as a result of the electrification of the West Coast Main Line. The entire station was rebuilt, with the exception of the train sheds (although those built in the 1880s were slightly shortened at the concourse end), with the 10-storey office block completed in May 1966. The curved office block – Gateway House – that replaced the ex-LNWR goods shed opened in 1969. The station was renamed Piccadilly on 12 September 1960.

To the south of Piccadilly station can be seen Manchester Mayfield station. This was opened by the LNWR on 8 August 1910 to provide additional capacity for services to and from Manchester. The station, which was raised above street level as a result of the approach viaduct into Piccadilly, was linked to the main station by a footbridge and had five main platforms, four of which were sited under the ridge-and-furrow-style train shed, plus two short bays. The Modernisation Plan of 1955, which envisaged the electrification of the ex-LNWR route to 25kV, excluded Mayfield from the scheme and passenger services were withdrawn from the station on 23 August 1960. For a decade the station was allowed to decay but work to convert it into a parcels depot was undertaken in the late 1960s; this work included its reconnection to the main line, the modification of its platforms and the refurbishment of its roof. The station reopened on 6 July 1970 and so was relatively new when recorded in this 1972 view.

Since the date of the photograph, Manchester Piccadilly has undergone further modernisation. In 2002 Manchester hosted the Commonwealth Games and the station, with its now Grade II listed train sheds, was refurbished, with the 1960s concourse area replaced by a new structure designed by the Manchester-based BDP Ltd. This work was undertaken between 1998 and 2002. Other work has seen the introduction of Manchester Metrolink services at street level. These first served Piccadilly on 20 July 1992 and have been subsequently extended to Ashton-under-Lyne. Also Grade II listed is the facade of the ex-LNWR goods offices on London Road.

Mayfield has been less fortunate. Parcels traffic ceased in 1986 and two years later the track was removed. The station has lain unused, in an increasingly derelict condition, for some 30 years. In 2005 the main building suffered serious fire damage, although at the time of writing it remains extant, while in 2013 the bulk of the train shed was removed. The long-term future of the structure is in some doubt and there are no definitive plans for its redevelopment at the present time.

EAW234676

When the Newcastle & Carlisle Railway opened from Blaydon to Redheugh on 1 March 1837, its terminus was on the south bank of the River Tyne. However, with the development of the Newcastle & Berwick Railway, authorised by an Act of Parliament of 31 July 1845, as well as the existing Newcastle & North Shields Railway, opened from Carliol Square to North Shields on 19 June 1839 and taken over by the Newcastle & Berwick on 31 July 1845, there was pressure for the construction of a new central station on the north bank, with a link across the river via the High Level Bridge (a Grade I listed structure opened in late 1849). George Hudson (1800–71) was the driving force behind the Newcastle & Berwick; he saw it as part of his scheme for a line linking London with Edinburgh, under his control. As a result, his focus was on the construction of the main lines approaching Newcastle from north and south and it was left to the Newcastle & Carlisle Railway to be increasingly proactive in the plan for the construction of a central station.

In early 1846, John Dobson (1787–1865) was appointed architect. Thomas Elliot Harrison (1808–88) and Robert Stephenson (1803–59) are also cited as having an involvement in the design but, as detailed by Gordon Biddle (2011), Dobson regarded the work very much as his own. He was already involved in designing some of the redevelopment of central Newcastle envisaged by the entrepreneur Richard Grainger (1797–1861) and so was ideally placed to design the station in accordance with a broader plan for rebuilding the city centre. The new station as designed by Dobson was to sweep away much that remained of medieval Newcastle, leaving the castle extant – a structure that was to become a familiar feature in countless railway photographs over the years. Dobson's plans included the train shed, with its three 18.3m spans, with two through-platform roads allied to bays at both the east and west

ends and an impressive 182.9m neoclassical facade. The first contract for the work was let in August 1847 but the project was severely affected by the collapse of Hudson's empire two years later. After this collapse, the York, Newcastle & Berwick Railway – into which the Newcastle & Berwick had been merged with the York & Newcastle Railway in 9 July 1847 – reduced its funding for the station project. Although the train shed was substantially completed when the station opened, the facade was incomplete and Dobson had to modify the original design prior to its completion. It was left to Thomas Prosser (1817–88) to design the porte cochère, which was completed in 1863.

As a result of the growth in the number of services during the 1860s, the station layout was modified in 1871 to provide additional platform accommodation. This was achieved by sacrificing the carriage sidings that had been part of the original track layout under the train shed. By now the station was being run by the North Eastern Railway, into which the York, Newcastle & Berwick Railway had been merged. Further expansion occurred in the early 1890s, with the construction of two further train sheds, to the design of William Bell (1844–1919), the NER's then chief architect, on the south side of the existing station. This work was completed in 1904. Also in 1904, a further change came with the third-rail electrification of the suburban services from Central station.

This view, taken from the south, shows to good effect the five arches of the train shed. Since the date of the photograph, the track layout at the station has been simplified, particularly since the loss of the services towards Tynemouth as a result of the Tyne & Wear Metro and the closure of the original Newcastle & Carlisle route along the north bank of the river. However, Newcastle remains a hugely impressive station and one that has

benefited from considerable investment in recent years, resulting in improved facilities. This work has included the glazing in of the original porte cochère to create an enlarged concourse area.

EAC522512

Nottingham Victoria
June 1925

In 1893, the Manchester, Sheffield & Lincolnshire Railway, under the chairmanship of the ambitious Sir Edward William Watkin (1819–1901), obtained powers to construct the last great main line of the 19th century – the London extension via Nottingham, Leicester and Rugby. Nottingham was provided with a prestigious new station, designed by the local architect Albert Edward Lambert (1869–1929), who was also involved in the rebuilding of the Midland Railway's station in the town.

The new station was to be jointly operated by the Great Central and Great Northern railways via the Nottingham Joint Station Committee, a body instituted following the Great Central & Great Northern Railway Act of 1897. The two railways had separate booking offices at the station and, initially, could not agree on a name for the new station. The GCR – inevitably – favoured 'Central' whereas the GNR preferred to call it 'Joint'. The suffix 'Victoria' was a compromise suggested by the town clerk as the original proposed opening date coincided with the Queen's birthday.

The construction of the station was on a massive scale: it occupied some 5.25 hectares and required the demolition of some 1,300 houses as well as 24 pubs and one church. Situated in a cutting, with tunnels to both its north and south, some 460,000m³ of sandstone were excavated to permit completion of the work. Although services through the site commenced in 1899, it was not until 24 May 1900 that Nottingham Victoria station opened, without ceremony, when the GCR service from Manchester to Marylebone called at 1.12am.

The station was constructed in a Renaissance style in brick with Darley Dale stone detailing. The facade of the three-storey main buildings was dominated by a 30m clock tower that incorporated a weathervane. For passengers, there were effectively two large island platforms – one of 380m and the other of 390m in length. Each of these had two bay platforms at both the north and south ends, giving a total of 12 platform faces in all. To provide cover, a three-part glazed canopy extending for 140m was provided; the central span was 25.4m in width, with the two side spans each being 19.4m. Platform awnings, clearly visible in this 1925 view taken looking towards the south, were also provided.

By the date of the photograph, the original joint committee had ceased to function – it had become irrelevant following the Grouping of the railways in 1923, when both the GCR and GNR had become part of the London & North Eastern Railway. The ex-GCR main line, along with Nottingham Victoria station, passed to British Railways (Eastern Region) at nationalisation but was transferred to the London Midland Region in the late 1950s as part of BR's programme of rationalising regional boundaries. The ex-GCR main line was listed for closure in the *Reshaping* report of 1963 and the line ceased to carry through services on 5 September 1966. The section between Nottingham Victoria and Rugby Central retained passenger services thereafter but services were cut back in Nottingham from Victoria to a reopened Arkwright Street station on 4 September 1967, when Victoria closed completely. The remnant of the service to Rugby ceased on 5 May 1969.

Following closure, the bulk of Victoria station was demolished to permit the construction of the Victoria shopping centre. The clock tower, however, survived and was incorporated into the new building. This surviving fragment of the once grand station is now Grade II listed. To the north of the former station site, the south portal of the Mansfield Road Tunnel remains, albeit now gated, while the north portal of the Victoria Street Tunnel, to the south, also survives but is sited behind the shopping centre's car park.

EPW013017

Plymouth North Road
18 August 1962

When the South Devon Railway first opened its line through to Plymouth on 5 May 1848, it served a temporary station at Laira, to the east. The extension through to the railway's initial terminus followed on 2 April 1849. This terminus became known as Millbay from the late 1870s, following the opening of another station at North Road.

The impetus for the construction of North Road station came with the arrival of London & South Western Railway services from Lydford on 18 May 1876, via running powers over the Great Western Railway line from Lydford to Tavistock Junction. Initially LSWR services terminated at Plymouth's Mutley station, which had opened on 1 August 1871. On 28 March 1877 a new jointly controlled station at North Road opened and LSWR services were extended to terminate there. The station at North Road had two through platforms, with the station buildings constructed in wood.

The opening of the Plymouth, Devonport & South Western Junction Railway to passenger traffic on 1 June 1890 resulted in the LSWR gaining improved – and independent – access to North Road, this time from the west. This was, however, to be the LSWR's terminus for a relatively short period as, on 1 July 1891, the railway opened its own station – Friary – to the south-east. The increase in traffic led to the expansion of North Road station, with additional platforms being completed in 1908.

In 1938 work started on the rebuilding of the station; this included the rebuilding of one of the station's signal boxes and the relocation of a second. However, little progress was made on the rebuilding scheme before World War II caused its postponement. One consequence of the work in expanding North Road was the closure of Mutley station, to the east, on 3 July 1939 in order to permit the realignment of the approach tracks. The enforced closure of Millbay on 23 April 1941 (as a result of enemy action) resulted in more traffic being concentrated on North Road, but it was not until 1956 that work on the rebuilding of the station restarted.

With its proximity to the naval dockyard at Devonport, it was inevitable that Plymouth would be a major target for the Luftwaffe during World War II and in 1943 the architect Leslie Patrick (later Sir Patrick) Abercrombie (1879–1957) and James Paton Watson (c 1898–1979), the Plymouth city engineer and surveyor, published *A Plan for Plymouth*. This blueprint anticipated the wholesale redevelopment of the central area and one of the features of this plan was the construction of a new office block – now known as Intercity House – which was officially opened by the then chairman of the British Railways Board, Dr Richard (later Lord) Beeching (1913–85). North Road became the main passenger station serving Plymouth after the closure of Friary station on 15 September 1958. On that date the suffix 'North Road' was dropped. Two years later the station was completely resignalled with a new panel box replacing those dating from the 1930s; the new box, in service from 26 November 1960, was built at the west end of platform 1.

More than 50 years after the date of the photograph, taken from the north-east, much of the station as rebuilt in the late 1950s remains. The number of through platforms has, however, been reduced to five through the creation in 1974 of two bay platforms on the west and two dock roads on the east (for parcels and mail traffic until this ceased in 2003) by the extension of the concourse area across to link up with platform 4. The panel box built in 1960 is also still operational. The major change since 1962 has been the construction of a multistorey car park to serve the station.

EAW107232

Sheffield Midland
6 September 1963

Initially the Midland Railway served Sheffield with a branch line from Rotherham; however, in the early 1860s plans were drawn up to connect Chesterfield with Sheffield via Sheepbridge and Heeley. The 21.5km route was authorised by an Act of Parliament of 25 July 1864, with construction work commencing the following year. The work included the construction of a new station in Sheffield to replace the MR's original station – Wicker. The new station was located on Pond Street and opened with the line on 1 February 1870.

The station was designed by the MR's architect, John Holloway Sanders (1825–84). The two-storey structure was in an Italianate style and the station also included a twin-arched train shed. Sanders' building is now found between platforms 2 and 5 as a result of an enlargement project completed in 1905. This project included the construction of a new frontage and the provision of two extra platforms on the west side of the station; this is the building that is visible in the foreground of this 1963 photograph, taken from the west. The work was designed by the then chief architect of the MR, Charles Trubshaw (1840–1917), and included a spectacular porte cochère with ridge-and-furrow roofing. Similar ridge-and-furrow platform canopies

were also provided for the two new platforms completed at the same time. Two footbridges were provided, the bridge to the south for railwaymen and parcels and that to the north for passengers.

The original 1870 train shed roof suffered damage during World War II and was not repaired; it was dismantled during the second half of 1956 and replaced with the awnings visible in the view taken seven years later. Two years after the date of the photograph, British Rail constructed a modern office block – Sheaf House – close to the station to accommodate the headquarters of its Sheffield Division. This was demolished in 2006 as part of the project to upgrade the immediate vicinity of the station.

Sheffield station – the suffix 'Midland' was dropped after the closure of the ex-Great Central Railway Victoria station on 5 January 1970 – is now Grade II listed. It has recently undergone a major upgrade as part of the 'Gateway to Sheffield' project. This has included the conversion of the former porte cochère into a larger concourse, along with the restoration of much of the actual structure.

EAW119937

Southampton Terminus
17 May 1964

The London & Southampton Railway was authorised by an Act of Parliament of 25 July 1834 to construct a line from the coast to the capital. This was partly a response to concerns raised during the Napoleonic Wars about the vulnerability of shipping in the Channel, as well as the inadequacy of transport links to ports further west. The line's first engineer was Francis Giles (1787–1847) but progress was limited until his replacement by Joseph Locke (1805–60) and a further Act (of 30 June 1837) that permitted the railway to increase its funding. The first section of line – from Nine Elms (London) to Woking – opened on 21 May 1838. The sections from Woking to Basingstoke and from Winchester to Northam Road (Southampton) opened on 10 June 1839. By then the company's name had been changed to the London & South Western Railway, following authorisation of the branch to Portsmouth by an Act of Parliament of 4 June 1839. The final sections – from Winchester to Basingstoke and from Northam Road to the new terminus at Southampton – opened on 11 June 1840.

At Southampton the LSWR constructed a station designed by William (later Sir William) Tite (1798–1873). This was originally known simply as 'Southampton' but was renamed Southampton Docks in July 1858 and Southampton Town & Docks in September 1896. It was to become Southampton Terminus on 9 July 1923. The station had two platforms but the layout was modified during the 1860s and again in 1876. Alongside the station, a new hotel – initially called the Imperial but later the South Western after its purchase by the railway in 1882 – was constructed to a design by John Norton (1823–1904) and opened in 1867.

This view of the station and hotel complex, from the south-west, shows to good effect the original Tite building of 1840 and the scale of the later hotel on the corner. The final significant modification to the station came in the 1920s: in 1924 a number of the station's platforms were slightly cut back to permit the construction of a private road between the hotel and station and, in 1927, the concourse between the station and hotel was provided with a ridge-and-furrow canopy. However, the importance of Terminus to the LSWR started to decline with the opening of Southampton West (later Southampton Central) on 1 November 1895. Although Terminus was used by Great Western Railway services over the Didcot, Newbury & Southampton line from 1905, the main line services increasingly used West, particularly after that station was enlarged in the mid-1930s.

The demise of Terminus came with the electrification of the main line to Bournemouth. The station was not scheduled for closure in the *Reshaping* report of 1963 but was not included in the planned electrification of the route. Passenger and parcel services ceased on 5 September 1966, although mail traffic continued to be handled until December 1967, when the work was transferred to Central station. Work on removing the track commenced in 1968 and was completed in 1970, when the signal box was also demolished. The redundant platforms were subsequently infilled and the site used as a car park.

Although long closed as a station, Tite's three-storey Italianate main building, with its five-arch colonnade, remains, as does the two-storey extension to the north; this building is now listed Grade II* and is in use as a casino. The ridge-and-furrow overall roof covering the concourse also remains and provides cover over part of the surviving car park. North of the car park, the trackbed towards the surviving line into the port has been redeveloped as housing. The hotel, which was requisitioned by the military during World War II (and named HMS *Shrapnel*), was renamed South Western House and converted to offices after the war. It is now Grade II listed. To the east of the surviving line, the large goods shed, which was completed in 1891, also survives. In use as a car park, this structure is Grade II listed.

EAW128480

York
July 1921

Viewed from the south, the scale of the station at York at the junction of the lines towards Durham and Scarborough is evident. The railway first arrived at the city on 29 May 1839, courtesy of the York & North Midland Railway (authorised by an Act of Parliament of 21 June 1836). The first station, located outside the city walls, was a temporary structure, which closed when the first permanent station opened on 4 January 1841.

This new station, the train shed of which can be seen on the extreme right of the photograph, was designed by George Townsend Andrews (1804–55). The building was originally two-storey, constructed in stone in an Italianate style; a third storey was added in 1850. Andrews also designed the original station hotel, completed in 1853. In order to gain access to the station, the railway was permitted to construct an arch (and later a second) through the city walls, provided that the design for any such arch was approved by the corporation. The neo-Tudor arches were again designed by Andrews. The original station was shared with the Great North of England Railway; this had been authorised by two Acts of Parliament, of 4 July 1836 and 12 July 1837, to construct a line from York to Newcastle. Passenger services commenced on 4 January 1841 and required reversal into and out of the joint station in York. This position was further complicated by the opening of the York & North Midland line to Scarborough on 7 July 1845, which had been authorised the previous year.

By the 1870s, the operation of the original station was causing problems and the North Eastern Railway, as successor to both the York & North Midland and Great North of England railways, decided to construct a new station. This was designed initially by Thomas Prosser (1817–88) and Thomas Elliot Harrison (1808–88) and then by Prosser's successor Benjamin Burleigh (1820–76). The work was completed by William Peachey (1826–1912), who (briefly) succeeded Burleigh as the NER's architect in 1876, before being forced to resign the following year. The new station, with its 13 platforms, opened on 25 June 1877 and was, at the time, the largest station in the world. The structure included the three curved train sheds seen in the centre-left of this photograph: the longest was 242.3m in length with a maximum height of 14.6m; the central one had a span of 24.7m, with each of the outer ones being 16.8m. Additional sheds were provided over the bay platforms at both the north and south ends of the station. A 14th platform, constructed on the west of the station, outside the train shed, was added in 1900. The final expansion of the station – an island platform beyond the 1900 platform – post-dates this photograph, being completed in 1939. The old station remained in use thereafter as siding accommodation, with part used after 1927 as the London & North Eastern Railway's museum.

In addition to completing work on the new station, Prosser and Peachey also designed the Royal Station hotel, which opened on 20 May 1878 and included 100 bedrooms. The hotel was extended, by the addition of a west wing, in 1896. It was privatised in 1983 and, after passing through several hands, is now known as The Principal York. The Grade II listed building underwent major refurbishment in a project completed in 2016.

York, as a major railway centre, was an inevitable target for the Luftwaffe during World War II and suffered particularly during the Baedeker Blitz of April and May 1942. The station was badly damaged on 29 April 1942 when the locomotive and stock forming an Anglo-Scottish service were destroyed in the station, with damage also to the fabric of the train shed. The station was repaired in 1947.

York station is today Grade II* listed, as are the remains of the 1841 station. Although the bulk of the original 1841 iron train shed (visible on the extreme right of this 1921 photograph) has disappeared, a fragment survived and was relocated as part of a recent redevelopment of the old station site. Other railway structures close to the 1841 station that are also listed include a pair of houses – now converted into offices and known as Toft Street Chambers – designed by Andrews for railway officers and completed in the mid-1840s; these are Grade II listed. The massive offices designed as the NER's headquarters by William Bell (1844–1919) and completed in 1906 are Grade II* listed, while the National Railway Museum, slightly further away, now also occupies the Grade II listed ex-goods shed designed by Burleigh and completed in 1877.

EPW006634

Ashburton
July 1930

Promoted by the Buckfastleigh, Totnes & South Devon Railway and authorised by Acts of Parliament of 25 June 1864 (the line to Buckfastleigh) and 26 May 1865 (the extension to Ashburton), the broad gauge, 16km branch from Totnes to Ashburton in Devon was eventually opened on 1 May 1872. The small terminus at Ashburton had a station building and train shed, goods shed and engine shed, all of which are clearly visible in this view, taken from the south in 1930. The line was worked by the South Devon Railway but operation passed to the Great Western Railway on 1 January 1876 and the railway's independent existence ceased when it was purchased by the Great Western Railway on 1 July 1897. Five years earlier, over the weekend of 20 to 23 May 1892, the branch was converted to standard gauge.

By the date of the photograph, the branch's fortunes were in decline – the rise of the motor car and bus, along with a decline in the area's traditional industries, had seen a steady and inexorable decline in the level of passenger traffic. Annual ticket sales at Ashburton fell some 80 per cent in thirty years, from 24,688 in 1903 to only 4,843 in 1933. Freight traffic remained reasonably buoyant, however, and the line survived through the early years of nationalisation. The economics of the 1950s saw the line under threat and passenger services ceased on 3 November 1958. The small locomotive shed was closed by British Railways on the same date. Freight traffic continued until facilities were withdrawn on 10 September 1962.

This was not the end of the story. The first stirrings of standard gauge railway preservation had appeared and a group of businessmen came together to form the Dart Valley Railway Ltd, to reopen the line. Although the first rolling stock arrived on 2 October 1962, it was not until 5 April 1969 that the first services operated. The primary problem was in obtaining a Light Railway Order from the Ministry of Transport as the trackbed between Ashburton and Buckfastleigh had been identified for use in the modernisation of the A38. Pending a final decision on the road project, operation to Ashburton was permitted, but this ceased – and the station was closed for a second time – on 2 October 1971. Since that date, the preserved section from Buckfastleigh to Totnes (see p 189), now operated by the South Devon Railway, has prospered.

Today, all the main railway buildings – station with train shed, engine shed and goods shed – remain and are used for various commercial activities. However, the only building to be listed – at Grade II – is the goods shed. The long-term future of the site is subject to some doubt. In 2015 plans were put forward for the redevelopment of the station and the remaining section of the trackbed as part of the Chuley Road Masterplan. These plans were, however, the subject of a successful legal challenge by the Friends of Ashburton Station, with the support of the South Devon Railway Trust. These organisations are now campaigning for the restoration of the heritage line to the town – in a project estimated to cost £20 million – while the planning authorities, having withdrawn the proposals, will continue to consider planning applications for the area on a case-by-case basis.

EPW033030

Banbury

28 May 1924

Viewed from the north, this shows the Great Western Railway station in the town shortly after the Grouping of the railways in 1923. The former London & North Western Railway station – Merton Street – was located slightly to the east of the scene illustrated here, to the south of the GWR station. Merton Street was the first passenger station to serve the town: the branch from Buckingham – courtesy of the Buckinghamshire Railway – opened on 1 May 1850.

Authorised by an Act of Parliament of 3 August 1846, the Birmingham & Oxford Junction Railway was the target for takeover by both the LNWR and GWR. By the time the line opened – as a mixed gauge route – from Oxford to Banbury on 2 September 1850 it was the latter that had absorbed the Birmingham & Oxford (following an agreement of 12 November 1846). The line from Oxford was initially single track and broad gauge; it was converted to mixed gauge and doubled with the completion of the line northwards. The line from Banbury to Birmingham opened on 1 October 1852. While the majority of services were initially broad gauge, this was not to last and the broad gauge north of Oxford was abolished on 1 April 1869. The importance of the station grew with the authorisation of the Banbury & Cheltenham Railway on 21 July 1873. This headed west at King's Sutton, just south of the town, and opened from Chipping Norton to King's Sutton on 6 April 1887. The original station possessed an overall roof – as shown here.

The early 20th century witnessed a considerable increase in the size of the station, with a new through platform and bays being constructed. This was due to the completion of the link through to the Great Central Railway's London Extension at Woodford Halse: the Woodford Halse line opened to freight traffic on 13 August 1900 and to passenger traffic on 13 August

1901. The expansion work also included the construction of new signal boxes: North, visible in the foreground of this view, in 1900, and South, beyond the station, eight years later. Improved connections to London were gained in 1910 with the opening of the GWR's Bicester cut-off route. To the north of the station, work was undertaken on a new yard – opened in 1931 – to deal with the marshalling of freight traffic between the London & North Eastern Railway and the GWR.

In 1937 work was authorised on the reconstruction of the station building. However, this was deferred in 1940 and it was not until 1958 that the station that exists today was completed. As part of the station rebuilding, a new down-relief through platform was added on the west side of the station. This resulted in a line passing to the west of the North box (and a minor diversion of the River Cherwell at this point to accommodate it). The station – which had been given the suffix 'Bridge Street' to differentiate it from the LNWR station – was retitled 'Banbury General' between 1948 and 1961. It became simply Banbury following the closure of Merton Street on 2 January 1961. The closure of the routes to Cheltenham – on 4 June 1951 – and to Woodford Halse – on 5 September 1966 – resulted in its reverting to a station serving the routes from Birmingham to London via Bicester and via Oxford.

The 1958 station remains today; however, the two signal boxes were closed as a result of a resignalling project in 2016 and subsequently demolished. The site of the former engine shed (to the south) is, at the time of writing, being redeveloped as a new maintenance depot for Chiltern Railways.

EPW010473

Bank Hall
July 1936

Viewed from the south, this is Bank Hall station in the Kirkdale district of Liverpool. Immediately to the station's west is the Bankhall Works of British Ropes Ltd. British Ropes Ltd was established on 6 June 1924 by the merger of older companies; the Globe Works, Bankhall, of W B Brown, was one of a further nine companies absorbed during 1925 and 1926 that further expanded the business.

The origins of Bank Hall station lay with the Liverpool, Crosby & Southport Railway, which had been authorised by an Act of Parliament of 2 July 1847 to construct a 29.5km line linking Liverpool with Southport. By this date Southport had become a popular place for the businessmen of Liverpool to live and its beaches attracted day trippers from the city. The line, initially single track (but on a double-track formation), opened from Waterloo station (Merseyside) to Southport on 24 July 1848. The line opened south from Waterloo to serve the new station at Liverpool Exchange (*see* p 19) on 1 October 1850, but it was not until 1 July 1870 that the intermediate station at Bank Hall opened. The line was extended in Southport from the original terminus at Eastbank Street to Chapel Street on 22 August 1851. Such was the traffic, particularly on the section between Liverpool and Crosby, that plans for the line's doubling were produced in 1851, with work being completed during the summer of the following year. Ownership of the line passed to the Lancashire & Yorkshire Railway on 14 June 1855. The possibility of purchase by this larger railway, either on its own or in conjunction with the East Lancashire Railway, had been under consideration previously, but agreement over the terms of the purchase could not be reached.

By the end of the 19th century, the L&YR faced increased competition as a result of tramway development in Liverpool. In order to counter the threat posed by this new form of transport, the L&YR decided in 1902 to undertake the electrification of the Liverpool Exchange-to-Southport route using 600V DC with a live third rail. Work commenced on the project on 8 March 1903 and the first test train ran from Crossens to Liverpool on 6 March 1904; the full service commenced on 13 May 1904.

The Liverpool-to-Southport line initially passed to the London & North Western Railway following its amalgamation with the L&YR on 1 January 1922 and thus to the London, Midland & Scottish Railway at Grouping. The *Reshaping* report of March 1963 envisaged the rationalisation of the local railway network and the closure of Liverpool Central station. At this stage, there was no immediate threat to Exchange station but service reductions and the decision to construct the Merseyrail network, into which the Exchange-to-Southport service was to be integrated, resulted in the gradual running down of Exchange and its eventual closure on 30 April 1977. From the following Monday – 2 May – Southport services were diverted to serve the new Moorfields station and the underground line through to the low-level station at Liverpool Central.

Passenger services continue to serve Bank Hall on the Merseyrail service towards Southport. Only the easternmost island platform is still in use, however, and the platform facilities have been reduced to a simple shelter. The westernmost island platform remains, but is derelict and overgrown as the once four-track line has been reduced to two tracks only. The brick-built, road-level – unlisted – ticket office on the A1056 Bankhall Road is also still in use.

EPW051325

Berkhamsted
22 April 1953

Viewed from the south-west, with the ruins of the 11th-century castle in the background, Berkhamsted station is on the West Coast Main Line in Hertfordshire. In early years, the station was also known as Berkhampstead and Berkhamstead.

The origins of the station lay with the London & Birmingham Railway, which was authorised by an Act of Parliament of 6 May 1833 to construct the line from Camden, in London, to Birmingham. (The Euston extension was authorised by an Act of 3 July 1835.) The proposed line had not been without its opponents; there had been a number of meetings – including one held in Berkhamsted – to express opposition and a bill proposing construction of the line in 1832 had been rejected. The line's engineer was Robert Stephenson (1803–59) and work started on the line's construction in November 1833. One of the centres of railway construction was Berkhamsted – the number of navvies employed on the line led to overcrowding in the town and complaints about behaviour.

The line opened between Euston and Boxmoor (Hemel Hempstead) on 20 July 1837. Although trains now passed through Berkhamsted, it was not until the following year that the first station to serve the town opened. Further sections of the line opened over the next 12 months, including Boxmoor to Tring on 16 October 1837 and Curzon Street (Birmingham) to Rugby and Tring to Denbigh Hall (Bletchley) on 9 April 1838. (In order to capitalise on the potential traffic for Queen Victoria's coronation, the London & Birmingham Railway operated a coach service from Rugby to Denbigh Hall.) The line was opened throughout on 17 September 1838. The London & Birmingham merged with the Grand Junction and Manchester & Liverpool railways on 16 July 1846 to form the London & North Western Railway.

With the quadrupling of the main line through Hertfordshire, a new station at Berkhamsted was constructed in 1875, some 100m north-west of the original station. The old station closed the same year. The new station had four platforms and a brick-and-slate, two-storey main building. The railway passes through Berkhamsted at this point on a low embankment and access to the platforms was through the main building's first floor. The symmetrical facade of the building also included a three-bay canopy over the main entrance.

Today the unlisted main station building is still intact and remains in use; part of the building is now occupied by a fish-and-chip shop. All four platforms are also still extant (although stopping services generally use the slow lines only) and platform buildings, with canopies from the 1875 rebuilding, remain. The small goods yard, visible to the north in the 1953 view, is no more. Freight facilities were withdrawn on 6 February 1967 and the site is now used as the station car park. The former London & North Western Railway signal box, visible to the south of the middle platforms, has been demolished and the main lines through the station are now equipped with 25kV catenary; electric services over the section between Rugby and Euston were introduced on 6 November 1965. Access to the platforms, particularly for passengers with disabilities, was improved through the installation of lifts; these were opened on 13 March 2015.

EAW048761

Beverley
10 September 1948

Pictured from the south-west shortly after it celebrated its centenary, the extensive facilities provided at Beverley station are clearly illustrated in this view. Surveyed by William Bayley Bray (1812–85) in 1844, the Bridlington branch of the Hill & Selby Railway was authorised by an Act of Parliament of 23 June 1845. (Bray emigrated to New Zealand in 1851, where he was involved with a number of projects, including railway construction.) Although the 50km line was constructed on behalf of the Hull & Selby, the York & North Midland Railway took over operation of the main line on 1 July 1845 and formally leased the line from 27 July 1846. The Hull & Selby, however, retained its notional independence until being formally purchased by the North Eastern Railway on 1 March 1872.

Construction of the line was relatively straightforward as the land through which it ran was level. The main contractors were Thomas Jackson (1808–85) and Alfred William Bean (c 1825–90) and the line opened on 6 October 1846. At the same time, the section of line between Seamer and Filey also opened. The opening of the section from Filey to Bridlington on 20 October 1847 provided a through route from Hull to Scarborough.

For the stations along the route, George Townsend Andrews (1804–55) was employed. He designed a range of stations in brick with stone detailing; of these, the most significant on the southern section of the route were those at Beverley, Bridlington and Driffield. The station at Beverley had an 18m double-span train shed with cast-iron central columns to provide support. This was replaced in 1908 by the single-span train shed visible in this 1948 view.

Beverley station's importance grew on 1 May 1865 with the opening of the line to Market Weighton. Completion of this route provided Hull with a more direct connection through to York. The junction for the route was slightly to the north of Beverley station. This line was scheduled for closure in the *Reshaping* report of 1963 and passenger services ceased on 29 November 1965. Although the Hull-to-Scarborough line was not one of the threatened lines in March 1963, one of the consequences of other closures was that its economics deteriorated, and by 1966 its future was under discussion. However, the 1968 Transport Act, which permitted the subsidy of loss-making lines deemed to fulfil a useful social need, resulted in its retention, although a number of intermediate stations were closed and certain sections singled.

Beverley station, Grade II listed since 1985, remains substantially as rebuilt in 1908 and retains its overall train shed. Also remaining are the NER cast-iron footbridge, which can be seen immediately to the south of the train shed, and the Grade II listed signal box, which dates to 1911. The level crossing adjacent to the box has, however, disappeared, to be replaced by a road bridge. With the withdrawal of freight facilities, the track layout has been rationalised to plain double track and the trackside buildings north and south of the station, including the goods shed, have been demolished, as has the engineering works of the Armstrong's Patents Co Ltd in the foreground. Much of the latter has been redeveloped for housing, while the station forecourt and the area immediately to the north, on both sides of the line, now provide an extensive car park for station users.

EAW018619

With the River Mersey and the ferry terminal providing a backdrop in this view from the west, Birkenhead Woodside was the terminus of the Birkenhead Railway. The station, with its twin train shed and five platforms, opened on 31 March 1878 to replace an earlier station – Birkenhead Monks Ferry – that dated to 23 October 1844.

The Chester & Birkenhead Railway was authorised by an Act of Parliament of 12 July 1837 to construct a 23.5km line from Chester to Birkenhead. The line opened to Birkenhead Grange Lane on 23 December 1840 and to Monks Ferry four years later. The Chester & Birkenhead merged with the Birkenhead, Lancashire & Cheshire Junction Railway following an Act of Parliament of 22 July 1847. The unified company was retitled the Birkenhead Railway on 1 August 1859, shortly before ownership passed jointly to the Great Western Railway and the London & North Western Railway on 1 January 1860. The impetus for the construction of the new terminus was the need to enhance the inadequate facilities that Monks Ferry offered. Monks Ferry survived as a goods station until March 1961.

The new Woodside station, believed to have been designed by Robert Edward Johnston (c 1839–1913), was at the north end of a short tunnel under Chester Street, constructed using the cut-and-cover method. It was designed to serve the adjacent Mersey ferry terminal, although the development of Birkenhead's tram network from 1860 – the town was the first place in England to possess a street tramway (promoted by the American George Francis Train [1829-1904]) – and the lack of cooperation from the ferry owners meant that this facility was not exploited to its maximum extent. Thus, while in theory the main booking hall, with porte cochère, faced the dry docks to the south of the station, in reality the rear entrance was used primarily as the booking hall until closure, with the result that the station was known as being 'the wrong way round'. The splendour of the booking hall, with its timber roof trusses and sandstone fireplaces, has been described by David Atwell as 'of truly baronial proportions' (Binney and Pearce 1979).

As a joint station, Birkenhead Woodside passed to the control of the GWR and the London, Midland & Scottish Railway at Grouping in 1923. At nationalisation, and following the redrafting of the regional boundaries, it passed to British Railways (London Midland Region). Through the 1950s the station continued to see heavy usage for local services as well as expresses through to London Paddington and to the Southern Region. Its swansong came during the period when services were disrupted as a result of electrification work on the West Coast Main Line; even in early 1967 there were still six through services to Paddington each weekday. Closure of the station had been foreshadowed by the *Reshaping* Report of March 1963: Dr Richard Beeching advocated the closure of Woodside, along with Liverpool Exchange and the high-level platforms at Liverpool Central. Following the removal of the through London services in March 1967, only local services to Chester and Helsby remained. These were cut back to Rock Ferry, and Woodside closed on 5 November 1967.

The building was demolished two years later. The site of the station now forms a bus interchange and car park, although the tunnel remains under Chester Street. The dry docks have also disappeared, with the sites redeveloped. Where ships were once repaired, there is now the Land Registry. From the ferry terminal, the Birkenhead Tramway now provides a service through to the Wirral Transport Museum using a number of preserved Merseyside electric trams.

EAW000412

Blenheim & Woodstock
May 1929

Backed financially by the 8th Duke of Marlborough (1844–92), the Woodstock Railway was authorised on 25 September 1886 to construct a branch line, just over 3km in length, from a junction just north of Kidlington, on the Great Western Railway's Oxford-to-Banbury line, to the town of Woodstock. Prior to the line's opening, agreement was reached with the GWR for the larger company to operate the line. Passenger services from the junction to Blenheim & Woodstock were introduced on 19 May 1890 and on 4 August of the same year the GWR obtained powers to extend the branch about 2km southwards from the original junction through to Kidlington, parallel to the main line; the same Act of Parliament formally authorised the GWR to operate the branch. The Woodstock Railway retained its nominal independence until it was formally absorbed by the GWR following an Act of Parliament of 6 August 1887.

The station at Woodstock, as illustrated in this 1929 view taken from the north-west, was a relatively small affair, typical of many rural branch line termini. It had a single platform, main building and small goods shed. Despite it size, the station played host to many notable visitors who were making their way to the Duke of Marlborough's home at Blenheim Palace. These included Winston Churchill and Kaiser Wilhelm II. For the routine passenger, however, the service was relatively limited. In 1910, there were eight return services per day, one of which was a single-class railmotor, with trains allowed eight minutes for the 6.25km journey from Kidlington. By the summer of 1939 the service was nine trains per day, of which three operated to and from Oxford. A halt – at Shipston-on-Cherwell – had been added in 1929.

After World War II and nationalisation, when the branch passed to British Railways (Western Region), the service was reduced to six trains per day in 1952, often with poor connecting times at Kidlington. In September 1953 BR announced its intention to close the line, citing a decline in passengers from 17,500 per annum in 1947 to fewer than 9,000 five years later. Despite strong opposition, approval to close the line was given and notices went up in early 1954 to the effect that the line was to close on 1 March 1954. As there was no Sunday service, the last passenger trains operated on 27 February 1954. With freight facilities withdrawn on the same date, the last train to run over the line was a two-coach service hauled by Class 14XX No 1420. Following closure, the line was eventually lifted, with the last track recovered on 26 January 1958.

The station building at Woodstock survived in commercial use, initially as a garage, although much of the station site was redeveloped. More recently, the main building was under threat of demolition as plans were announced for a housing development. While efforts to get the station listed came to nought, West Oxfordshire District Council rejected the application to demolish the structure as: 'The former station building makes a positive contribution to the character and appearance of the Woodstock Conservation Area.' The building survives intact, now converted into small offices.

The station at Woodstock has one further claim to fame: in 1952 it was used in the classic Ealing comedy *The Titfield Thunderbolt* as the location for the scenes where the supposed '14XX' locomotive breaks through the station gates and runs out into the street under the control of an inebriated Stanley Holloway and Hugh Griffith.

EPW026925

Bletchley
26 April 1938

When the London & Birmingham Railway (authorised by an Act of Parliament of 6 May 1833) opened from Tring to a temporary terminus at Denbigh Hall (to the north of Bletchley) on 9 April 1838, there was no station at Bletchley itself. It was not until the completion of the branch eastwards to Bedford that the first station serving the town opened on 17 November 1846. The line west, towards Buckingham, followed on 1 May 1850. The east–west line eventually formed part of the London & North Western Railway line linking Oxford and Cambridge.

The original station was substantially rebuilt in 1858, with a new main building designed by John William Livock (1814–83) in a neo-Jacobean style with a five-bay stone portico. It is this building that dominates the foreground in this view, taken shortly before the outbreak of World War II, looking towards the east. In 1859 a third running line – for freight traffic – was added, but it was not until 1876 that the lines south from Bletchley were finally quadrupled; the four-track section was eventually extended northwards to Roade. Initially the slow lines were used for freight only but passenger services were operated over them from 1882. The platform accommodation at the station was modified in 1881, at which date the footbridge shown here was completed in place of the earlier subway. Later in the decade a building was constructed at right angles to the main station building; this was occupied by the General Post Office.

Immediately to the north of the station, on the Down side, was the locomotive shed. The original wooden structure dated to 1851 but had been blown down in 1872. A new, brick, six-road shed opened the following year and it is this structure that is illustrated here. The building was reroofed in 1954 and closed on 15 July 1965. The shed was subsequently demolished and the site is now used as the station car park.

In 1957 gale-force winds so seriously damaged the canopies on platforms 5 to 8 that they had to be dismantled; this was to foreshadow a much more radical redevelopment of the station in connection with the electrification of the West Coast Main Line. Work commenced in July 1963, with the work including the construction of a new footbridge and the demolition of Livock's main station building. The new station building was completed in the spring of 1966, shortly after the launch of the new electric services from Euston to Rugby via Weedon on 6 November 1965 and those via the Northampton loop on 22 November 1965. The Oxford-to-Cambridge line was one of those scheduled to receive a modified service under the *Reshaping* report of 1963, with most intermediate stations due to be closed. In the event, passenger services to Oxford ceased on 1 January 1968 but those east as far as Bedford St Johns were reprieved.

As part of the Modernisation Plan, a new flyover was constructed immediately to the south of the station. This connected the slow lines at Denbigh Hall Junction and the line from Bedford with the route to Oxford, thus permitting freight traffic to traverse these routes without having to cross the main lines through Bletchley. This was completed in late 1961, some two years late, and was a white elephant almost from opening as the associated Swanbourne marshalling yard closed in March 1967.

Bletchley remains an important intermediate station on the West Coast Main Line and a junction for the branch to Bedford. It retains platforms on both the main and slow lines, as well as those that serve the route to Bedford (now numbered 5 and 6). Of the buildings illustrated in the 1938 view, only two remain: the stationmaster's house (a two-storey brick-and-slate dwelling located to the south-west of the main station)

and the old goods shed visible to the north-east of the Bedford line platforms. The flyover also survives, having been out of use for some years, and is to be integrated into the proposed new service from Oxford to Milton Keynes over the reopened route from Bicester to Bletchley. There are plans, eventually, for the restoration of the full link between Oxford and Cambridge.

EPW056947

Blisworth

12 June 1950

The London & Birmingham Railway, authorised by an Act of Parliament of 6 May 1833, was originally empowered to construct a main line from Camden in London to Curzon Street in Birmingham. The new railway employed Robert Stephenson (1803–59) as its engineer. The line opened from Euston (*see* p 25) to Hemel Hempstead on 20 July 1837, Hemel Hempstead to Tring on 16 October 1837 and Tring to Denbigh Hall (north of Bletchley) and Curzon Street to Rugby on 9 April 1838. The central section, from Rugby to Denbigh Hall, was delayed as a result of the complexity of the construction of the 2.25km-long Kilsby Tunnel, where unexpected quicksand caused flooding and the collapse of the tunnel roof during work. Although there were limited services over the line from 24 June 1838 – primarily to capitalise on traffic to London to witness Queen Victoria's coronation on 28 June 1838 – it was not until 17 September 1838 that the Rugby-to-Denbigh Hall section was officially opened. One of the intermediate stations that opened at the same time was Blisworth, which acted as the station serving Northampton until the opening of the London & Birmingham's Northampton and Peterborough line.

The Northampton & Peterborough Railway was authorised by an Act of Parliament of 4 July 1843 and was again engineered by Robert Stephenson. The line opened from Blisworth to Northampton on 13 May 1845 and, to provide a good interchange for the new branch, Blisworth station was relocated 800m to the north. The line, along with the London & Birmingham, became part of the London & North Western Railway on 16 July 1846. A second station – the terminus seen immediately to the west of the through platforms in this view from 1950, taken from the east – was constructed by the Northampton & Banbury Junction Railway. This had been authorised by an Act of Parliament of 28 July

1863 and opened its line from Blisworth to Towcester on 1 May 1866. This company was taken over by the Stratford-upon-Avon & Midland Junction Railway on 1 July 1910 following an Act of Parliament of 29 April 1909. The Northampton & Banbury constructed a small shed at Blisworth, out of view to the west, in 1882. This was officially closed by the London, Midland & Scottish Railway on 10 August 1929, with the shed dismantled and reused as a goods shed at Towcester, although basic servicing continued in the yard until November 1955.

By the date of the photograph, the ex-Northampton & Banbury Junction Railway station was approaching the end of its operational life – the final services via Towcester to Stratford were withdrawn on 7 April 1952. The end for the ex-LNWR station came on 4 January 1960, with the withdrawal of local passenger services over the line from Northampton Bridge Street. The station was demolished shortly after as work was undertaken on the electrification of the West Coast Main Line. Freight traffic over the line towards Towcester ceased beyond a private siding at Blisworth on 3 February 1964; the final stub was closed on 30 September 1967. The end of the Northampton Bridge Street-to-Blisworth line came with the withdrawal of through services on 6 January 1969.

Today, the railway – now electrified at 25kV – continues to pass the site of the stations. Of the stations themselves there is nothing left other than a siding on the Down side. The impressive building to the south of the stations still exists, as the Walnut Tree Inn, and provides a useful reference to the location. The land to the west of the stations is now dominated by the A43 dual carriageway, which crosses the railway to the north and uses the trackbed of the closed line to Northampton for its route. The fields beyond the Walnut Tree Inn now form a housing estate.

EAW030228

Bournemouth Central
10 October 1950

The first railway to reach the town of Bournemouth was an extension of the Ringwood, Christchurch & Bournemouth Railway. This company had originally been authorised by an Act of Parliament of 8 August 1859 to construct a 12.5km line linking Ringwood to Christchurch, on the London & South Western Railway's line from Southampton to Dorchester. The line opened from Ringwood to Christchurch on 13 November 1862 and was operated by the LSWR from the start. On 13 July 1863 the company was empowered to construct a 5.5km extension to a new station on the east side of Holdenhurst Road, Bournemouth. This station opened on 14 March 1870. The Ringwood, Christchurch & Bournemouth Railway was acquired by the LSWR on 1 January 1874, following an Act of Parliament of 16 June 1873.

During the latter half of the 19th century Bournemouth grew rapidly, aided by the arrival of the railway, and the original link proved increasingly unsatisfactory. The LSWR obtained powers to construct a direct line from Brockenhurst to connect with the line from Ringwood just east of Christchurch, to double the line from Christchurch to the existing Bournemouth station, to construct a new line towards Poole and to construct a new station at Bournemouth. The new station, designed by William Jacomb (1831–87), chief engineer of the LSWR, opened on 20 July 1885, the doubled line to Christchurch on 30 May 1886 and the line westwards on 6 March 1888. The station, initially known as Bournemouth East (to differentiate it from Bournemouth West, which had opened on 15 June 1874), was renamed Bournemouth Central on 1 May 1899. The suffix 'Central' was abandoned on 10 July 1967 following the closure of West.

This view from the north-east shows the station with the now demolished church of St Paul's in the background. In the station a London-bound service awaits departure, headed by one of Bulleid's unrebuilt Pacific classes (probably one of the 30 'Merchant Navy' class locomotives; all were rebuilt between 1956 and 1963). To the west of the station, on the north side of the line, can be seen the turntable that served the locomotive shed. The first shed here opened in 1885 and was a small building between the turntable and station. This was closed in 1921 and the building was subsequently demolished as it was largely supplanted by a new – larger – shed located slightly further to the west, which opened in March 1888. This later shed underwent considerable expansion in 1936 and was reroofed 20 years later. The shed closed on 9 July 1967 with the end of Southern Region steam services.

Bournemouth station, which is now Grade II listed, was designed as a grand structure, befitting an increasingly fashionable town. The train shed extends over some 107m, with a height of 13m and a span – over four tracks – of 29m. The main walls, which extend over 22 bays, are constructed in brick with stone detailing, with the station's main entrance on the north – Up – side. The roof suffered severe damage during the storm of October 1987 and, after being in a state of disrepair for a number of years, was fully refurbished by Network Rail in 2000. The building survives, with the major changes since the 1950 view being the electrification of the route (initially only to Bournemouth in 1967 and eventually through to Weymouth) and the removal of the through – non-platform – roads.

EAW033403

Bromley North
August 1929

The short – just over 2.5km – branch from Grove Park to Bromley North was promoted by the locally based Bromley Direct Railway and backed by the larger South Eastern Railway, which saw the line as a means of competing with the London, Chatham & Dover Railway in the area. Authorised by an Act of Parliament of 16 July 1874, the line, with its one intermediate station at Grove Park, opened on 1 January 1878. The line's construction was handled by the contractors Lucas & Aird (who were also working on the SER's line from Greenwich to Maze Hill at the same time). Operated by the SER from the outset, the Bromley Direct was formally absorbed by the SER on 21 July 1879. In 1899 the SER and LCDR formed the South Eastern & Chatham Railway. This was not a complete amalgamation – the two companies retained their separate legal status through to the Grouping in 1923 – but was a management committee that oversaw joint marketing and operation of the two companies' lines. At Grouping, ownership of the line passed to the Southern Railway and thus to British Railways (Southern Region) at nationalisation.

This photograph, taken in the summer of 1929, views the station from the south-west. The date is significant as it shows the station shortly after its rebuilding by the Southern Railway during 1925 and 1926. The original SER structure had been small and constructed in wood. The new building – designed by the SR's chief architect, James Robb Scott (1882–1965) – was built as part of the SR's plans for the electrification of the branch. Trial running of the new electric services commenced on 19 November 1925 and the new station, albeit not wholly complete, opened on 27 December 1925. Full electric services were introduced on 28 February 1926.

The new station, which has been listed as Grade II since 1990, was one of the last constructed by the SR in the late Edwardian red-brick style that dominated much corporate architecture in the immediate post-World War I era. The building, with its prominent cupola and pediment over the entrance, is clearly seen in the centre of the photograph, with the awning running along much of the platform. To the west of the station is the goods yard; until 1926 there was a private siding here that served Bromley Council. Visible at the northern end of the station is the signal box.

Bromley North remains operational; however, there have been some significant changes since the photograph was taken. Most notably, freight facilities over the branch were withdrawn on 20 May 1968. The site of the goods yard was converted into car parking for the station. An office block – Northside House – has been built on the land immediately to the west of the main station building, although the latter – still boldly proclaiming 'Southern Railway' over its entrance – remains, as does the substantial platform awning. The signal box was replaced in 1962 by a modern electro-mechanical box; this too has been subsequently replaced and demolished.

EPW028346

Bromyard

13 August 1938

The Worcester, Bromyard & Leominster Railway was authorised by an Act of Parliament of 1 August 1861 to construct a 39.5km line from Leominster Junction, just west of Worcester, to Leominster, on the Shrewsbury-to-Hereford line. However, with progress slow, the company abandoned the section north of Bromyard in 1869. The line opened from Leominster Junction to Yearsett (a station that closed in 1877) on 2 May 1874 and to Bromyard on 22 October 1877. In the meantime, a second company – the Leominster & Bromyard Railway – was authorised to construct the 18km section from Bromyard to Leominster on 30 July 1874. The line opened From Leominster to Steens Bridge on 1 March 1884 and, like the original line from Bromyard southwards, was operated from opening by the Great Western Railway. The two railways, never financially secure, passed to the GWR on 1 July 1888; the Worcester, Bromyard & Leominster was in the hands of the liquidator at the time and cost the GWR £20,000 to acquire. The new owners eventually completed the link between Steens Bridge and Bromyard, which opened on 1 September 1897.

Viewed from the north-east, this photograph shows a two-coach passenger train, hauled by a GWR '2251' Class 0-6-0 (one of 120 built between 1930 and 1948) on a Worcester-bound service. In the foreground is one of the town's two gasworks – Broad Bridge. Linking the gasworks to the railway goods yard is a short section of narrow gauge track and it is possible to see coal being transferred from the main line wagon into a smaller wagon for shipment into the gasworks.

Passenger services between Leominster and Bromyard did not survive World War II by many years; they were withdrawn – and the section of line closed completely – on 15 September 1952. The line was not immediately dismantled, however, as it was traversed by a railtour as late as 26 April 1958. The remaining section – from Bromyard to Leominster Junction, Worcester – was listed for closure in the *Reshaping* report of 1963 and services were withdrawn from 7 September 1964. Freight facilities were withdrawn from the branch at the same time and thus the line closed completely from that date.

Today, little remains of the railway's presence in the town; the station site has been converted into an industrial estate, although it is still possible to trace the trackbed east from the station. North of the town, the trackbed is more readily identifiable and at two of the privately owned stations – Rowden Mill and Fencote – short sections of track through the stations have been relaid and the station buildings restored.

EPW058622

Buckingham
18 September 1964

Most traditional county towns still have a railway station; indeed, the vast majority also still have through services to and from London. One of the few exceptions is Buckingham. This is slightly ironic considering the proximity of Buckinghamshire to the metropolis, but the three main lines that headed north through the county all bypassed the town, leaving it to be served by a branch line from Banbury to Verney Junction. Originally the London & Birmingham line was to have served the town, but opposition from the then Duke of Buckingham resulted in the route running to the east through Wolverton.

The origins of the line through Buckingham lay with the Buckinghamshire Railway. This was created on 22 July 1847 from a merger of two earlier railways – the Buckingham & Brackley Junction and the Oxford & Bletchley Junction – that had both been authorised in 1846, with powers to extend from Brackley to Banbury. The company was backed by the London & North Western Railway, which feared that the line, if operated by another railway, might threaten its Birmingham traffic. The line was engineered by Robert Stephenson (1803–59) with Thomas Brassey (1805–70) contracted to act as contractor. The line opened from Bletchley to Banbury on 30 March 1850 and from Verney Junction to Oxford on 20 May 1851. It was operated from opening by the LNWR, being leased by the larger company on 1 July 1851 and being formally absorbed on 21 July 1879.

The station, illustrated here from the south-west, was the second to serve the town; the original building was constructed in wood, with access from the Down side, which was inconvenient. A new road – Chandos Road – was constructed from the town and a new station

building – designed by John William Livock (1814–83) – was completed in 1861. This is the structure illustrated in this 1964 view.

The passenger service between Banbury (*see* p 53) and Buckingham was selected following the Modernisation Plan of 1955 for the experimental use of lightweight single diesel units. However, through passengers were expected to change trains at Buckingham for a connecting steam-hauled service southwards. Although the new diesel units, introduced in 1956, resulted in a significant increase in traffic, it was not enough to save the passenger service. This ceased on the Buckingham-to-Banbury section on 2 January 1961, with the diesel units transferred to operate the remaining section south to Verney Junction. The line from Verney Junction to Buckingham was scheduled for closure in the *Reshaping* report of 1963 and passenger services were withdrawn on 7 September 1964. The section north of Buckingham closed completely in December 1964 and that south to Verney Junction followed on 5 December 1966, when freight facilities were withdrawn from Buckingham. Lifting of the line took place early in 1967.

Today, the trackbed through the town remains as the Buckingham Railway Walk as far as the A421, although the station itself has been demolished. While the platforms remain, the trackbed has been infilled through the platforms. Inevitably in the 50-plus years since the photograph was taken, the town itself has grown significantly.

EAW140779

Budleigh Salterton
September 1928

To the east of the River Exe estuary, the London & South Western Railway possessed a number of main and branch lines; of these, the only survivors are the main line from Exeter to Salisbury and the Exmouth branch. Among those stations once served by the LSWR that are nothing more than a distant memory is Budleigh Salterton, on the line from Sidmouth Junction to Exmouth.

The genesis of the branch through Budleigh Salterton was the Sidmouth Railway. Authorised by an Act of Parliament of 29 June 1871, this railway's route from Sidmouth Junction to Sidmouth via Tipton St John's opened throughout on 6 July 1874. Although there had been earlier proposals, it was not until 20 July 1894 that the Budleigh Salterton Railway was authorised. The 10.5km line from Tipton St John's, with its intermediate stations at Newton Poppleford (opened 1899) and East Budleigh, opened on 15 May 1897. The station was originally a terminus – known as Salterton (the name was changed to Budleigh Salterton on 27 April 1898) – with a single platform and main single-storey station building constructed in brick. Operation of the line from opening was in the hands of the LSWR. The Budleigh Salterton Railway retained its independence until being formally absorbed into the LSWR following an Act of Parliament of 18 August 1911.

The westward extension to Exmouth was undertaken by the LSWR and opened on 1 June 1903. The opening resulted in a number of changes to the station, all of which are reflected in this 1928 view. A second platform was completed on the north side; this was to become the station's Up platform, with the original platform becoming the Down. At the same time, a footbridge was installed, as was the small – 20-lever – ground-level signal box. The limited freight facilities, with a small goods shed located to the west of the station, already existed but traffic was always relatively light. After the date of the photograph, taken from the south-east, the only significant change prior to the station's decline came in 1938, with the installation of a 2-ton yard crane that replaced an earlier crane within the goods shed.

Passenger traffic over the line remained reasonably strong until the 1950s but, as elsewhere, the rise of the motor car and the long-distance coach resulted in an inexorable decline post-World War II. The *Reshaping* report of March 1963 listed all of the ex-LSWR branches in east Devon and west Dorset for closure and, despite the introduction of DMUs to the route on 4 November 1963, formal announcement of the proposed closure of the line was made on 20 August 1964, with ministerial consent being given by the then Minister of Transport, Tom Fraser, on 22 December 1965. Remaining through services were diverted from the route at the end of the 1966 summer season and the passenger service ceased on 6 March 1967. With freight traffic having already ceased – facilities had been withdrawn from Budleigh Salterton on 27 January 1964 – the line closed completely on 6 March 1967 and demolition followed soon after.

Today, little remains to remind locals and visitors that there was once a station in Budleigh Salterton. The station site and much of the trackbed west of the station has been redeveloped for housing. East of the Leas Road bridge – visible at the eastern extremity of the station in 1928 – the road overbridge remains and it is still possible to trace the trackbed north of Budleigh Salterton.

EPW023991

The twin stations of the Midland Railway and the London & North Western Railway stand adjacent to each other in this view of Buxton, taken from the north-west shortly after the once-fierce rivalry between the two companies had been replaced by common ownership by the London, Midland & Scottish Railway. That on the right is the ex-MR station, which was given the suffix 'Central' in 1924, while that on the left is the ex-LNWR; this was known as Buxton South from the same date.

The LNWR-backed Stockport, Disley & Whaley Bridge Railway was authorised to extend to Buxton by an Act of Parliament of 27 July 1857. With work commencing in 1859, the Buxton extension was due to open throughout on 1 June 1863, although full services to Buxton did not operate until 15 June. The LNWR formally absorbed the Stockport, Disley & Whaley Bridge Railway following an Act of Parliament of 23 July 1866. Parallel with the development of the LNWR line to the town, the MR was backing a separate route into the town courtesy of the Manchester, Buxton, Matlock & Midland Junction Railway, an ambitious scheme authorised by an Act of Parliament of 16 July 1846 to construct a line from Ambergate through the Peak District. In the event, the money ran out and the company only achieved the opening of the section from Ambergate to Rowsley in 1849. The MR obtained new powers in an Act of Parliament of 25 May 1860 to extend the line from Rowsley to Buxton. Work started in September 1860 and the line opened contemporaneously with the LNWR, with the first services operating on 1 June 1863.

The two stations were, as is evident, in close proximity, and were designed to be very similar, with wrought-iron glazed train sheds and identical stone-built frontages with semicircular glazed panels. The architect of the two stations was J Smith, but Joseph (later Sir Joseph) Paxton (1803–65), who was the then

Duke of Devonshire's agent, assisted as the Duke had a financial interest in the two railways. The ex-MR station, which had been modified with an extended roof in the late 1880s, closed on 6 March 1967 and the building was subsequently demolished. Although the ex-LNWR station remains open, it has lost its train shed but retains the end gable, which was restored in 2009, and the main station buildings, which are now Grade II listed.

Also visible in this 1930 view is the ex-LNWR Hogshaw Lane Viaduct, constructed in around 1890 as part of the LNWR's planned connection, via a section of the Cromford & High Peak line, to the North Staffordshire Railway at Ashbourne. Passenger services commenced to Parsley Hay on 1 June 1894 and to Ashbourne on 4 August 1899. Passenger services over the section from Buxton to Rocester via Ashbourne ceased on 1 November 1954, but the line over the viaduct remains open for freight traffic as far as Hindlow. The viaduct, 320m in length, is built in both millstone grit and limestone with brick soffits; the dividing point between the two types of stone is the tenth arch. The bridge's arches are of varying spans and include a skewed arch over Spring Gardens and plate girder spans over the former MR route.

To the east of the ex-MR station is the two-road engine shed built by the MR and opened in 1867. The shed was extended in 1884 and, as can be seen, the facilities included a turntable. By the date of the photograph, the shed was coming to the end of its life; it closed on 19 August 1935, with the town's locomotive allocation being concentrated thereafter at the ex-LNWR shed.

EPW034108

Chertsey
September 1928

Viewed from the east, this photograph shows the station at Chertsey, in Surrey, on the loop line that links Virginia Water with Weybridge. The first railway to serve the town was a branch, authorised by an Act of Parliament of 16 July 1846, promoted by the London & South Western Railway to link Weybridge with Egham. This opened from Weybridge to the first station in Chertsey – located to the south of the level crossing – on 14 February 1848 but the section northwards was not initially progressed as a second company – the Windsor, Staines & South Western Railway – had been authorised on 25 June 1847 to construct a line from Staines to Pirbright, along with a branch from Virginia Water to Chertsey. In the event, this line was not completed and it was almost two decades before the line north opened.

On 8 July 1853 another company – the Staines, Woking & Wokingham Railway – was authorised to build a line westwards from the existing Windsor line at Staines. The line opened from Staines to Ascot, via Virginia Water, on 4 June 1856 and was worked from opening by the LSWR. Leased by the LSWR from 28 August 1858, it was formally absorbed by the larger company following an Act of Parliament of 4 July 1878. Although the distance between Chertsey and Virginia Water was only 4km, it was not until 23 June 1864 that the LSWR received powers to build the connection. The new line opened on 1 October 1866 and served the new – but incomplete – Chertsey station from that date. The new station, derived from the earlier designs of Sir William Tite (1798–1873) for the LSWR, was constructed in London stock brick with stucco architraves to the windows and a slate roof. It was completed in 1868. The local railway network was finished by the addition of a north-to-west curve at Weybridge (opened on 20 August 1883) and a south-to-west curve at Virginia Water (opened on 10 August 1885); the former makes the loop a useful diversionary route for the ex-LSWR London-to-Woking main line. The later spur at Virginia Water closed in 1966. Services over the loop line were electrified almost nine years after the date of this photograph, on 3 January 1937.

Today, the main station building – listed Grade II since 1986 – remains. To the west of the station, the railway is now crossed by a road overbridge carrying the A320. This has significantly reduced the traffic using the level crossing that still crosses the road to the east of the station. The sidings and goods yard have disappeared; general freight facilities were withdrawn from the station on 5 October 1964. The area has been redeveloped for industrial use on the north side and for residential purposes on the south.

EPW023380

Colchester St Botolph's
29 March 1968

Although the Colchester, Stour Valley, Sudbury & Halstead Railway was primarily authorised by an Act of Parliament of 26 June 1846 to construct a line linking Colchester with Cambridge, its powers also extended to the construction of a short branch south from Colchester station to serve Hythe Quay. This line, which initially carried freight traffic only, opened on 1 April 1847. The extension of this line to Wivenhoe and subsequently onwards to Walton-on-the-Naze came with the promotion of the Tendring Hundred Railway.

The Tendring Hundred Railway, which was heavily backed financially by the Great Eastern Railway, was authorised by an Act of Parliament of 13 August 1859 to construct the line from Hythe to Wivenhoe. Although only some 4km in length, the work also included the upgrading of the existing line from Colchester to Hythe and its opening to passenger services. Passenger services to Wivenhoe were introduced on 6 May 1863, when a station at Hythe also opened. The line was operated by the GER from its opening. The original station at Colchester was some distance from the town centre and the new branch opened up the opportunity of developing a more central station. The new St Botolph's station opened on 1 March 1866. The station had a two-storey, brick-built main station building, with a full-width canopy along the facade. Integrated into the station and converted into a station house was a pre-existing late-Georgian two-storey brick-built house. The station had a single island platform with two platform faces. A short canopy along the platform provided shelter for the passengers.

The Tendring Hundred Railway's independence ceased on 1 July 1883, when, following an Act of Parliament of 29 June 1883, it was vested in the GER. As such, the station passed to the London & North Eastern Railway in 1923 and to British Railways (Eastern Region) at nationalisation. The lines from Colchester to Walton and to Clacton were part of the planned electrification of the Eastern Region route out of Liverpool Street in the 1950s. Following experience elsewhere, it was decided to convert these lines, as well as the route into St Botolph's, to 25kV. Work started on the conversion in 1957 and the new electric services were introduced on 13 April 1959.

This view, taken from the north-west, shows the station as it existed at the end of the 1960s. On 8 July 1991 the station became known as Colchester Town, and today its building is largely unchanged from its original form. It retains both the canopy over its entrance and along the platform, although the number of operational platforms has been reduced to one. While the main station building is currently unlisted, the late-Georgian station house is now Grade II listed. To the south of the station, the area has recently been redeveloped and now accommodates the town's magistrates' court.

EAW179247

Cullompton
12 October 1950

Promoted by businessmen in both Bristol and Exeter, the Bristol & Exeter Railway was surveyed by Isambard Kingdom Brunel (1806–59) and his assistant William Gravatt (1806–66) and was authorised by an Act of Parliament of 19 May 1836. However, despite the earlier enthusiasm, raising funds for the construction of the 121km route proved difficult and, before the first section of line opened, the company entered into an agreement with the Great Western Railway that the latter would operate the line. The GWR did so until the expiry of its lease on 30 April 1849. The GWR leased the Bristol & Exeter again from 1 January 1876, before formally absorbing it on 1 August 1876 following an Act of Parliament of 27 June 1876.

The first section of the broad gauge route, from Bristol to Bridgwater, opened on 14 June 1841. The line opened from Bridgwater to Taunton on 1 July 1842 and Taunton to a temporary station at Beam Bridge on 1 May 1843. Work was completed on Whiteball Tunnel, and thence to Exeter, on 1 May 1844. The Taunton-to-Exeter section included a number of intermediate stations when it initially opened – Wellington (1843), Tiverton Junction (1844), Cullompton (1844) and Hele & Bradninch (1844) – but the temporary station at Beam Bridge closed on 1 May 1844 when the line was opened throughout. Subsequently additional stations were added at Norton Fitzwarren (1873), Burlescombe (1867), Sampford Peverell (1928), Silverton (1860) and Stone Canon (1860; relocated in 1894). The original station at Cullompton was a relatively small affair, with short platforms alongside the two running lines. The lines were subsequently modified in 1876 for mixed gauge working and finally to standard gauge only in 1892.

This view, taken from the west, shows Cullompton station with the Culm Leather Pressing Co Ltd works in the foreground. The station as shown was the result of work undertaken during 1931 and 1932 on the Bristol-to-Exeter line. At several stations, including Cullompton, the number of running lines was increased to four. At Cullompton, as shown in this view, two new and longer platforms were constructed; these were set back from the original location to serve the two loops. The station buildings were replaced at the same time with the single-storey structure as illustrated here, on the Up side, with a second shelter on the Down side. The platforms were linked by a new footbridge.

The *Reshaping* report of March 1963 advocated the closure of the surviving intermediate stations between Exeter and Taunton. With the exception of Tiverton Junction (subsequently relocated and now known as Tiverton Parkway), all closed. Cullompton lost its passenger services on 6 October 1964. Freight facilities were removed on 6 May 1967. The station was subsequently demolished, although the platforms survived for a number of years, set back from the now rationalised double-track layout.

This once-rural scene has now been wholly transformed: running parallel to the railway on its east side is the M5 and the motorway's Junction 28 links into the road overbridge – now much enlarged – that sat to the south of the station. The goods yard on the Down side has been redeveloped and now forms the site of the Cullompton motorway services. The site of the leather works has also been redeveloped, although it remains in a variety of commercial uses.

EAW033588

Dawlish
17 June 1947

There were few more mercurial engineers in the 19th century than Isambard Kingdom Brunel (1806–59) and the station at Dawlish was the product of one of his schemes – the South Devon Railway.

West of Exeter, the challenge facing any railway engineer was topography: any potential route between Exeter and Plymouth faced the prospect of steep gradients and severe curves. In an era when steam locomotive technology was still relatively primitive, there was no guarantee that steam would prove capable of handling the trains. There was a potential alternative, however. From the 1830s there had been experimentation in the possibilities of the construction of atmospheric railways. The first commercial exploitation of the principle was an extension of the Kingstown & Dalkey Railway in Ireland, which opened on 29 March 1844 and was inspected by Brunel and Daniel Gooch (1816–89). The timing is significant as, on 4 July 1844, the South Devon Railway – which was backed by the Bristol & Exeter, the Bristol & Gloucester and the Great Western railways – received its parliamentary approval. The South Devon's board agreed to adopt the atmospheric system, following a further inspection on 19 August 1844 and an inspection by the shareholders on 28 August 1844.

The new railway was authorised to run from Exeter via Dawlish, Teignmouth and Newton Abbot to Plymouth and to be built to Brunel's favoured broad gauge. Following construction, the first section – including the original station at Dawlish – opened from Exeter to Teignmouth on 30 May 1846 and on to Newton Abbot on 30 December 1846. As the atmospheric equipment was not yet complete, services were initially steam-hauled, using locomotives hired from the GWR. It was not until 13 September 1847 that the first revenue-earning passenger trains operated with the atmospheric

equipment, although experimental running had commenced earlier in the year. Full atmospheric operation through to Newton Abbot commenced on 10 January 1848 but, by this date, it was apparent that Brunel had not ordered the engine house equipment for the line west of Newton Abbot – the section to Totnes had opened on 20 July 1847 – and that serious doubts about the operation of the Exeter-to-Newton Abbot section were beginning to surface. In March 1848 the board instructed Brunel to cease work on the installation project west of Newton Abbot and, following a further board decision on 29 August 1848, the last atmospheric service operated on 10 September 1848. In theory, this was just a temporary suspension pending improvements and repairs, but these were never carried out and the equipment was never used again.

When opened in 1846, Dawlish station possessed a single platform on the northern – Up – side with a loop on the south; it was not until 1 May 1858 that the Down platform opened. One of the engine houses required by the atmospheric equipment was situated at Dawlish, slightly to the east of the station on the landward side; demolished by the date of this 1947 photograph, part of one wall with bricked-up windows is still visible in the station car park. The original station was constructed in wood but this was destroyed by fire on 14 August 1873. The new station – constructed by the Tavistock-based contractor Blatchford & Son – opened on 12 August 1875. The South Devon Railway was operated by the GWR on 1 January 1876 and formally absorbed by the larger railway on 1 August 1878. The line through the station was finally converted from broad to standard gauge on 20 May 1892.

The stucco-finished station, listed Grade II in 1951 and seen from the east in this photograph, remains open. There have, however, been some changes since

1947. The cast-iron-and-glass platform canopies were removed in 1961 and replaced with canopies supported by concrete beams. Freight facilities were withdrawn from the station on 17 May 1965 and the goods shed demolished; the site of the goods yard is now the station car park. The signal box was closed on 27 September 1986; although there were efforts to use the building commercially, these proved unsuccessful and the structure was demolished between 2 and 5 July 2013.

EAW007656

Derby Friargate
10 June 1952

While the railway history of Derby is inevitably dominated by the story of the Midland Railway and its antecedents and successors, there was a second railway – the Great Northern – that played an important role in the railway development of the city. As elsewhere, the dominance of one company gave rise to concerns about the monopoly that this represented and the lack of competition in terms of rates, particularly for freight. As a result, the GNR was encouraged to open a line west from Nottingham to serve Derby and then head south towards Burton-upon-Trent.

Construction of the new line was enshrined in the Great North (Derbyshire and Staffordshire Extension) Act of 25 July 1872. The contractor for the construction of the 65km-long line was the local company of Benton & Woodiwiss. Freight traffic over the line commenced on 28 January 1878, with passenger services following on 1 April 1878. The GNR station, which was more conveniently located for the centre of town than the existing MR station, had a main island platform, which catered for most timetabled services. Two outer platforms were generally used for excursion traffic or for freight services passing through the station when the main through roads were occupied. With the station built upon a viaduct, as shown in this view, the main station offices were located at ground level on the western side, with access to the platforms gained via a subway.

Timetabled passenger services south of Derby Friargate were a relatively early casualty, being withdrawn by the London & North Eastern Railway on 4 December 1939, although post-war excursion traffic continued to serve this section until the early 1960s. The *Reshaping* report of March 1963 recommended the withdrawal of passenger services from Friargate to Nottingham via New Basford and these were withdrawn on 7 September 1964. Freight traffic, which

had remained significant through the 1950s, gradually declined or was transferred to alternative routes. Freight facilities were withdrawn from Friargate on 4 September 1967 and the line from Friargate northwards to Stanton Junction closed completely on 6 May 1968. The Stephenson Locomotive Society organised a farewell tour of the line on 4 May 1968; this was the last passenger service over the route. The section south from Friargate to Egginton Junction was retained as a test track for use by the Railway Technical Centre. The section from Mickleover to Friargate was, however, closed on 26 November 1971 in order to permit road improvement work, while the final section of the ex-GNR line, from Egginton Junction to Mickleover, was finally closed on 9 July 1990.

Of the GNR presence in Derby, very little now remains. The most substantial survivals are two of the bridges produced by the local iron founders Andrew Handyside & Co – the double bridge over Friargate immediately to the north of the station, as illustrated in this 1952 view taken from the east, and that over the River Derwent further to the north and now used to carry a footpath across the river. Both are now Grade II listed. Also Grade II listed is the substantial red-brick warehouse constructed by the GNR to the south of the station and thus not visible in this view. At the time of writing this structure is in a very poor condition, although there are plans for its conversion into an apartment block. Also remaining but unlisted is a small hydraulic pump house. The upper-level station buildings have been demolished, although the platform survives, albeit highly overgrown. The ground-level buildings also survive as they are built into the viaduct at this point. Again, these are in a derelict condition. To the south of the station, running past the derelict warehouse, the trackbed is visible as far as Uttoxeter Old Road. North of the bridge over

Friargate, the viaduct on which the railway ran has been demolished and substantially redeveloped.

EAW044086

Dover Marine
10 September 1971

During the latter half of the 19th century the port of Dover underwent significant expansion, a reflection of its use by the Admiralty and the burgeoning cross-Channel traffic. During the first decade of the 20th century, the new Admiralty Pier was constructed, and the opportunity arose for the South Eastern & Chatham Railway to build a new terminus to handle the passenger traffic for the cross-Channel steamers. Work started in 1909 on the reclamation of four hectares of the dock at the northern end of the new pier; this required the sinking of some 1,200 ferro-concrete piles into the seabed. Once completed, in 1913, work started on the new station. It was designed by Percy (later Sir Percy) Crosland Tempest (1860–1924), chief engineer and later general manger of the SECR, and comprised a steel-and-glass train shed, 240m long and 51.8m wide, which accommodated two island platforms, 18.3m wide, that stretched 213.4m. The facade of the station, facing north, was completed in a French Beaux-Arts style. This section of the station was not completed until after the end of World War I.

Although the new station was substantially complete in 1914, the outbreak of war meant that initially it was used only for military traffic; it was not until 18 January 1919 that civilian use commenced. At the western side of the new station (viewed here from the south-east), a four-road carriage shed was completed.

With the outbreak of World War II in September 1939, ferry services were reduced but the station received many thousands of those evacuated from Dunkirk in May and June 1940. Civilian passenger traffic ceased thereafter, although the station was used by the military again from mid-1941 onwards and suffered damage during German raids on a number of occasions.

After the war, the station was returned to civilian use but the rise of the private motor car resulted in a gradual decline in traffic. The next significant alteration to the station came in the late 1950s with the Kent Coast electrification. To accommodate 12-coach EMUs, the platforms were extended by 33.5m at the northern end. This required modification of the track layout at the northern end before services commenced on 15 June 1959.

Linked to the station by a footbridge is the Lord Warden Hotel (the square building at the northernmost point of the quay). This was designed by Samuel Beazley (1786–1851) for the South Eastern Railway and was formally opened on 7 September 1853. The hotel, now Grade II listed, was requisitioned for military use in World War II, when it became known as HMS *Wasp*. When it was decommissioned on 19 November 1944, the Admiralty returned the building, which had been used as the headquarters of the Coastal Forces Base, to the Southern Railway on 18 September 1945 but little repair work was undertaken before the building passed to British Railways at nationalisation. Renamed Southern House, the building remained offices, being occupied by HM Customs & Excise from 1956. By the early 1990s the condition of the building was a cause for concern and, after four years of ownership by the shipping line Stena, the building was acquired by the Dover Harbour Board in 1998. Subsequently renamed Lord Warden House, the building has recently undergone a major refurbishment and remains in use as offices.

The construction of a train ferry terminal at Dover (separate from the Dover Marine rail terminus) was undertaken following the rejection of earlier plans for the construction of a fixed link and a decision that Dover was a more suitable location than Richborough. It was designed to permit the loading of carriages and wagons onto train ferries for onward travel to France. In the summer of 1933, contracts were let for the work to Edmund Nuttall, Sons & Co Ltd and John Mowlem & Co Ltd. The new dock was 126.5m by 21.9m and was located between the original Admiralty Pier and the South Pier. Between May 1940 and May 1945 services were suspended due to the war. Used by both passenger ferries – most notably the 'Night Ferry' until 31 October 1980, when the service ceased – and freight stock, the facility was last used for the maintenance of the MS *Nord Pas-de-Calais* between 28 and 30 December 1988.

Dover Marine station was renamed Dover Western Dock on 14 May 1979. However, with the development of the Channel Tunnel, its future was in doubt and, on 25 September 1994, the station closed officially, although a non-timetabled service continued to operate until 19 November 1994. Following closure of the signal box on 5 July 1995, work on track removal commenced in 1996. Although the harbour board had hoped to demolish the station, which had been Grade II listed in 1989, it was decided to convert the building into a cruise terminal and it reopened for this purpose in 1996. Recently, the harbour board has undertaken a major renovation, restoring the building, including the SECR war memorial, to a very high standard.

EAW215113

Elstree & Borehamwood
12 June 1952

Recorded from the north-west in 1952, with the twin northern portals of the 980m Elstree Tunnel in the distance, Elstree & Borehamwood station was a familiar sight to the staff of Aerofilms, as the company's offices were located for many years at Gate Studios, the industrial estate south-east of the station. The studios, initially based in a single building, opened in 1928 and were acquired by Arthur Rank in 1950. Seven years later the site was purchased by Andrew Smith Harkness and the industrial estate developed. Later, the site was acquired for redevelopment and, despite a campaign for its preservation, the original studio, along with the remainder of the site, was cleared for residential development in 2006. The Aerofilms archive transferred to Potters Bar, prior to its purchase by English Heritage (now Historic England), the Royal Commission on the Ancient and Historical Monuments of Scotland and the Royal Commission on the Ancient and Historical Monuments of Wales. At the time of writing, the gas holders still remain, along with a small single-storey brick building on Station Road, but the rest of the site – along with the fields beyond – has been redeveloped for housing.

The first Midland Railway services to reach London were operated using running powers over the London & North Western Railway from Rugby into Euston (*see* p 25). However, this was not ideal as capacity was limited and the MR initially undertook the construction of a line southwards from Leicester via Bedford to Hitchin. With the opening of the Bedford-to-Hitchin line, MR services to London then operated into King's Cross station (*see* p 27) from 1 February 1858. However, the MR was determined to gain its own independent access to the metropolis as capacity south of Hitchin was also an issue and, in 1862, sought parliamentary approval for the construction of a London extension. The line was authorised by an Act of Parliament of 22 June 1863.

The new line opened throughout on 1 October 1868 and a new London terminus – St Pancras (*see* p 27) – was provided. One of the intermediate stations that opened at the same time as the route was Elstree. Over the years, the name has fluctuated, with '& Borehamwood' (with variants) being carried between 1 June 1869 and 1 April 1904, from 21 September 1953 until 6 May 1974, and from about 1988.

The MR four-platform station, with its ridge-and-furrow platform canopies and single-storey main building, dates from the opening of the line. In addition to the station, there was a small goods yard with shed. Freight facilities were withdrawn from the station on 19 June 1967. By that date, however, the station itself had been completely rebuilt. In 1959, at a time when the St Pancras-to-Bedford local service was being converted to diesel (timetabled DMU services were launched on 4 January 1960), the existing station was modernised. At the same time, the main station building was transferred from the Down to the Up side. New platform structures and canopies were also installed.

Today, the station retains its four platforms, with services provided by Thameslink. Electric services over the line to Bedford were initially introduced on 28 March 1983, with the full timetable commencing on 11 July 1983. Although the work had been completed two years earlier, a dispute over the operation of one-person-operated trains led to industrial action and a 12-month delay in the introduction of the new services. Facilities at the station now include a new footbridge with lifts; this was completed in 2014.

EAW044079

Fareham
August 1928

Recorded from the north, this view of Fareham station includes the junction, just south of the station, between the lines to Gosport and to Portsmouth. Slightly north of the station, and not recorded, are the junctions off the Eastleigh main line for the lines to Southampton and Alton.

Promoted by the London & Southampton Railway, the line from Basingstoke to Gosport was authorised by an Act of Parliament of 4 June 1839 (the same Act also saw the London & Southampton become the London & South Western Railway). The London & Southampton had initially wished to serve Portsmouth but local opposition and the opening of a floating bridge between Gosport and Portsmouth made Gosport a cheaper option. The line opened throughout on 29 November 1841. Gosport, which was used by Queen Victoria and her family for journeys to and from the Isle of Wight, was provided with a suitably grand neoclassical station designed by William (later Sir William) Tite (1798–1873). After many years of disuse, the remains of this station were restored between 2008 and 2011. Tite also designed the original station at Fareham; this is the small single-storey yellow-brick building at the southern end of the station.

Fareham became a junction on 1 October 1848 with the opening of the line to Portcreek Junction via Cosham; this was to allow LSWR services to reach Portsmouth for the first time. The line from Fareham to Netley opened on 2 September 1889; the LSWR-backed Southampton & Netley Railway had opened from Netley westwards on 5 March 1866. The final link – the Alton-to-Fareham line (the Meon Valley Railway) – opened on 1 June 1903. The 1928 view records the scene shortly after the LSWR's incorporation into the Southern Railway in 1923.

Contraction of the local railway network commenced soon after nationalisation, with the withdrawal of passenger services over the original line to Gosport on 8 June 1953. The line remained open for freight traffic until 30 January 1969; and for military traffic – latterly the northern section to serve a Royal Navy depot at Bedenham only – until this traffic ceased in 1991. Passenger services were withdrawn on the Meon Valley line on 5 February 1955, with freight services over the section from Fareham to Droxford withdrawn on 30 April 1962.

Today, Fareham remains a significant station on the routes to Portsmouth, Eastleigh and Southampton; passenger services through the station were electrified in May 1990. The station and platform buildings – not currently listed – and platform awnings are still extant, although the northern end of the platforms have seen the erection of a new footbridge and lifts in order to make the station suitable for passengers with disabilities. The trackbed of the Gosport branch remains intact, albeit heavily overgrown, while south of the station, the bridge has been lengthened to accommodate the widened A27. The goods yard, which lost its main freight facilities on 1 June 1970 but still retains a small stone terminal on the eastern side, is now largely a car park. Although the station itself is unlisted, there are two railway viaducts in the town that are: Quay Street and Cams Hill (*see* p 221), on the line to Portsmouth. These were both designed by Joseph Locke (1805–60) and opened in 1848.

EPW023072

Gidea Park
12 April 1927

When the Eastern Counties Railway was first authorised (by an Act of Parliament of 4 July 1836) and opened (from Devon Street, in London's Mile End, to Romford on 20 June 1839), much of the line passed through countryside. However, with the arrival of the railway, there was a stimulus to develop these areas, a process that was aided by the Great Eastern Railway's policy of running frequent services to and from the suburbs. As new centres of population emerged, so the railway opened up new stations to cater for this traffic. One of these was Gidea Park. Opened initially on 1 December 1910 as Squirrels Heath & Gidea Park, the station's name was changed on 1 October 1913 to Gidea Park & Squirrels Heath (the '& Squirrels Heath' suffix was dropped on 20 February 1969). The station, as shown in this 1927 view from the south, had two island platforms with four platform faces. The main station building, constructed in brick and slate, was located on – appropriately – Station Road. Single-storey structures with canopies were provided on both platforms. As a relatively late addition to the network and serving primarily the passenger trade, Gidea Park was, like a number of these suburban stations, never provided with freight facilities.

By 1927 the station, along with the rest of the GER, had passed to the London & North Eastern Railway. Prior to the Grouping, the Great Eastern Railway had had plans for the electrification of its intensive suburban services out of Liverpool Street. However, this did not progress and it was left to the LNER to start the programme, in conjunction with plans by the London Passenger Transport Board to extend the Central Line east of Liverpool Street. Following the recommendation of the Weir Committee, the LNER decided to adopt 1,500V DC for the work and initial plans foresaw electrification of all four lines as far as Gidea Park, but only two onwards to Shenfield. Although work started, the onset of war in September 1939 resulted in its suspension and work did not recommence until January 1946. Although initial services were introduced on 26 September 1949, the full electric timetable was not introduced until 7 November that year. This timetable resulted in three workings per hour operating all stations to Gidea Park, with a further three per hour operating semi-fast to Shenfield. Although the route was initially electrified as planned at 1,500V DC, it was subsequently upgraded to 6.6kV and later to 25kV.

Today, Gidea Park is undergoing an upgrade as part of the Crossrail project. The original main station building on Station Road, as shown in the 1927 view, on the Up side, remains. However, there is now a modern – but temporary – addition on the eastern side. There is still a footbridge; that illustrated in 1927 has been replaced and the bridge is now fully enclosed and stretches across the lines to connect the station platforms with a car park, which is now sited on the Down side. Also still extant are the platform-level buildings with their platform canopies. None of the station buildings are currently listed. The most spectacular change over the past 90 years, other than the electrification of the lines, is the scale of urbanisation. All of the once open land is now developed, primarily for housing. One of the few constants is the structure built immediately to the north of the road overbridge. This is now occupied by a dry cleaning business.

EPW017574

Gloucester
3 July 1986

Following the closure of the Eastgate station on 1 December 1975, all passenger services in Gloucester have been concentrated on the ex-Great Western Railway Central station, which is recorded in this view from the east in 1986.

The first railway to serve the site of the future Central station was the Birmingham & Gloucester Railway. The railway, authorised by an Act of Parliament of 22 April 1836, opened into the city from Cheltenham on 4 November 1840. The newly opened line was leased by the Midland Railway on 1 July 1845 and formally absorbed by the larger railway on 3 August 1846. The next arrival was the Bristol & Gloucester Railway. This had been authorised by an Act of Parliament of 1 July 1839 to take over the existing Bristol & Gloucestershire Railway (a 16km line linking Bristol with various collieries to the north of the city), convert it to a main line and extend it through to Gloucester itself. Originally planned as a standard gauge route, the decision was made to construct it to broad gauge and the line was formally opened on 6 July 1844. The Bristol & Gloucester was worked by the MR from 7 May 1845 and formally absorbed the following year. This meant that the MR was now operating both standard and broad gauge trains to and from Gloucester. This problem was not resolved until powers were obtained by the MR to build standard gauge lines to Bristol. These opened on 22 May 1854, although the company had to maintain its broad gauge tracks for some years thereafter.

The gauge complexity was compounded by the arrival of a third railway, the Cheltenham & Great Western Union, which had been authorised by an Act of Parliament of 21 June 1836 to construct a broad gauge line from Swindon to Gloucester. This railway, which was operated by the GWR from opening (and was formally absorbed by it on 10 May 1844), opened from Kemble to Gloucester. A second Gloucester station, slightly to the north of the original, was provided on 12 May 1845, via a broad gauge connection to Standish Junction, built by the Birmingham & Gloucester. A further broad gauge line, the South Wales Railway (authorised by an Act of Parliament of 4 August 1845), opened from Chepstow to Gloucester on 19 September 1851. The line was operated by the GWR from opening and formally absorbed on 1 August 1863. The new arrival meant that, for the first time, Gloucester was now a through station and a new, two-platform station was constructed for the purpose. This was relatively short-lived as a new, single-platform station was constructed to replace it four years later.

The Tuffley loop, which formed part of the MR's 1854 standard gauge line to Bristol, was not initially provided with a station so MR trains continued to use the existing station. This required through services to be reversed into and out of the station – a similar problem affected GWR through services heading to and from Cheltenham. However, the opening of a second station on the loop on 12 April 1896 meant that MR through services were diverted to the new station. The ex-GWR station was given the suffix 'Central' and the ex-MR became Gloucester Eastgate on 17 September 1951. The original GWR station retained only a single platform until 1914, when a second platform was added.

This view, taken in 1986, shows the impact of the rationalisation locally. The 1914 platform at Central was converted to handle parcels traffic only in the late 1960s, while Eastgate station closed on 1 December 1975, with all services concentrated on Central. In 1975 a contract was let to the Evesham-based contractor Espley Tyas Construction Ltd for the rebuilding of the surviving station. The new structure was formally opened by the Mayor of Gloucester on 8 March 1977. The new structure included a 54.9m-long steel canopy constructed by Conder Hardware of Winchester. The platform was lengthened to 602.7m as part of the work. Capable of accommodating two HST sets, the platform is the second longest in Britain. In 1984 the 1914 platform was restored to passenger use and a new footbridge provided to access it.

Today, despite a fire in 2010 that caused serious damage, Gloucester station retains most of the features visible in the 1986 view, including the 1914 platform and its canopy. The most significant change is the upgrade to the footbridge, including lifts; this was completed in 2013.

EAW504192

Guisborough
July 1932

Backed by the Stockton & Darlington Railway, which operated the line from opening and amalgamated with it on 23 July 1858, the Middlesbrough & Guisbrough (sic) Railway was authorised by an Act of Parliament of 17 June 1852 to construct the 16km line on the south side of the Tees estuary. Work started on 30 October 1852 and the line opened for freight traffic on 11 November 1853 and to passenger services on 25 February 1854.

This view of Guisborough station from the south shows to good effect the station building, with its single platform, train shed, goods shed and engine shed. All dated originally to the line's opening, with the exception of the engine shed. Although a shed was provided with the opening of the line in 1854, this was destroyed by fire on 27 February 1903 and the North Eastern Railway – as successor to the Stockton & Darlington – replaced it in 1908. Between the late 1880s and 1922 a small turntable was sited to the south-west of the shed. The shed closed on 20 September 1954. There was also a small signal box located south-west of the turntable; the box was closed on 16 March 1932 when the box at Hutton Gate was renamed Guisborough. This resulted in the splitting of the former double track into two separate single tracks: the former Up line was used exclusively for passenger services, with the former Down route for freight traffic. A small ground frame sited at the outer end of the platform replaced the box.

From Hutton Gate towards Saltburn, the Cleveland Railway, authorised on 23 July 1858, completed an alternative route between Guisborough and Middlesbrough. Initially freight only, from 1 November 1878 a passenger service from Middlesbrough to Saltburn via Hutton Gate was introduced. This was linked into the existing Guisborough service and required a number of reversals to achieve a through trip. The use of steam railmotors, Sentinel units and, eventually, DMUs made this process of reversal more straightforward. The year after this photograph was taken, services via Loftus from Whitby were diverted to terminate at Middlesbrough rather than Saltburn. As a result, rules were put in place to permit the propelling of longer trains – up to seven coaches – to and from Guisborough.

Passenger services over the Hutton Gate-to-Saltburn route ceased on 2 May 1960 and for the remainder of its life Guisborough reverted to being a simple branch terminus. The *Reshaping* report of March 1963 listed the Guisborough line for closure. British Railways applied to close the line on 14 June 1963 and, following a public enquiry held in Middlesbrough on 23 August 1963, approval for closure of the Nunthorpe-to-Guisborough section was given on 27 November 1963. Passenger services were withdrawn on 2 March 1964, with the last trains operating on 29 February. The line remained open for freight until 31 August 1964; the remaining limited private siding traffic ceased soon afterwards.

Today, little remains of the railway's presence in Guisborough as the station was demolished in 1967 and a road now cuts through the site. Much of the trackbed to the west of Hutton Gate Junction is now a footpath, as is a section of the former Cleveland Railway towards Saltburn. It is still possible to trace part of the route from Hutton Gate towards Guisborough, although the northern half has disappeared under a retail park and a care home. A section of the original Middlesbrough & Guisbrough Railway line to Nunthorpe remains open for passenger services, providing part of the surviving route to Whitby.

EPW038956

Harold Wood

6 June 1951

The Eastern Counties Railway was authorised by an Act of Parliament of 4 July 1836 to construct the 200km line from London to Great Yarmouth. At the time this ambitious project was the single longest railway in the country to be authorised but only the section through to Colchester was completed. The line opened from Mile End to Romford on 20 June 1839 and was extended eastwards to Brentwood on 1 July 1840. It was not, however, until 1 December 1868 that the original two-platform station at Harold Wood opened. The station, as seen in this 1951 view, is the result of work undertaken by the London & North Eastern Railway in the early 1930s. The ex-Great Eastern main line through Harold Wood was quadrupled in 1934 and the station was substantially rebuilt. The single-storey main station building is largely constructed in brick with stone detailing, with 'LNER' carved into the stone above the main entrance on Gubbins Lane. The footbridge and platform-level buildings were rebuilt by the LNER as part of the quadrupling work.

Clearly evident in this 1951 view, taken from the south-west, is the electrification of the line. Although the Great Eastern Railway had plans in the early 20th century to electrify its suburban routes, lack of finance prevented this progressing and it was not until the mid-1930s that this work began. This was partly the result of the London Passenger Transport Board's New Works programme, which included the extension of the Central Line east of Liverpool Street, and partly the LNER's work to introduce 1,500V DC, as recommended by the Weir Committee, to the main line as far as Shenfield; this has been subsequently upgraded initially to 6.25kV and finally to 25kV. Work on electrification commenced in 1939 but was suspended when World War II intervened. Work resumed in early 1946 and by the end of 1948 the overhead was being erected. Initial test running of the new EMUs commenced on 23 March 1949 and public services started on 26 September of the same year.

Harold Wood station has undergone modernisation as part of the project to deliver Crossrail. In order to accommodate the 200m-long trains delivered for use on the new service, the platforms have been extended at the country end. In addition, the footbridge installed by the LNER has been replaced by a new structure that incorporates lifts, to provide step-free access to each platform. However, the LNER-built main station building at road level remains, as do the platform-level buildings, with their canopies on the island platform and on the Down slow. The building on the Up fast platform has been demolished. None of the station is currently listed.

EAW036993

Harrogate
5 June 1926

The town of Harrogate experienced significant growth during the 19th century, largely as a result of the mineral water springs that were a popular draw. A number of significant hotels were constructed to serve the people who came to take the waters, and the railway played a considerable part in bringing these visitors to the town. The first railway to serve Harrogate was the branch of the York & North Midland that opened to a terminus, Brunswick, opened on 20 July 1848. This line connected Harrogate with Church Fenton via Wetherby. While this connected the town to the railway network, it was a somewhat circuitous route to Leeds. This was partially resolved by the Leeds & Thirsk Railway (the Leeds Northern Railway from 3 July 1851), which was authorised by an Act of Parliament of 21 July 1845 to construct a line north from Leeds to Thirsk, skirting to the east of Harrogate to achieve an easier route. The line opened in stages: from Thirsk to Ripon on 31 May 1848, from Weeton to Wormald Green (via a station at Starbeck for Harrogate) on 1 September 1848, from Wormald Green to Ripon on 13 September 1848 and finally, following the completion of Bramhope Tunnel, from Weeton south to Leeds on 9 July 1849. The line from York to Knaresborough, constructed by the East & West Yorkshire Junction Railway (authorised by an Act of Parliament of 16 July 1846 and subsumed into the York & North Midland Railway on 1 July 1851), opened in two stages: from Poppleton Junction to Knaresborough on 30 October 1848 and on to a junction with the Leeds Northern on 1 October 1851.

Following the creation of the North Eastern Railway, of which both the Leeds North and the York & North Midland railways were constituents, the new company sought to improve connections into Harrogate. An Act of Parliament of 8 August 1859 authorised the NER to construct three lines in Harrogate that permitted the building of a more central station. This work involved the construction of a cutting through parkland known as The Stray, and the new line and station opened on 1 August 1862. The new station, as illustrated in this 1926 view from the west, was designed by Thomas Prosser (1817–88), and constructed in red brick and slate. The footbridge was added in 1873 and the platforms extended in 1883 to cater for additional traffic.

The local passenger network remained largely intact until the 1960s. However, the *Reshaping* report of 1963 saw a number of lines that served the town threatened with closure: the lines from Harrogate to Church Fenton and to Cross Gates closed on 6 January 1964, while the Leeds Northern line closed north of Harrogate on 6 March 1967. The line from Harrogate to York was threatened with closure as well, which would have resulted in the town being served solely by services to and from Leeds via Weeton, but the route to Poppleton Junction was reprieved in 1966, with the basic service being formed thereafter by trains running between Leeds and York via Harrogate.

Of the station recorded in 1926 little now remains. The significant survival is the bulk of the two-storey structure visible facing onto Station Parade, to the north-west of the main station building, along with the five-bay single storey that links the main station building with the two-storey structure. This structure, which is unlisted, has recently undergone refurbishment and is now a pub. There are also fragments of the exterior wall to the north of the modern footbridge that connects the station with the Victoria shopping centre. The bulk of the Victorian station was demolished in the early 1960s and a replacement was designed by the locally based architects Taylor, Bown & Miller. As a result of the rationalisation of the local network, the new station had only two platforms.

EPW015798

Havant
August 1928

This view, taken from the south-west, records the station at Havant in Hampshire. Following the completion of the London & Brighton line to Shoreham, a further extension westwards to Chichester was authorised by an Act of Parliament of 4 July 1844. The Brighton & Chichester Railway was completed in three stages: from Shoreham to Worthing on 24 November 1845, Worthing to Littlehampton on 16 March 1846 and Littlehampton to Chichester on 8 June 1846. While work on the original line was in hand, the company was authorised on 8 August 1845 to construct a further westwards extension to Havant and Portsmouth. Work started on the section from Chichester to Havant in early 1846, shortly before the company was formally merged, following an Act of Parliament of 27 July 1846, into the new London, Brighton & South Coast Railway. The Chichester-to-Portsmouth section opened on 14 June 1847. The section from Havant to Portsmouth was made eventually into a joint line with the London & South Western Railway – albeit after some controversy and inter-railway politics – with the completion of the 'Portsmouth Direct' line in 1859.

The first station to serve Havant was about 500m to the east of the station illustrated in this view. Known as Havant Halt, it opened with the line on 15 March 1847. This was replaced by a new station about 300m to the east of this station, which opened in 1859 with the LSWR line from Petersfield. Finally, the station was relocated again with the opening of the Hayling Island branch on 16 July 1867. This is the station illustrated in this 1928 view. The station at the time possessed two main platforms plus a bay platform at the east to serve the Hayling Island branch. However, major reconstruction meant that the station was completely rebuilt during the following decade.

During the 1930s the Southern Railway undertook a programme to extend its network of third-rail electrified services; among the routes converted during the period was the main line from London Waterloo to Portsmouth via Havant. Electric services over the section from Guildford to Portsmouth commenced on 29 May 1937. As part of the work, the station at Havant was replaced. The work included the quadrupling of the line through the station, with the provision of two through roads and two platform roads. The new station possessed longer platforms, being extended to the west, with the result that the level crossing that linked North Street and Leigh Road was closed. Work on the new station, largely constructed in red brick, was completed in 1938. Never electrified, the steam-operated passenger service to Hayling Island was withdrawn on 4 November 1963. Although there were proposals for its preservation – indeed an electric Blackpool tramcar was moved to Hayling with a view to its possible operation over the line – the branch was subsequently lifted.

Today, Havant station remains operational, with services on the Portsmouth-to-London Waterloo main line and on the ex-LBSCR line towards Brighton. Although the Hayling Island branch is no more, the trackbed south from the station is now in use as a footpath almost as far as Langstone. The track through Havant station has been rationalised, with the loss of the two through roads, and the goods yard has also closed (freight facilities having been withdrawn on 6 January 1969). The main station itself is unlisted but remains very much as rebuilt by the SR in the 1930s (although the footbridge has been modified to include lifts). The ex-LBSCR signal box that once controlled the New Lane level crossing slightly to the east of this view remains; constructed by Saxby & Farmer in 1876, this box, which is now out of use, is Grade II listed.

EPW023038

Henley-in-Arden
August 1930

Situated in Warwickshire, Henley-in-Arden is one of the intermediate stations on the former Great Western Railway line from Birmingham to Stratford-upon-Avon. The station seen in this view, taken from the west, was the second to serve the town and dated to the early years of the 20th century.

The first station in Henley was promoted by the Birmingham & Henley-in-Arden Railway, which was authorised by an Act of Parliament of 7 August 1888 to assume the powers held originally by the abandoned Henley-in-Arden & Great Western Junction Railway (originally authorised on 5 August 1873 and renewed on 23 June 1884) to construct a 4.5km line from Rowington Junction, between Hatton and Lapworth, to Henley. Backed and worked by the GWR, the new company opened its branch to passenger traffic on 6 June 1894 and to freight on 2 July of that year. The railway was formally absorbed by the GWR on 1 July 1900.

Almost from the date of its opening, the branch was living on borrowed time. On 25 August 1894 the Birmingham, North Warwickshire & Stratford-upon-Avon Railway was authorised to construct a line from Tyseley, via Henley, to Stratford. However, lack of finance meant that little had been achieved before the GWR stepped in and took over on 30 July 1900 (confirmed by an Act of Parliament of 6 August 1900). With a slight revision to the route, the line opened from Tyseley to Bearley North Junction (for Stratford) to freight traffic on 9 December 1907 and to passenger services on 1 July 1908. It was on this date that the station illustrated here opened. A short connection was constructed between the original branch and the new station, allowing services to be diverted to the new station. The original Henley station closed on the same day, although it remained open for freight traffic. Passenger services over the original branch ceased as a wartime economy measure during World War I and the tracks were removed from Rowington Junction through to the junction with the 1908 spur; the latter section survived until 31 December 1962, when freight facilities were withdrawn from the original station.

As can be seen, the station had three platforms; two were used for the through services, while the third was for services from Birmingham that terminated at the station (and, briefly, for the branch service to Rowington Junction). Today, the two through roads remain operational, although the buildings on the island platform have been removed, as has the footbridge. This was replaced in 2014, with the original being donated to the Gloucestershire Warwickshire Railway. While the main buildings on the Up side, built in brick and slate, remain, they are currently out of use and boarded up as the station is now unstaffed.

EPW034340

Henley-on-Thames
August 1928

Known simply as Henley when it first opened on 1 June 1857, the suffix 'on-Thames' was added on 1 January 1895. The 7.5km broad gauge branch from Twyford was built by the Great Western Railway. Originally single track, the line was doubled in 1898, following the abolition of the broad gauge. The railway regarded Henley as an important destination, particularly for traffic to the annual regatta, and a sizeable station – as illustrated in this 1928 view from the north-east – was the result. Three platforms were provided, with a small overall roof at the concourse end. The platforms were lengthened in 1891 and the train shed roof was extended by about 60m in 1910. The small single-track engine shed with turntable, adjacent to the station, opened with the branch. The turntable was originally located immediately to the north of the engine shed but by the date of this photograph had been relocated to the east. South of the station, there were extensive sidings for the stabling of carriages.

Rationalisation of the extensive facilities seen in the 1928 view commenced in the late 1950s. The engine shed closed on 5 October 1958. In 1961 the branch was singled; at the same time, a new – experimental electronic interlocking – signalling system was installed in the signal box. The majority of passenger services were DMU-operated by the early 1960s, but the last steam-operated passenger services – through trains to and from London Paddington – ran on 14 June 1963. Freight facilities were withdrawn on 7 September 1964. The number of platforms was reduced to two in 1969 and the signal box closed on 20 March 1972. In 1975 the original station, with its overall roof, was demolished and the site sold; at the same time the branch was cut back slightly to the south, using the country end of the surviving platforms.

Reduced to a single platform in 1985 and with a new station building completed the following year, Henley is still the terminus of the branch from Twyford. The once extensive goods yard to the south and west of the station now forms the station car park, while the area between the original station and Station Road has been redeveloped, as has the land to the west of the goods yard.

EPW022753

Hereford
September 1929

The impressive station at Hereford was one of three that originally served the city. The first railway to arrive was the Newport, Abergavenny & Hereford Railway, which was authorised on 3 August 1846. This railway opened a station – the future Hereford (Barton) – on the western side of the city on 16 January 1854.

The impetus for the development of a new station (that shown in this photograph) came with proposals for the Shrewsbury & Hereford Railway. The existing station was too small to cope with the additional traffic and its site was too cramped to permit expansion. Three other railways – the Hereford, Ross & Gloucester, the Hereford, Hay & Brecon and the Worcester & Hereford – also eventually reached the city.

The Shrewsbury & Hereford was authorised on 3 August 1846 but construction did not commence until 1850, when Thomas Brassey (1805–70) was appointed engineer. The first Shrewsbury & Hereford train reached the new Hereford Barr's Court station on 28 October 1853 but it was not officially opened until 6 December the same year. The Hereford, Ross & Gloucester line opened from Hopesbrook on 2 June 1855; the Worcester & Hereford from Malvern Wells to Shelwick Junction (just north of the city) followed on 17 September 1861. The Hereford, Hay & Brecon line to Eardisley opened to passenger services on 30 June 1863; from then until 1874 it served a separate station – Hereford (Moorfields). Although the majority of services, including those of the Newport, Abergavenny & Hereford, were concentrated on Barr's Court, it was not until 2 January 1893 that the last passenger services operated out of Barton. Following Barton's closure, the surviving station lost its 'Barr's Court' suffix.

The impressive main station building visible in this view from the west was designed by Thomas Mainwaring Penson (1818–64) in a red-brick neo-Tudor style. The ground floor included a booking office, separate refreshment rooms for first- and second-class passengers, and various waiting rooms and offices; the first floor provided accommodation for the stationmaster and further offices. The station was controlled by the Shrewsbury & Hereford Railway, which was jointly owned by the Great Western Railway and the London & North Western Railway; at the Grouping in 1923 it passed to the London, Midland & Scottish Railway and the GWR.

Post-nationalisation, there was some rationalisation of services; the former Midland Railway route to Brecon via Hay-on-Wye lost its passenger services on 31 December 1962, and those on the ex-GWR line to Gloucester via Ross-on-Wye followed on 2 November 1964. Today, passenger services operate through Hereford on the line from Shrewsbury to Newport and from Shelwick Junction to Great Malvern (for Worcester and beyond). Although the main station building (now Grade II listed) is intact, that on the island platform has been significantly reduced, with only the southern third still extant. The original buildings have been replaced by flower beds. To the south of the station, slightly out of range in this view, an ex-Shrewsbury & Hereford signal box also remains. This was built in 1884 and modernised in 1938 and again in 1984. To the north of the station, but again out of view, the goods shed also survives; this has been reused as a ten-pin bowling alley.

EPW029907

Hove
27 November 1931

The London & Brighton Railway was authorised by an Act of Parliament of 15 July 1837 to construct a line that linked the existing London & Croydon Railway's line at Selhurst to Brighton and to build a branch west from Brighton towards Shoreham. The line's engineer was John Urpeth Rastrick (1780–1856). The first section of the railway to open was that from Brighton to Shoreham, with services commencing on 11 May 1840. Among the stations that opened with the line was Hove.

The original station at Hove, designed by the London & Brighton's architect David Mocatta (1806–82), was east of the station illustrated in this 1931 view (taken looking towards the west). This station closed on 1 March 1880 and was converted into a goods depot – Holland Road – that survived until 14 June 1971. A small halt – Holland Road (constructed in wood) – opened in 1905, closing on 7 May 1956. This site has been redeveloped and, apart from the railway line from Brighton towards Hove, nothing now survives.

The station illustrated in this view dates to 1 October 1865, when it was opened as Cliftonville. The station was renamed West Brighton on 1 July 1879 and Hove & West Brighton on 1 October 1894, before becoming simply Hove on 1 July 1895. The new station had an Italianate-style two-storey building on the south side, possibly designed by Frederick Dale Bannister (1823–97), who had been appointed chief resident engineer of the London, Brighton & South Coast Railway in 1860. This was originally completed by a porte cochère, but it was demolished shortly after the completion of a new station entrance, again with a porte cochère, in 1904. This was constructed to the west of the 1865 station building and separated from it by a long footbridge, constructed in the 1880s, that stretches across the station platforms to Hove Park Villas.

Hove remains an important intermediate station on the line from Brighton westwards. The line was electrified from 7 July 1935 as part of the Southern Railway's major expansion of the third-rail network during the interwar years. Although freight traffic was extensive in 1931, this declined and freight facilities were withdrawn on 4 November 1967. However, a coal concentration depot was established at Hove on 14 June 1971; this has closed and the site of the former goods yard has been redeveloped. Some of the sidings on the north side of the station remain, however, and are now used for the stabling of EMUs. Of the station buildings, listed Grade II, the 1865 block is still extant, albeit now in commercial use, while the 1904 building remains, as does its substantial, and recently restored, porte cochère. The footbridge also remains, although the island platform has lost its traditional ridge-and-furrow canopy, having been completely reglazed.

EPW037247

Hulme End
July 1930

The number of passenger-carrying narrow gauge railways in England was relatively limited and all ceased to carry passengers – indeed most any sort of traffic – during the interwar years. This is a view of Hulme End, terminus of the North Staffordshire Railway's Leek & Manifold line, taken from the south some four years before the line's closure.

In 1898 the Leek & Manifold Valley Light Railway was authorised under the Light Railways Act of 1896 to construct a 13.25km 2ft 6in (762mm) line from the NSR's terminus at Waterhouses to Hulme End. The railway's engineer was Everard Calthrop (1857–1927), who had had considerable experience of building narrow gauge railways (particularly in India). The Light Railways Act sought to encourage the development of railways through abandoning the necessity of obtaining a specific Act of Parliament – the application of a Light Railway Order gave sufficient powers for the construction and operation of the line – and permitted reduced standards of construction. The Act was the result of an economic downturn in the 1880s and the desire of the government to encourage development of railways in areas that had not previously been considered sufficiently commercial.

The line opened throughout on 27 June 1904 and, for the bulk of its life, the main traffic was milk transported to Waterhouses for onward shipment. Passenger traffic – other than day trippers at weekends and bank holidays – was relatively limited as the stations were some distance from the communities they purported to serve (and thus susceptible to competition from road traffic after World War I). The railway ran in the deep valley bottom, while human habitation lay on the heights to each side. The line was operated by the NSR initially and by the London, Midland & Scottish Railway from 1923. By the end of the 1920s, the line's economic position was deteriorating but the final closure was largely the result of the decision of Express Dairies to close its Ecton creamery in 1932. This resulted in the line's temporary closure; it reopened briefly in 1933 before finally ceasing operation on 10 March 1934.

Today, the site is remarkably unchanged. The main station building was retained after closure and was later converted into an information centre for the footpath – now called the Manifold Way – that was built by Staffordshire County Council following the transfer of the railway property from the LMS to the council on 23 July 1937. Although the engine shed also still stands, this is a modern replica built using part of the original framework. It is possible to walk the entire length of the long-closed railway, although for a short section between Butterton and Redhurst, walkers have to share the trackbed with a diverted B road.

EPW034239

Kidderminster

3 July 1989

The two railway stations that serve Kidderminster are portrayed in this view looking towards the north. The station on the east serves the main line between Worcester and Birmingham; the station to the west of this is the terminus built to serve the preserved Severn Valley Railway.

The railway first reached the town, courtesy of the Oxford, Worcester & Wolverhampton Railway (authorised by an Act of Parliament of 4 August 1845), when the section from Droitwich to Stourbridge opened on 1 May 1852. Although the line's Act specified the use of the broad gauge, the route was actually constructed to standard gauge – leading to disputes with the Great Western Railway – with the OWWR claiming that it was its intention – never completed – to construct the line to mixed gauge throughout. The OWWR merged with the Worcester & Hereford and Newport, Abergavenny & Hereford railways to form the West Midland Railway on 1 July 1860; this amalgamated with the GWR on 1 August 1863.

The original station at Kidderminster was replaced in 1859, but this new structure was short-lived, being destroyed by fire four years after completion. It was replaced by a two-storey structure, in a mock-Tudor domestic style, that survived until the late 1960s. Following the discovery of rot, the building was demolished in 1968 and replaced by the small brick-built single-storey structure illustrated in this view (in the east).

Kidderminster became a junction with the opening of the short branch to Bewdley on 1 June 1878. By the date of this photograph, however, passenger services between Kidderminster and Bewdley had been withdrawn – on 5 January 1970 – and, following

the cessation of traffic to the British Sugar Corporation factory at Foley Park (in April 1982; the factory itself closed in 2002), the line had been reopened by the Severn Valley Railway. The preserved railway acquired the line east of Foley Park and leased the goods yard site, including the large goods shed (visible between the two stations; unlisted and now in use by the railway for carriage repairs and restoration), in 1982. The goods yard site was purchased outright in 1994. The railway constructed a new terminus to the west of the existing station – called Kidderminster Town – based on the design of the brick-built station at Ross-on-Wye, which had been completed in 1890. The station included a single island platform with two faces. When planned, the railway envisaged the incorporation of platform canopies from Birmingham Moor Street. These were, however, retained in situ and so the platform remains uncovered. The original Town station, which opened on 30 July 1984, eventually had a main building and a western wing. The latter was completed by the end of 1984 and the former during the following year. Subsequently an eastern wing and a steel canopy over the concourse were completed in 2006. To the west of the station, an ex-GWR warehouse is now occupied by the Kidderminster Railway Museum.

The station built by British Railways to serve Kidderminster (the station in the east in this photograph) is shortly to be consigned to history. In July 2017 plans for a new £4.3-million structure were announced. At the time of writing, it is expected that the new station will be completed during the summer of 2019.

EAC570872

Kingsbridge
September 1928

Kingsbridge in Devon was served by a 20km branch – nicknamed the 'Primrose Line' – from Brent on the Great Western Railway main line linking Exeter with Plymouth. The Kingsbridge & Salcombe Railway was authorised by an Act of Parliament of 24 July 1882. Backed by the GWR, the new company inherited certain powers granted to an earlier company – the Kingsbridge Railway – by an Act of 29 May 1864. However, construction work was again delayed and it was not until 19 December 1893 that the line to Kingsbridge was completed; the proposed link through to Salcombe was never built. By the date of the line's opening, the Kingsbridge & Salcombe Railway's independent existence had ended; it had been formally absorbed by the GWR on 13 August 1888.

The station as illustrated in this 1928 view from the south-west includes the main station building. This was constructed in stone and provided facilities for passengers as well as accommodation for the stationmaster. The station building was slightly extended on its western side during the 1940s. The small engine shed, capable of housing a single 2-6-2T, was on a spur off the bay platform road. This closed in September 1961 some two years before the final demise of the line. Visible to the north of the main platform is the two-coach carriage shed. This was constructed in corrugated iron and had originally been sited adjacent to the signal box – located to the west of the goods shed – prior to alterations to the track layout at the station. A second corrugated iron shed is also visible, further to the north; this was a shed that accommodated fodder and bedding for the cattle awaiting transportation from the station. The goods shed can be seen at the west of the station site. The line retained substantial freight traffic through to its final closure.

Although the line saw some increase in traffic during World War II, particularly during the build-up to the D-Day landing of 6 June 1944, post-war the growth in private car ownership resulted in a decline in passenger traffic. The line was one of those already proposed for closure prior to the publication of the *Reshaping* report in March 1963. The line's last year saw an increase in passenger traffic – aided by the summer through service to and from London Paddington – but there was to be no reprieve. All traffic – both passenger and freight – was withdrawn on 16 September 1963. There might have been a future for the line as opposition to its closure had led to a campaign for its preservation. However, this failed, leading to the preservation of the Ashburton line (*see* p 51) instead.

Today, although some of the trackbed forms a footpath, the line's approach to Kingsbridge itself has disappeared under new housing. The site of the station yard was converted into an industrial estate but it was not until 2009 that the main station building was finally demolished. Of the railway structures, only one – the stone-built goods shed – remains intact, although traces of the platform can still be identified.

EPW023737

Kingswear
September 1928

When the South Devon Railway opened its broad gauge branch to Torquay (a station later renamed Torre) on 18 December 1848, the area around the estuary of the River Dart was left without railway services and it was down to an independent company – the Dartmouth & Torbay Railway, authorised by an Act of Parliament of 27 July 1857 – to obtain powers to construct a line south from Torre to serve the district. Construction of the line proved difficult and it was not until 2 August 1859 that the section from Torre to Paignton opened, with that from Paignton to Brixham Road (later renamed Churston) following on 14 March 1861. The potential crossing of the River Dart was problematic and a second Act, of 7 July 1862, permitted a deviation of the route to serve Hoodown and ultimately Kingswear on the eastern bank of the river, as well as an extension to the time limit for the line's construction. The broad gauge line finally opened through to Kingswear on 16 August 1864. The 15.5km line was operated by the South Devon from opening and it was leased to the larger company on 1 January 1866, being formally absorbed by the South Devon in 1872 and thus passing to the Great Western Railway on 1 February 1876. The broad gauge line survived until the final conversion to standard gauge in May 1892.

The station provided by the Dartmouth & Torbay at Kingswear was designed by Robert Pearson Brereton (1818–94), who had been appointed chief assistant to Isambard Kingdom Brunel (1806–59) in 1847 and who completed work on a number of projects that Brunel had started, following Brunel's death. At Kingswear, a single platform with two platform faces was provided, with a 30m wooden train shed and a single-storey timber station building (seen here between the two jetties). An archway provided a link through to the adjacent Royal Dart Hotel. From the quay, a ferry service, owned

by the railway, offered a connection across the river to Dartmouth. Freight services to Kingswear commenced on 2 April 1866 and there was considerable traffic through to the quay and to the adjacent jetty (which was accessed by two wagon turntables). A small goods shed was built adjacent to the western side of the train shed.

The date of the photograph (viewed from the east) is significant as it was taken before major work was undertaken at the station. The small engine shed, out of shot slightly to the north, had closed on 14 July 1924. During 1929 the GWR extended the platform to a length of 259m and added a platform canopy beyond the train shed to the north. This combined with a slight realignment of the line to the north and the reconstruction of Hoodown Viaduct, just to the north of the station, into a steel-double-track structure (completed in 1928), resulting in the operation of longer and heavier trains, including the through 'Torbay Express' to London Paddington. One of the consequences of this work was the loss of the lines serving the jetty; these and one of the turntables can be seen in this view located at the junction on the L-shaped jetty adjacent to the small guiding light, although, given the lack of rolling stock, it appears that they were out of use at the time of this photograph.

The Kingswear branch passed to British Railways (Western Region) in 1948 and survived largely intact until rationalisation began in the 1960s. General freight traffic was withdrawn on 4 May 1964 and private siding traffic ceased on 14 June 1965. The signal box closed on 20 October 1968, as did the shorter platform 2. By that date, much of the redundant track had been removed. The line to Kingswear was scheduled as one of those to receive a modified service in the *Reshaping* report of 1963 and, in November 1968, formal closure proposals for the section south of Paignton were issued. In the

event, the line from Paignton to Kingswear was sold to the owners of the preserved Dart Valley Railway for £275,000 on 30 December 1972.

Kingswear station, now Grade II listed, remains the southern terminus of the preserved Dartmouth Steam Railway. The new owners have reinstated track to platform 2 (completed in 1976). The quayside lines, which were filled with wagons in the 1928 view, are now in use as a car park.

EPW024180

Lancaster Green Ayre
June 1933

Viewed looking towards the west along the River Lune, Lancaster Green Ayre station can be seen in the right foreground. The electrified line is heading across the river towards Morecambe, while the connecting line to Lancaster Castle station is running along the south bank of the river before heading south to the former London & North Western Railway station.

The Morecambe Harbour & Railway was authorised on 16 July 1846 to construct a railway between Morecambe and Lancaster. The line's independent existence was short as it was taken over by the North Western Railway later the same year. The route opened throughout on 12 June 1848 to a new station – originally simply called Lancaster – designed by Edmund Sharpe (1809–77). Green Ayre became a through station on 17 November 1849 with the opening of the North Western Railway line from Wennington. The company had been authorised on 26 June 1846 to construct the line from Skipton to Ingleton and the route from Clapham to Lancaster via Wennington. Also authorised was the link line between Green Ayre and Castle stations; this opened on 18 December 1849. Operation of the lines passed under lease to the Midland Railway on 1 January 1859, with the larger company purchasing the North Western on 1 June 1871. The original Greyhound Bridge across the Lune was constructed in wood; this was replaced by a wrought-iron viaduct between 1862 and 1864, which itself was replaced by a third viaduct in 1911.

Clearly visible on the Greyhound Bridge is the catenary installed by the MR for the electrification of the services from Castle via Green Ayre (where services reversed) to Morecambe and Heysham. The MR had plans – never progressed – for the electrification of the Derby-to-Manchester line and the need to improve local services in the Lancaster area provided an ideal opportunity to test the use of the equipment. Adopting 6.6kV at 25 cycles AC – the MR was the first railway in Britain to use alternating current – services first operated between Morecambe and Heysham on 13 April 1908; they were extended from Morecambe to Lancaster on 1 July 1908. The final section – Green Ayre to Castle – was inaugurated on 14 September 1908. Electric services were suspended on 11 February 1951 to allow British Railways to upgrade the equipment to 6.6kV at 50 cycles – again as a test bed for a future project (in this case the West Coast Main Line) – and were reintroduced on 17 August 1953.

Passenger services from Wennington to Morecambe and from Green Ayre to Castle were scheduled for withdrawal in the *Reshaping* report of 1963 and ceased on 3 January 1966. The route from Green Ayre, across the River Lune, to White Lund (Morecambe) closed completely on 5 June 1967, as did the route from Wennington to Green Ayre. Freight continued to serve the former MR goods yard – visible in the middle of the 1933 photograph – until this traffic ceased. The line between Castle and the goods yard closed on 17 March 1976. Today, although Green Ayre station has been demolished, much of the trackbed of the line exists as a footpath. More significant, however, is the survival of the third Greyhound Bridge. After the closure of the railway in 1967, it was converted to form a further road crossing of the river and reopened as a road bridge in 1972.

EPW042035

Leamington Spa

24 May 1937

This view of the two stations in Leamington Spa, taken from the west, sees the Great Western Railway station (to the right in this photograph) in the process of being rebuilt. Work on the station's reconstruction commenced in late 1936, having been authorised in November 1934. The new three-storey main station building located on the Down side was constructed with a steel frame clad in white Portland stone and was completed in late 1938, while the new buildings on the Up platform were completed the following year. Evidence of the new platform canopies under construction can be seen at the western end of the Down platform.

The GWR main line through Leamington had originally been authorised as the Birmingham & Oxford Junction Railway by an Act of Parliament of 3 August 1846. Constructed to the broad gauge, the line opened from Oxford to Banbury on 2 September 1850 and on to Birmingham on 1 October 1852. Operation of the line was undertaken by the GWR, which had formally absorbed the Birmingham & Oxford Junction following an agreement dated 12 November 1846. The section north of Banbury was constructed to mixed gauge; broad gauge operation between Oxford and Birmingham ceased on 1 April 1869. Leamington station opened with the line on 1 October 1852 ('Spa' was added to its name on 12 July 1913). The main station building was constructed in brick, with wooden platform buildings. Originally there had been a wooden train shed across the running lines, but this was cut back during the first decade of the 20th century to leave the two platforms with steeply angled canopies.

The London, Midland & Scottish Railway station (to the left in this photograph) owed its origins to a branch of the London & Birmingham Railway, which opened a line from Coventry to a station between Warwick and Leamington Spa (although this station was initially called Leamington) on 9 December 1844. This station had various names during its career, including Milverton; it was relocated slightly to the south in 1883 and closed on 18 January 1965.

The Rugby & Leamington Railway was authorised by an Act of Parliament of 13 August 1846 to construct a line from Rugby to Leamington and to construct a new station in Leamington Spa into which services over the branch from Coventry were to be extended from the original Leamington (Milverton) station. The Rugby & Leamington was acquired by the London & North Western Railway on 17 November 1846, before construction work on the line had started, and the line opened on 1 March 1851. It was not until February 1854 that the new LNWR (later LMS) station opened. The station, which also acquired the 'Spa' suffix in 1913, was set at a slightly lower level than the GWR station, with the line to Rugby, originally single track but doubled throughout by 1884, running parallel to the GWR line towards the south. A connection between the LNWR and GWR routes opened on 26 January 1864.

Although both stations had carried various suffixes during their lives, they were renamed Leamington Spa General (the former GWR station, on 25 September 1950) and Leamington Spa Avenue (the former LNWR/LMS station, on 27 June 1951) by British Railways. Avenue closed on 18 January 1965 following the withdrawal of passenger services to Coventry; those eastbound to Weedon and to Rugby had ceased on 15 September 1958 and 15 June 1959 respectively. The connection between the ex-GWR and ex-LMS lines was abandoned on 2 July 1961. This was followed, on 4 April 1966, by the closure of the ex-LMS line from Leamington to Marton Junction (the section beyond Marton to Rugby remained open for cement traffic). Following closure, Avenue was demolished and the surviving station lost its 'General'

suffix on 18 April 1966. A new connection between the line to Coventry and the ex-GWR route to the west of the station opened on 27 May 1966, with passenger services being restored over the route on 2 May 1977.

Today, Leamington Spa station, which is now Grade II listed, remains very much as rebuilt by the GWR in the 1930s; indeed structures on both the Up and Down platforms have undergone recent refurbishment that has enhanced and restored the art deco features that were a mark of the GWR rebuilding work. The platforms were extended in 1946. The site of Avenue station, which was derelict for a number of years, is currently undergoing redevelopment. East of the station, it is still possible to trace the route of the closed line as it parallels the surviving route, although the various bridges have lost their girder sections.

EPW053218

Leicester Central
11 April 1926

There were few more ambitious railway chairmen during the latter half of the 19th century than Sir Edward William Watkin (1819–1901), who converted the provincial Manchester, Sheffield & Lincolnshire Railway into the Great Central Railway and, in so doing, oversaw the construction of the last great main line to be built in Britain for almost a century.

The MS&LR was authorised in 1893 to construct its 'London Extension'. The 148km route extended southwards from Annesley, in Nottinghamshire, through Nottingham, Leicester, Rugby and Brackley south to a new terminus at London Marylebone. Construction started in 1895 and, on 1 August 1897, the MS&LR became the Great Central Railway. Although coal traffic commenced over the new main line on 25 July 1898, it was not until 15 March 1899 that passenger services were introduced.

In order to serve the new line, the GCR constructed a number of significant stations; of these the most important were those at Nottingham (see p 41), which was set into a cutting, and Leicester, as illustrated in this view from the west, which was sited on a wide viaduct. In all, the city was crossed by a viaduct about 2.5km in length. Constructed in brick, the viaduct was at its widest – almost 60m – at the point at which Central station was constructed. This 1926 view, taken shortly after the GCR had been absorbed into the London & North Eastern Railway, shows to good effect the facilities at the station. It possessed two through platforms and four bay platforms – two at both the north and south ends – based around what was effectively one large island platform. The through platforms were capable of handling the major expresses – such as the 'Master Cutler' that operated over the ex-GCR route between its launch on 6 October 1947 and its transfer to serve London King's Cross (see p 27) on 15 September 1958.

The engine shed visible on the east side of the station closed in 1964. Through express services over the ex-GCR main line were withdrawn, as recommended in the *Reshaping* report, on 5 September 1966, although a residual DMU-operated service ran between Rugby and Nottingham Victoria until 5 May 1969. The withdrawal of this service resulted in the final closure of Leicester Central station. Following closure, the bulk of the platforms – part of them survive at the north end of the site – and platform-level buildings were demolished and replaced with industrial buildings. Part of the space, including that of the former engine shed, was used as a car park. However, the street-level buildings remained virtually intact. These included the parcels office and booking hall – the latter still with its ticket windows – and in 2016 it was announced that the building will be refurbished as part of a project to regenerate Leicester's waterside area. North and south of the station, the viaducts that once carried the GCR through the city have been largely demolished and traces of the route are difficult to find. At the former Belgrave & Birstall station – now renamed Leicester North – the preserved Great Central Railway operates over the line to Loughborough.

EPW014908

Lincoln
July 1926

Viewed from the south, the proximity of the two stations in Lincoln, St Marks and Central, is evident (St Marks is the southernmost of the two). The first railway to reach the city was that promoted by the Midland Railway, which opened on 4 August 1846 from Nottingham to the future St Marks station (the suffixes 'St Marks' and 'Central' were not carried until 15 September 1950, after nationalisation). The line was engineered by Robert Stephenson (1803–59) and the design of the station, in a neoclassical style, is attributed to I A Davies. It became a through station when the connection to the Great Grimsby & Sheffield Junction Railway (authorised by an Act of Parliament of 30 June 1845) line to Barnetby opened on 18 December 1848.

The second station was the result of the Great Northern's arrival in the city. The GNR had been authorised by an Act of Parliament of 26 June 1846 to construct a main line from London to Doncaster, with an alternative route from Peterborough to Doncaster via Lincoln. The route from Peterborough to Lincoln opened on 17 October 1848; the line was extended northwards to Gainsborough on 9 April 1849. At Lincoln the GNR constructed a separate station; this was built in a neo-Tudor style to a design produced by the London-based John Henry Taylor (1791–1867). As illustrated here, the ex-GNR station had glass-and-iron train sheds; these were removed in the early 1950s and replaced by steel and asbestos awnings, which were themselves later refurbished and modified.

Visible in the view immediately to the west of St Marks station, to the south of the main line, is the former MR engine shed. This two-road structure was built by the MR in 1867 and replaced an earlier shed built on the same site, which dated to the opening of the line in 1846. The shed, as illustrated here, was reroofed by the London, Midland & Scottish Railway during World War II

and survived until closure in January 1959. The building was subsequently demolished. On the north side of the MR main line can be seen the MR's goods shed; general freight facilities were withdrawn from the yard on 3 May 1965. Further north, on the south side of the main line west from Central, can be seen the ex-GNR engine shed. This brick-built four-road structure dated to 1875 and replaced an earlier shed built to the east of the GNR station. This shed was reroofed by British Railways in the mid-1950s but closed in October 1964. Although the building was still standing at the end of the 20th century, it has been subsequently demolished and replaced by a modern pub called, appropriately, The Engine Shed. Immediately south of the ex-GNR shed, the ex-GCR grain and goods warehouse is also visible; known as Lincoln West, the freight facilities were withdrawn on 4 January 1965. This red-brick (and unlisted) building – heavily modified – has been converted into a library for use by the University of Lincoln, with its eastern gable still proudly proclaiming 'Great Central Warehouse'.

The train shed at St Marks was removed in the late 1950s and replaced with simple platform canopies. Subsequently the two through roads were removed, leaving the station simply with the two platform lines. St Marks station finally closed on 11 May 1985, with services transferred via a new curve to serve Central station, in order to reduce the number of level crossings in the city centre. Although the bulk of the station site has been cleared and redeveloped as a shopping centre, the brick (with stone detailing) facade of the 1846 station, with its portico, which is now Grade II listed, has been restored and incorporated into the new structure.

Lincoln Central station has retained the suffix despite the closure of St Marks. Grade II listed, the station has recently undergone considerable restoration work, including the careful reroofing of the main building.

Also listed Grade II are two ex-GNR signal boxes on the line: East Holmes of 1873 and High Street of the following year. The two boxes no longer have any operational role, however – both were taken out of use in 2008.

EPW016192

Littleborough

August 1926

Situated just to the west of Summit Tunnel, Littleborough station was briefly the terminus of the Manchester & Leeds Railway when that pioneering trans-Pennine line initially opened. The railway was authorised by an Act of Parliament of 4 July 1836 to run from a station at Oldham Road in Manchester through to Goose Hill Junction at Normanton, where access to Leeds was to be achieved via the North Midland route from Derby. A second Act, in 1839, permitted the extension in Manchester to connect into the Liverpool & Manchester Railway at Hunt's Cross (the site of the future Manchester Victoria station). The line's surveyor was George Stephenson (1781–1848), who was assisted by Thomas Longridge Gooch (1808–82), the brother of Daniel Gooch (1816–89) of the Great Western Railway, who oversaw the line's actual construction. The Manchester & Leeds Railway amalgamated with a number of other local railways to form the Lancashire & Yorkshire Railway on 9 July 1847.

The first section of the Manchester & Leeds, from the original terminus at Oldham Road to Littleborough, opened on 4 July 1939 (Oldham Road station closed to passenger services in 1844 when the line to Victoria opened, but was retained for freight traffic). The section from Normanton to Hebden Bridge followed on 5 October 1840. The final section – from Hebden Bridge to Littleborough – opened on 1 March 1841 following the completion of Summit Tunnel between Littleborough and Todmorden. The tunnel extends for some 2.6km and was, when completed, the longest railway tunnel in the world. Constructed through shale, coal and limestone, the tunnel's interior was lined with six courses of brick. The strength that these courses provided was demonstrated when, on 20 December 1984, a train laden with petrol derailed into the tunnel, causing a massive fire. The temperatures generated melted the outer layers of brick and resulted in the temporary closure of the tunnel while repairs were undertaken. The repair work included coating some of the surviving brickwork with cement. The tunnel reopened on 19 August 1985. The tunnel has three sections: the main section, Summit West (50m) and Summit East (37.5m). The latter two are located to the south and north of the main tunnel respectively. The south portal of West, which includes a Manchester & Leeds Railway monogram, and the south portal of the main tunnel are now both Grade II listed.

As can be seen in this view taken from the south-east, Littleborough had staggered platforms and a substantial main building (made from stone) on the eastbound platform. There was also a goods shed and signal box. Today, the main station building remains, although the building on the westbound platform has been replaced. While the station, rebuilt in the 1870s, is unlisted, the five-arch stone viaduct immediately to the east of the station (and partially visible in this view), which was designed by Stephenson, is now Grade II listed. Freight facilities were withdrawn from the station on 7 September 1964 and the goods shed was subsequently redeveloped; the bulk of the yard is now occupied by a supermarket. The signal box, which was constructed in 1897, was closed in January 1971 and subsequently demolished.

EPW016766

Louth

9 September 1971

The railway route through Louth was promoted by the East Lincolnshire Railway. This line, which was backed by the Great Northern Railway, was authorised by an Act of Parliament of 26 June 1846 to construct a 76km line from Grimsby to Boston. The northern section, from Louth to Grimsby, opened on 1 March 1848. The line from Louth to Firsby opened on 4 September 1848 and on to Boston on 2 October of the same year. Although the Manchester, Sheffield & Lincolnshire Railway, fearing the potential competition, attempted to negotiate a lease of the line, the GNR operated the line from opening and leased it on the same day as the Boston extension opened; the lease was formally approved by an Act of Parliament of 9 July 1847. The East Lincolnshire Railway, however, retained its independence through to the Grouping in 1923 and had its headquarters in the station at Louth. Louth became a junction station with the completion of the GNR branch from Bardney; this opened from Donington on Bain to Louth on 28 June 1876 for freight traffic and on 1 December 1876 for passenger services. This was followed by the branch to Mablethorpe, which opened on 16 October 1877.

The East Lincolnshire Railway employed the Sheffield-based architects Matthew Ellison Hadfield (1812–85) and John Grey Weightman (1809–72) to design the station buildings along the line, including that at Louth. The foundation stone for the station was laid on 8 July 1847 and the building was completed in a red brick with stone detailing in a neo-Jacobean style, with a stone triple-arched arcade forming its main entrance.

By the date of this photograph, taken from the west, passenger services through Louth had ceased. The first casualty had been the Bardney branch. This did not survive nationalisation for long, with services withdrawn on 5 November 1951. The section between Louth and Donington on Bain closed completely on 17 December 1956. Passenger services to Mablethorpe ceased on 5 December 1960, resulting in the complete closure of this section of line. The *Reshaping* report of March 1963 presaged the elimination of the bulk of the ex-GNR network in east Lincolnshire. Despite considerable opposition, passenger services from Peterborough to Grimsby were withdrawn on 5 October 1970, on which date the section south from Louth to Firsby Junction closed completely. The section north from Louth to Grimsby survived for freight traffic until this too was withdrawn on 3 October 1980.

The main station building was Grade II listed in 1974, but its condition deteriorated for a number of years after closure. More recently, however, the structure has been converted into residential accommodation. The bulk of the station site has been redeveloped for housing and a supermarket occupies the alignment immediately to the north of the station. Also still surviving is the former Louth North signal box. This structure, situated out of view in this photograph at the level crossing on Keddington Road (where one gate also survives), was constructed by the GNR in 1890 and was in a near derelict condition before being purchased for preservation and restoration in 1992. The trackbed through the town itself has been largely obliterated by modern development, although north of Keddington Road it is still extant and there are long-term plans by the preserved Lincolnshire Wolds Railway to extend to a new station using this alignment.

EAW215260

Malton
July 1935

Controlled by the 'Railway King', George Hudson (1800–71), the York & North Midland Railway was authorised by an Act of Parliament of July 1844 to construct a 67km line from York to Scarborough, along with the 9km branch from Rillington Junction, just north of Malton, to connect with the pre-existing Whitby & Pickering Railway at Pickering. Construction was rapid and the entire line opened on 7 July 1845. The most important intermediate station was at Malton, which is seen in this view, taken from the south in 1935. The station was designed by George Townsend Andrews (1804–55); completed for the line's opening, the building was extended in 1855.

The importance of the station was increased by the opening of the Malton & Driffield Junction Railway. This had been authorised by an Act of Parliament of 26 June 1846 and the steeply graded 31km line opened throughout to public traffic on 1 June 1853. At Scarborough Road Junction, the line connected into the line from Thirsk via Gilling, which had opened on 19 May 1853 (the date of the Malton & Driffield's official opening). All of the railways at Malton eventually passed to the North Eastern Railway and thus at Grouping to the London & North Eastern Railway. Although Malton station possessed more than one platform, there was no footbridge or subway linking the platforms. Instead, there was a drawbridge, which was interlocked with the signalling and could be rolled out between the main and island platform. This facet of the station's operation survived until rationalisation in the 1960s.

The passenger service north to Gilling and Thirsk did not last long into the Grouping era, ceasing, except for summer services to Scarborough, on 1 January 1931. Passenger services south of Scarborough Road Junction to Driffield were withdrawn on 3 June 1950, although they were temporarily restored in February 1953 and again in February 1958 as a result of heavy snow. The line closed completely on 20 October 1958. The section from Malton station to Scarborough Road Junction remained open to permit the summer seasonal passenger services from Thirsk to reverse into the station at Malton, until these were withdrawn on 8 September 1962. This section of line closed completely on 19 October 1964 with the withdrawal of freight services. The line to Pickering lost its passenger services on 6 March 1963 and closed completely on 4 July 1966.

Today, Malton is still served by trains on the York-to-Scarborough line. The main station building was listed as Grade II in 1986 and still survives. However, the loss of the drawbridge in 1966, following the withdrawal of the Pickering service, resulted in the station becoming effectively a single-platform station and the island platform has been subsequently removed. All passenger services now use the old Down platform, although double track remains through the station. The train shed was demolished in 1989 and replaced by ex-NER platform awnings salvaged from the redundant bay platform. The site of the goods yard has been redeveloped, while the engine shed site is overgrown. A signal box, which dated originally to 1873, still exists; this is located to the east of the view recorded here and controls the Castlegate level crossing.

EPW048561

Market Drayton
30 August 1947

Viewed from the north with the line stretching south-west towards Tern Hill station and eventually Wellington, this is a view of Market Drayton in Shropshire. The first railway to reach the town was the Nantwich & Market Drayton Railway. This was authorised by an Act of Parliament of 7 June 1861 to construct a 17.5km line south from Nantwich, on the London & North Western Railway's Shrewsbury-to-Crewe route. The single-track line opened on 20 October 1863. Although initially it was planned that the LNWR would operate the branch, it was the Great Western Railway that actually undertook the work. This line was followed by the Wellington & Drayton Railway. This was authorised by an Act of Parliament of 7 August 1862 as part of a broader scheme to provide links through to Knutsford and beyond. The Wellington & Drayton Railway was backed by the GWR, which saw the line as a means of gaining access to Manchester. The presence of the Nantwich & Market Drayton, allied to running powers over the LNWR to Crewe, rendered the proposals for a northern extension unnecessary. A further Act, of 14 July 1864, authorised the GWR's takeover of the Wellington & Drayton on the line's completion, although this was not finalised until some time later.

The 26km double-track line from Wellington to Market Drayton opened throughout on 16 October 1867. Prior to the line's completion, the earlier link to Nantwich was also doubled, thus providing the GWR with a double-track line throughout. The Nantwich & Market Drayton retained its notional independence until being formally absorbed by the GWR on 1 July 1897. The North Staffordshire Railway, fearing that the GWR had designs on its Staffordshire heartland, had opposed the Wellington & Drayton scheme; with that approved, it moved to secure its own position by promoting a link from its existing line at Silverdale through to Market Drayton. This was authorised by an Act of Parliament of 29 July 1864 and the line opened on 1 July 1870. The junction for the branch to Silverdale was located to the east of the view recorded here. In order to accommodate the new arrival, Market Drayton station was rebuilt. The NSR took over the existing Nantwich & Market Drayton Railway engine shed and enlarged it slightly in 1877. The shed, with a small turntable, was located on the east side of the line at the northern end of the station. These facilities were, however, closed in the early 1930s and the only evidence of their existence is the overgrown turntable.

Rationalisation of the railways at Market Drayton commenced with the withdrawal of passenger services on the ex-NSR line on 7 May 1956 and the cessation of freight traffic over the westernmost section of the line. Although the Nantwich-to-Wellington line proved to be a useful diversionary route during the electrification of the West Coast Main Line, withdrawal of passenger services was already under consideration at the time of the *Reshaping* report and services ceased on 9 September 1963. Freight traffic over the route continued until 1 May 1967.

Today, there is little evidence that the railway ever served Market Drayton. The station site itself was cleared and redeveloped as a supermarket. It is possible still to trace evidence of both the GWR and NSR trackbeds to the east of the station site, although the route of the former is incorporated into a trading estate and milk processing plant. There are again traces of the line west of the station for a short distance, but housing development and the construction of the A53 have eradicated the trackbed to the town's outskirts.

EAW010376

Meltham
August 1926

The Lancashire & Yorkshire Railway's 5.6km-long Meltham branch, in the West Riding of Yorkshire, was authorised by an Act of Parliament of 7 June 1861. It was not, however, until 16 February 1865 that the first tenders were accepted and construction work commenced. The original Act had specified an opening date no later than 1 June 1866 but problems in construction, notably a collapse in Netherton Tunnel, resulted in delays. A second Act, of 18 May 1866, permitted an extension but even after this there were further delays. It was not until 8 August 1868 that the first freight traffic operated over the branch, but a landslip resulted in the line's temporary closure soon after and it was not until 6 February 1869 that the line reopened for freight. A further landslip resulted in a second temporary closure, from 17 February 1869 to 5 July of the same year; it was on the same day that passenger services commenced.

As can be seen in this view from the west, Meltham had a sizeable goods yard and stone-built goods shed. The latter was extended prior to World War I by the side canopy visible on the building's south side. The northernmost siding in the yard was used as a private siding by the Meltham Silica Fire Brick Co following an agreement of June 1900 and a short tramway, again visible in the view, linked the loading platform with the company's works. The main station building, on the north side of the single platform, was a single-storey structure constructed in stone that provided a booking office, waiting rooms and other facilities. Immediately to the east of the station building can be seen the engine shed. This single-track structure opened with the line in 1868 but was closed, and its access track removed, in 1889 when the station platform was extended. The building was subsequently used as a store but was later

largely dismantled, with only traces surviving by the early 1950s. Behind the station and dominating this 1926 view are the mills of the Meltham Spinning Co.

The economics of the passenger service deteriorated once Huddersfield Corporation bus services were extended to serve Meltham from 1924. The establishment of a joint undertaking between the corporation and the London, Midland & Scottish Railway gave the railway a half-share in the Huddersfield Joint Omnibus Committee and the railway legally owned a number of the buses operated. The LMS's share in the committee passed to British Railways in 1948. Passenger services over the Meltham branch were withdrawn on 23 May 1949. The line, however, remained open for freight traffic for a further two decades.

One factor in the line's survival was the purchase, in 1939, of Meltham Mills, slightly to the east of the view seen here, by the David Brown company. This business had entered into a joint venture in 1936 to start the construction of tractors and, following a split with its original partner, had sought its own premises for tractor construction. The decline in the West Riding textile industry resulted in Meltham Mills becoming available but the outbreak of World War II almost immediately after the purchase meant that, initially, much of the production from the factory was wartime related and it was only after 1945 that bulk tractor production commenced, with the production being shipped out over the Meltham branch.

Tractor production at Meltham Mills ceased in March 1988, but use of the Meltham branch had ceased long before this. The line closed completely on 5 April 1965. Today, although the trackbed survives as a footpath, there is little evidence that a railway once served the town. The station site and that of the former Meltham

Spinning Co have been redeveloped as a supermarket, car park and housing. The brickworks has also disappeared under a housing estate.

EPW016485

Melton Mowbray

11 May 1953

The Syston & Peterborough Railway was one of the multitude of schemes promoted by the 'Railway King', George Hudson (1800–71), as he sought to extend the influence of his empire towards Peterborough and East Anglia. The line was authorised by an Act of Parliament of 30 June 1845, with George Stephenson (1781–1848) and Charles Liddell (1813–94) as engineers. The line opened from Syston to Melton Mowbray on 1 September 1846 and from Stamford to Peterborough on 2 October the same year. However, the centre section was delayed due to the sixth Earl of Harborough, owner of Stapleford Park, who had objected to the original bill. Although he had failed to get the line rejected, the resulting Act had included a tunnel under his Cuckoo Plantation. The collapse of this tunnel during construction further soured relations and resulted in a second Act, in 1847, to permit a deviation from the original alignment. As a result, it was not until 20 March 1848 that the Melton Mowbray-to-Stamford section opened to freight traffic; passenger services commenced on 1 May 1848. The line was operated by, and part of, the Midland Railway from opening. Melton Mowbray station became more significant with the opening in 1880 of the MR's route via Old Dalby that allowed the railway to serve Nottingham while bypassing Leicester.

The original station at Melton Mowbray, viewed here from the south-west as an '8F'-hauled freight train trundles through, is credited to the architect Sancton Wood (1815–86). However, Gordon Biddle (2011) doubts this attribution on the basis that it is not up to the same standard as much of his other work and speculates that, if it is by Wood, financial constraints must have been a causal factor. The station was constructed in brick and was originally provided with a train shed; this collapsed in 1876 following a heavy snowfall. The station seen here was the result of much rebuilding during the last decades of the 19th century. The exterior of the main station building was modified during 1879–81 by the construction of a three-arch Italianesque colonnade. This was designed by the MR's then architect John Holloway Sanders (1825–84). The platform canopies were added at the same time, while the footbridge was constructed in 1897.

Today, Melton Mowbray serves trains on the Peterborough-to-Leicester route. While unlisted, the historic station buildings have recently undergone refurbishment, as have the platform canopies (although these are now shorter than when recorded in 1953) and the 1897 footbridge. The signal box, which was rebuilt by the London, Midland & Scottish Railway in 1942, also remains; however, the wooden structure is coming towards the end of its operational life as the line is scheduled for resignalling. The goods yard has disappeared and the site now forms the station car park, although there is still track towards its west end in connection with the use of the former main line towards Nottingham as a test track.

EAW049203

Minehead

July 1930

Now a station familiar to many as the terminus of the preserved West Somerset Railway, Minehead station is viewed here from the north with the Queen's Hall Theatre in the foreground. This building dates to 1914 and is today used as a bar and restaurant. To the right of the theatre is the Strand private hotel, again of 1914, and adjacent to the railway goods shed are the Gaiety Theatre and the public conveniences (now demolished).

Although authorised by an Act of Parliament of 14 August 1857, it was not until 1859 that construction of the broad gauge West Somerset Railway commenced. The line opened from the junction at Norton Fitzwarren to Watchet on 31 March 1862. The extension to Minehead was first authorised on 5 July 1865, but the Minehead Railway failed and the company was dissolved in 1870. A second attempt – backed by the West Somerset Railway – was authorised on 29 June 1871. This was more successful, with the line – operated by the Bristol & Exeter Railway – opening on 16 July 1874. The Great Western Railway leased the Bristol & Exeter from 1 January 1876 and, following an Act of Parliament of 27 June 1876, the two railways were formally amalgamated on 1 August of the same year. Built as a broad gauge line, the final broad gauge services operated on 28 October 1882 and, following conversion to standard gauge, services resumed on the afternoon of Monday 30 October.

The layout at Minehead was modified shortly before the date of the photograph. In 1928 a carriage siding was added immediately to the west of the turntable road; this is clearly evident in this 1930 view, as is the lengthened platform. It seems likely that the roofing of the station, which is now Grade II listed, was altered to its current form at the same time. The signalling visible was slightly modified four years later. The small engine shed, a single-road structure constructed in wood,

dated to the opening of the line. It had previously stood at Watchet and was slightly modified when relocated to Minehead. The shed closed in November 1956 and was subsequently demolished.

Although the station was capable of taking long excursion trains, much of the traffic was seasonal and the route was one of those listed for closure in the *Reshaping* report of March 1963. Freight facilities were withdrawn from the station on 6 July 1964 and passenger services ceased on 4 January 1971. This was not, however, the end of the story, as a preservation society was formed the following month and, two years later, the line from Norton Fitzwarren was purchased by Somerset County Council and leased to the new West Somerset Railway. Services were progressively reintroduced from 28 March 1976, when the Minehead-to-Blue Anchor section opened. Services now operate between Minehead and Bishops Lydeard, although there remains a main line connection at Norton Fitzwarren used by occasional through excursions. Today, the station building at Minehead remains largely as seen in the 1930 view. The goods shed – now extended – also remains in use by the railway. The signal box is, however, a replacement; the original box was demolished by British Rail in 1966 and in 1977 the redundant box from Dunster was relocated to Minehead as a replacement. The original 45ft (13.7m) diameter turntable also disappeared but, in 1974, the West Somerset Railway acquired the then disused 55ft (16.7m) turntable from Pwllheli. Extending it to 65ft (19.8m), the railway installed the turntable in a project completed in 2008.

EPW033299

Morpeth
18 October 1927

Viewed from the south, this photograph shows clearly the stations constructed to serve the Northumbrian town of Morpeth. Situated on the main line is the station built for the Newcastle & Berwick Railway, while to the south is the later station constructed for the Blyth & Tyne Railway. The latter, which was also used by trains operated by the North British Railway on the branch from Scots Gap between 1862 and 1872, closed on 24 May 1880. After the station's closure, all passenger services, including those on the Blyth & Tyne route, moved to the Newcastle & Berwick station.

The Newcastle & Berwick was authorised by an Act of Parliament of 31 July 1845 to construct a line from Newcastle to connect with the North British Railway at Berwick. The route opened from Newcastle to Morpeth on 1 March 1847 and on to Berwick on 1 July 1847. The company was not independent for long; it merged with the York & Newcastle on 9 July 1847 to form the York, Newcastle & Berwick Railway, becoming part of the North Eastern Railway on 31 July 1854. The now Grade II listed station at Morpeth – like others along the Newcastle & Berwick – was designed by the Newcastle-based architect Benjamin Green (1813–58) in a neo-Elizabethan style.

The Blyth & Tyne Railway was authorised by an Act of Parliament of 30 June 1852 to combine a number of pre-existing wagonways between the River Tyne and the River Blyth. A further Act of 4 August 1853 authorised the construction of a branch from Bedlington to Morpeth and the construction of a second station in the town; this opened on 1 April 1858. The importance of the station grew with the opening of the North British line from the west on 23 July 1862. However, the construction of a connection a decade later resulted in North British

services using the North Eastern Railway station from 1872. The Blyth & Tyne was bought by the NER on 7 August 1874, although passenger services continued to use the old Blyth & Tyne station until a connection was constructed, and a bay platform installed to the original Newcastle & Berwick station. The Blyth & Tyne station was originally built in stone and was later modified by the NER to provide accommodation for railway officers. Immediately to its east, and clearly visible in this 1927 view, the NER constructed a new goods shed in 1879. Freight facilities at Morpeth survived until the 1980s.

Timetabled passenger services over the ex-Blyth & Tyne route were withdrawn on 3 April 1950, although excursion trains continued to operate until 10 August 1953. Freight traffic, however, has continued to use the line, which remains open. There have been campaigns – although no concrete proposals – for the restoration of a passenger service. Passenger services over the ex-North British line via Scots Gap to Rothbury were withdrawn on 15 September 1952, with the line west of Morpeth to Woodburn closing completely on 3 October 1966, with the withdrawal of the remaining freight traffic.

Today, Morpeth station is still open; as well as the main station building, a section of platform awning, dating to the 1880s, is still extant on the Up platform. The main line is now electrified; the work was completed between Newcastle and Edinburgh in 1991. Also still extant are the ex-Blyth & Tyne station, now listed Grade II, and the 1879 goods shed; both of these are now in commercial use. The main station building itself is, at the time of writing, undergoing a major restoration programme.

EPW019776

Needham
9 October 1928

Situated on the Ipswich-to-Norwich main line, the station at Needham – as it was called until closure in 1967 – typifies the neo-Jacobean style adopted by Frederick Barnes (1814–98) for the Ipswich & Bury Railway. The station is built in red brick, with white-brick and Caen-stone detailing.

The railway was authorised on 21 July 1845 to construct a 42.25km line from Ipswich to Bury St Edmunds via Stowmarket. At Ipswich the line formed a connection with the Eastern Union Railway, another of the chain of companies that was eventually to complete the London to Norwich main line. Work on the new line started on 1 August 1845 and the line was officially opened throughout on 7 December 1846, with a through service from London. Following the Board of Trade Inspection on 15 December 1846, normal services commenced on Christmas Eve of the same year. At the time, not all of the Barnes-designed stations were complete. It was not until 1847 that the contractor Daniel Revitt, who worked closely with Barnes on a number of the latter's schemes, finished the work. The Ipswich & Bury and Eastern Union railways were worked as a single entity from 1 January 1847, with a formal amalgamation authorised on 9 July 1847. The enlarged Eastern Union Railway was worked by the Eastern Counties Railway from 1 January 1854, a move authorised by an Act of Parliament of 7 August 1854, before being formally merged into the Great Eastern Railway in 1862.

This view, taken from the west, shows to good effect the station building. Barnes designed buildings in a similar style for a number – but not all – of the other intermediate stations along the line. Apart from Needham, other survivors are Thurston and Stowmarket; all are now Grade II listed. The station building as illustrated here has been slightly modified from the original: a 1912 photograph shows elaborate Dutch-style gables and ogee caps on the end square towers, as opposed to the plain gable ends and the castellated parapets visible in 1928. This work seems to have been carried out shortly after the London & North Eastern Railway took over in 1923 and so would have been relatively newly completed when this photograph was taken. More recent work has seen modified steps, including a ramp for disabled access, at the main entrance.

Although not listed for closure in the 1963 *Reshaping* report, Needham was one of a number of intermediate stations between Ipswich and Norwich that were to close. Services were withdrawn from the station on 2 January 1967 but, in the case of Needham, the loss was relatively short-lived: passenger services were restored – with the station renamed Needham Market – on 6 December 1971. However, by that date the main station building had been leased out. The building was fully restored in the early 21st century and, more recently, work has been undertaken on an upgrade to the operational part of the station.

EPW024993

Newbury
15 August 1928

The Berkshire town of Newbury was an early target for both the Great Western Railway and the London & South Western Railway, but it was the former – through the nominally independent Berkshire & Hampshire Railway – that proved triumphant. This railway was authorised by an Act of Parliament of 30 June 1845 and, following a further Act of 14 May 1846, was formally absorbed by the GWR. The broad gauge line opened from Reading, through Newbury, to Hungerford on 21 December 1847. The route was converted to standard gauge in late June and early July 1874. The importance of the station grew with the opening of the Didcot, Newbury & Southampton Railway's lines north to Didcot (on 10 August 1882) and south to Winchester (on 1 May 1885). The new railway was operated by the GWR from opening but retained its independent existence through to Grouping in 1923. The last addition to the local railway network came courtesy of the Lambourn Valley Railway. This was originally authorised on 2 August 1883 but it was not until 2 April 1898 that services commenced on this 19km-long branch. While the Lambourn Valley initially operated its own services, these were taken over by the GWR in 1904. The larger company formally absorbed the smaller following an Act of Parliament of 4 August 1905.

With the opening of the routes north and south, as well as the Lambourn branch, the original station at Newbury was no longer adequate, particularly as it acted as a bottleneck for expresses using the Berks & Hants route on through services to and from the West Country. As a result, Newbury station was rebuilt between 1908 and 1910, with two through roads for the express services and with platform loops; this is the station recorded in this 1928 view from the south-west. Rationalisation of the local network predated the *Reshaping* report of 1963: passenger services to Lambourn ceased on 4 January 1960, those to Winchester on 7 March 1960 and those to Didcot on 10 September 1962. The lines closed completely, following the withdrawal of freight traffic, to Winchester on 31 December 1962, to Didcot on 10 August 1964 and, finally, to Welford Park – the Lambourn Valley line had closed beyond there completely on 4 January 1960 – on 5 November 1973.

Today, the railway station retains much of the ambience that resulted from the rebuilding immediately prior to World War I. The main red-brick building remains, as do the platform awnings. The goods yard – visible beyond the road overbridge in the 1928 view – is, however, no more; the site has been redeveloped and now accommodates a Sainsbury's supermarket. The footbridge remained in use until 2018, when a replacement was constructed at the opposite end of the station as part of work to electrify the line.

EPW022626

Newport Pagnell
August 1928

Viewed from the north-west, this is the terminus at Newport Pagnell of the short – 6.25km – branch from Wolverton. Promoted by the Newport Pagnell Railway, the line's construction was authorised by an Act of Parliament of 29 June 1863. This permitted the new railway to purchase the existing branch of the Grand Junction Canal – which had opened in 1817 – to the town and to enter into a working agreement with the London & North Western Railway for the line's operation. Work commenced on the line's construction in August 1864 and, on 30 September 1865, a trainload of navvies traversed the completed line. Initially, there was a dispute with the LNWR over access to Wolverton station with the result that, although freight traffic over the completed branch commenced on 24 July 1866, it was not until 2 September 1867 that passenger services began. Although powers were obtained for the extension of the branch northwards towards Wellingborough and some limited work was undertaken, this was never completed and the powers lapsed in 1871.

The branch possessed two intermediate stations – Bradwell and Great Linford – while the terminus, as shown in this 1928 view, had a single platform with a station building constructed in brick. The line ran beyond the passenger terminus through to Shipley Wharf, which had served the canal basin. The latter had been filled in to accommodate the railway's goods yard and a number of the buildings that served the railway post-1866 had their origins with the canal. Apart from the normal freight traffic, the terminus also had two private sidings to serve local flour mills. Both of these are visible in this view. The mills of Price & Goff can be seen on the north side of the goods yard; this was rail-connected in 1870. The second site – originally Hives & Sons but taken over by Francis Coales & Sons in 1885 – was served by a siding, visible in the photograph, that ran to the south of the platform. Another significant source of traffic arrived after World War II when the new owners of Aston Martin relocated manufacture of the cars to a factory in Newport Pagnell. Making use of the cattle dock, the railway delivered engines and chassis, and took away completed cars.

Operated by the LNWR from opening, the branch was formally taken over by the larger railway in 1875; it thus passed to the London, Midland & Scottish Railway in 1923 and to British Railways (London Midland Region) in 1948. The line was scheduled for closure in the *Reshaping* report of 1963. This was strongly opposed locally and resulted in a public inquiry being held on 7 June 1964. Despite numerous objections, permission to close the line was given and the final passenger services operated on 5 September 1964. Freight traffic continued for a further three years, until 22 May 1967, and the track was lifted later the same year.

Today, although the station site at Newport Pagnell and the goods yard have been redeveloped, the trackbed towards Wolverton is largely intact and part has been incorporated into the Milton Keynes 'redway' system, a network of paths designed for pedestrians and cyclists within Milton Keynes. Although the buildings at both Bradwell and Great Linford have been demolished, the platforms remain. With the significant population growth since the line's closure, there have been suggestions that the line's reopening could be a useful contribution to passenger transport provision within Milton Keynes.

EPW022488

Norwich City
6 July 1949

The city of Norwich possessed three terminal stations: Thorpe, which is still open, Victoria, which closed on 22 May 1916, and City, which is also now closed. The first two were operated by the Great Eastern Railway; the latter by the Midland & Great Northern Railway and it is this station that has been photographed here from the west by the Aerofilms cameraman.

The branch from Melton Constable to Norwich opened on 2 December 1882 under the auspices of the Lynn & Fakenham Railway. This company merged with Yarmouth Union and Yarmouth & North Norfolk railways on 1 July 1883 to create the Eastern & Midlands Railway. Construction work on the original City station was clearly still in hand at this date as the new building incorporated reference to the Eastern & Midlands Railway rather than to the Lynn & Fakenham. The Eastern & Midlands was to become the Midland & Great Northern Joint Railway – jointly controlled by the Great Northern and Midland railways – on 1 July 1893 following the opening of the line to Cromer and the connection to the Midland Railway at Saxby. The Midland & Great Northern passed to the joint control of the London, Midland & Scottish Railway and the London & North Eastern Railway at Grouping in 1923, but became solely run by the latter on 1 October 1936. By the date of this photograph, the station was controlled by British Railways (Eastern Region).

Norwich City was a substantial neoclassical main building complete with pediment over the main entrance. However, the city of Norwich suffered two nights of devastating German attacks on 27 and 28 April 1942 as part of the Luftwaffe's 'Baedeker Raids' on cities of cultural and historical importance. Among the buildings largely destroyed was Norwich City station. The view in this photograph, therefore, records the station in the aftermath of the wartime destruction. The once impressive building was replaced by a temporary structure that sufficed through to the closure of the line to passenger services on 2 March 1959. Freight traffic continued to serve the freight yard until 3 February 1969, when the section south from Drayton closed completely. The bulk of the station site has been demolished and much of it now lies under a roundabout on the A147 inner link road. There are, however, traces of the platforms, and the trackbed northwards forms part of Marriott's Way, a footpath that commemorates the Midland & Great Northern's engineer, William Marriott (1857–1943), who was involved with the railway and its predecessors for some 40 years.

Pictured in the station is Class D15 4-4-0 No 62538. This was one of the last survivors of the class. The locomotives were designed by James Holden (1837–1925) and built at Stratford. By this date, No 62538 was approaching the end of its life; it was withdrawn for scrap in April 1952, having achieved almost 50 years of service.

EAW024414

Padgate

May 1934

With a concrete pipe works in the background, this view records Padgate station (on the Cheshire Lines Committee route from Liverpool, via Warrington, to Manchester) from the north-west. The CLC was formed by the Great Northern Railway and the Manchester, Sheffield & Lincolnshire Railway on 5 July 1865, following the passing of the Cheshire Lines Transfer Act of that date, with the Midland Railway joining the following year. The Cheshire Lines Act of 15 August 1867 established the CLC as an independent company under the control of the three railway companies.

The station at Padgate was the result of the CLC's desire to construct an independent main line between Manchester and Liverpool. The powers to construct the line were, in fact, obtained by the MS&LR in two Acts of Parliament: the Manchester, Sheffield & Lincolnshire Railway (Extension) Act of 6 July 1865 and the Manchester, Sheffield & Lincolnshire Railway (New Works) Act of 16 July 1866. The completed lines were vested in the CLC on opening. The former permitted the construction of the main line and the latter a deviation to provide a more central station in Warrington following complaints that the original line was too far to the north. However, it was not until 1869 that major construction work started. The delay was caused by the economic downturn in the mid-1860s (the cotton industry and much other trade in the north-west suffered adversely from the trade embargo on the export of cotton from the Confederate states during the American Civil War) and by the offer, which was refused, by the London & North Western Railway to share traffic on its own route to Garston. Had work started promptly following the

passing of the Acts, construction was to have been handled by Thomas Brassey (1805–70), but the delay resulted in the work being handled by Abraham (later Sir Abraham) W Woodiwiss (1828–84) and his brother George (died *c* 1886).

Construction of the new line was more complex and expensive than anticipated but, in March 1873, the first freight traffic operated over the route, with passenger services commencing on 1 September 1873. Padgate station was located just to the east of the junction between the line through Warrington Central station and the avoiding line (which opened for freight traffic on 13 August 1883 and initially carried no passenger trains). It was one of the intermediate stations that opened with the line itself. The CLC – controlled by the London, Midland & Scottish Railway and the London & North Eastern Railway after the Grouping in 1923 – remained a joint operation until nationalisation in 1948.

Today the station is still open, albeit unstaffed, and retains its buildings on both platforms. The main station building is in commercial use – as a fish-and-chip shop and garden retailer at the time of writing – and is not listed. The concrete pipe works has disappeared, as have the open fields beyond; all have succumbed to residential development. General freight facilities were withdrawn from Padgate on 9 August 1965, while the direct line, from Padgate Junction to Sankey Junction avoiding Warrington Central, closed completely on 22 July 1968.

EPW044423

Pickering
15 May 1947

Viewed from the north-east and with the town's castle dominating the foreground, Pickering station, with its overall roof, can be seen on the extreme left of this view, with the line towards Whitby heading off towards the north.

The town was one of the earliest in Yorkshire to be connected to a passenger railway; the Whitby & Pickering Railway was authorised by an Act of Parliament of 6 May 1833 to construct the 38.5km-long line linking Pickering with the harbour at Whitby. The line was surveyed and engineered by George Stephenson (1781–1848) and included a rope-worked incline into the Esk Valley (this survived until a new alignment opened on 1 July 1865). The horse-operated line opened from Whitby to Grosmont on 8 June 1835 and on to Pickering on 26 May 1836. The original station at Pickering was slightly to the north of the train shed seen in this 1947 view. The railway was acquired by the York & North Midland Railway on 30 June 1845. The new owners constructed a line southwards to connect with the line from York to Scarborough at Rillington Junction and converted the existing line for the operation of steam locomotives. The first section of converted track, from Pickering to Levisham, was operational from 1 September 1846. In connection with the extension southwards, a new two-platform station with train shed was completed to a design by George Townsend Andrews (1804–55). The York & North Midland became part of the North Eastern Railway on 31 July 1854.

Pickering became a junction with the opening of lines westwards to Kirbymoorside on 1 April 1875 and eastwards to Seamer on 1 May 1882. The junctions for these lines were immediately to the south of the station. The local network of lines remained intact until nationalisation, but the first closures occurred shortly afterwards. Passenger services were withdrawn on the Seamer line on 5 June 1950, on which date the line east of Thornton Dale closed completely (the short section from Pickering to Thornton Dale became freight only until final closure on 10 August 1964). Passenger services through Kirbymoorside to Gilling ceased on 2 February 1953, on which date the section from Pickering to Kirbymoorside closed completely. In the *Reshaping* report of March 1963 it was anticipated that all routes to Whitby – from Middlesbrough, Rillington Junction and Scarborough – would be withdrawn. Although that from Middlesbrough survived, passenger services through Pickering were withdrawn on 8 March 1965, on which date the line north from Pickering closed completely. The section south to Rillington Junction remained open for freight traffic until final closure on 4 July 1966 (the last demolition train over the line southwards operated on 2 November 1969).

This might have been the end of the story but for the creation of the North Yorkshire Moors Railway Society in June 1967. Although the first working northwards from Pickering since closure occurred on 2 February 1969, it was not until 24 May 1975 that passenger services were officially relaunched to Pickering.

The preserved railway acquired the Grade II listed station at Pickering; however, the station was devoid of its overall roof, which had been removed in 1952 and replaced by platform canopies. As part of the preserved railway's 'Train of Thought' project, a replica train shed was installed at Pickering, with work completed in April 2011. In addition to the station there are two other Grade II listed railway buildings in the town that are now in alternative use. Immediately to the south of the station is the former engine shed; this dated to the York & North Midland Railway in 1845 and was enlarged in 1876. The shed originally had a turntable but, towards the end of the 19th century, this was relocated north of the station and the replacement 45ft (13.7m) turntable is clearly visible in the 1947 view. Andrews also designed a gasworks for the railway. Latterly used by the railway as a warehouse, this also survives and is now known as 'The Ropery'. Both of these structures are to the south of the station.

EAW005712

Pudsey Greenside
September 1928

When the Great Northern Railway line from Leeds to Bradford opened in 1854 it bypassed the small town of Pudsey, which was an important centre of the West Riding woollen trade. In order to serve the town, the GNR obtained powers in an Act of Parliament of 24 July 1871 to construct a short branch from Stanningley through Pudsey towards Bradford. Initially, only the section from Stanningley to Pudsey was completed. Although built to accommodate double track, the branch was initially constructed with only a single line and opened to freight traffic during the summer of 1877. Passenger services from Stanningley to Pudsey were introduced on 1 April 1878. There were two passenger stations: Pudsey Lowtown and Pudsey Greenside. It is the latter station that is illustrated, looking towards the north, in this 1928 view.

The GNR had ambitious plans for exploiting traffic in the West Riding and, consequently, a further Act was obtained on 16 July 1885 to extend the line from Pudsey to Cutlers Junction, south of Laisterdyke in Bradford, and to construct a curve from south to east at Bramley, thus allowing, for the first time, direct services from Leeds to Pudsey. The new lines opened on 1 November 1893 and the work included the doubling of the existing branch to Greenside. With the opening of the south-to-east curve at Bramley, the original link to Stanningley was closed. Among engineering work on the extension was a 565m tunnel immediately to the west of Pudsey Greenside station. The extensive goods yard, visible on the south side of the station, is testament to the amount of freight traffic generated by the textile mills of the town.

As with the rest of the GNR, the Pudsey loop line passed to the London & North Eastern Railway in 1923 and to British Railways (Eastern Region) at nationalisation. Like many lines in predominantly urban areas, passenger services over the loop suffered from the rise of the tram and the bus. Despite the competition, both stations survived until being listed for closure in the *Reshaping* report of March 1963. Passenger services over the branch from Bramley, via Pudsey, to Laisterdyke ceased on 15 June 1964. Freight facilities were withdrawn from the two intermediate stations on 6 July of the same year, resulting in the complete closure of the line from Cutlers Junction to Bramley.

Since the line's closure, the station site at Greenside has been fully redeveloped with warehousing and housing, although the Carlisle Road overbridge remains, illustrating where the railway once ran. Greenside Tunnel still survives – just – as planning permission has been granted to fill it in, along with the cutting between it and Carlisle Road. It is still possible to trace part of the route to the east of Greenside station. Much more extensive are the physical remains of the line to the west of Pudsey towards Cutlers Junction. Pudsey is now served by a station on the Leeds-to-Bradford line called New Pudsey. This opened on 6 March 1967 and was one of the earliest stations built to incorporate a significant car park. Located about 2km from Pudsey's town centre, it is, however, much less convenient for local residents than the two stations closed in 1964.

EPW023822

Redruth

24 June 1928

The first line to serve Redruth was the Hayle Railway. This standard gauge line was authorised by an Act of Parliament of 27 June 1834 to construct a number of lines in west Cornwall. Mineral traffic to Redruth commenced on 11 June 1838 but it was not until 23 May 1843 that a passenger service between Hayle and Redruth began. On 3 August 1846, the West Cornwall Railway was authorised to take over and use the Hayle Railway as part of the former's proposed line from Truro to Penzance; the actual purchase took place on 3 November 1846. The new line, built again to standard gauge (following an amendment to the original West Cornwall Act) but with provision for the use of the broad gauge, opened from the original Hayle Railway station in Redruth to Penzance on 11 March 1852. The line to Truro, over a Brunel-designed timber viaduct and through to a temporary station in the city, opened on 25 August the same year. At this date the original terminus in Redruth closed and the new through station (shown in this view taken from the south) opened. The original station, situated at the end of a short branch, reopened as a goods yard until closure on 6 May 1967.

Broad gauge rail was added to the West Cornwall Railway in November 1866, making it mixed gauge; this permitted, for the first time, the operation of through trains east of Truro. In 1888 the wooden viaduct at the southern end of the station was replaced by one constructed in stone. While accommodating only a single line at this stage, it was built of a sufficient width to permit the operation of double standard gauge track once the broad gauge was eliminated. Following the abolition of the broad gauge in 1892, doubling of the section west from Redruth to Carn Brae was completed during the first half of 1896 but it was not until December 1911 that the section east from Redruth was finished. The following year, Redruth underwent significant modification. A new goods yard – Drump Lane – opened to the east of the short tunnel and freight facilities at the station illustrated in this view were withdrawn on 17 June 1912. Two sidings on the Down side had existed, as had a goods shed on the Up, but these had been removed by the date of this photograph. In addition, the signal box was relocated from the northern end of the Down platform to the southern end, as recorded in this view. The next significant change to the station came in 1938, when the Great Western Railway replaced the main station buildings on the Up platform with a more modern structure constructed in brick with concrete banding. The signal box was closed in December 1955, when the block telegraph section was modified to simply Drump Lane to Redruth Junction.

Today, the station retains the 1938 block. Two elements visible in the 1928 view remain, however, and these are both now Grade II listed. The older of these two structures is the monogrammed lattice footbridge, which dates to 1888. The wooden platform shelter on the Down side dates to around 1900; the building's roof is extended over the platform, supported by iron brackets, to form a canopy.

EPW021734

Selby

September 1932

Pictured from the east, Selby station can be seen immediately to the south of the River Ouse. The station illustrated in this photograph is the third to have served the town, with the first, dating to the opening of the Leeds & Selby Railway, visible immediately to the east of the newer station.

The Leeds & Selby Railway was authorised by an Act of Parliament of 1 June 1830, with construction commencing four months later. The line opened throughout from a terminus in Marsh Lane in Leeds to the first station in Selby on 22 September 1834 for passenger traffic, with freight following on 15 December 1834. The brick-built station at Selby was designed by James Walker (1781–1862) and George Smith. The station was effectively a large warehouse, 75m in length and 29m in width, with three wooden-trussed spans on cast-iron columns. The building catered for both passenger and freight traffic, with the track for the latter being extended beyond the station to serve a quay on the river once it ceased to cater for passenger traffic (this is indicated by the date 1841 being cast into a beam inserted into the brick wall at the northern end).

The 1834 station had a relatively short life as, with the opening of the Hull & Selby Railway (authorised by an Act of Parliament of 21 June 1836) on 1 July 1840, a new through station was provided. The new station was constructed to the west of the 1834 station and the original station was converted to handle freight traffic only. This station was itself replaced in the early 1870s when Selby became an important junction station on the East Coast Main Line, following the opening by the North Eastern Railway of the lines from Shaftholme Junction (6km north of Doncaster) to Selby Old West Junction, and from Barlby Junction (north of the swing bridge) to Chaloners Whin Junction (just south of York).

The new station, designed by Thomas Prosser (1817–88), opened in 1873.

The increased traffic across the River Ouse bridge led to the replacement of the cast-iron bascule bridge built for the Hull & Selby Railway. The new swing bridge was designed by the NER's chief engineer, Thomas Elliot Harrison (1808–88), and opened, slightly to the east of the original bridge, on 1 February 1891. The hydraulic equipment for the new bridge was supplied by Armstrong Mitchell & Co; the ironwork and the foundation work was handled by the Cleveland Bridge & Engineering Co and the actual construction was completed by the York-based Nelson & Co.

In order to gain access to the new bridge, the alignment of the 1873 station was slightly modified. This work was completed to the design of William Bell (1844–1919). The Down platform, on the west, was largely unaltered but the platform on the Up side, to the east, was realigned, with Prosser's platform canopy reused and extended. This was the position as recorded by the Aerofilms photographer almost a decade after the NER had been subsumed into the London & North Eastern Railway.

Much of the railway infrastructure illustrated here still exists. The swing bridge remains operational and is now Grade II listed. Although the Prosser-designed single-storey main station building of 1873 has been replaced – by a more modern structure of 1964 – the bulk of the 1873 station as modified by Bell remains intact. This includes the platform canopies on both platforms, as well as the cross-braced iron footbridge and the Up station buildings. The station is also Grade II listed. Another survival is the original station of 1834; the final traffic to use the building ceased in 1984 and the structure has been in commercial use since then.

The building is also Grade II listed. Situated on Ousegate between the old and current stations, are two brick structures: a two-storey office block and a 17th-century building acquired by the Leeds & Selby Railway to accommodate the station superintendent. These structures are both Grade II listed. In many respects the most significant change has been the loss of the East Coast Main Line traffic; the development of the Selby coalfield and the construction of the diversionary route resulted in the closure of the Selby-to-York line on 24 September 1983.

EPW040264

Sevenoaks

8 June 1920

The first railway to serve Sevenoaks was the appropriately named Sevenoaks Railway. Backed by the London, Chatham & Dover Railway, this was authorised by an Act of Parliament of 1 August 1859 to construct a 9.6km line from Swanley to a station slightly to the north of Sevenoaks town centre (the future Bat & Ball station). The line opened on 17 July 1862. The station illustrated in this view, taken from the west just before the Grouping, was the result of the South Eastern Railway wishing to reduce the length of its London-to-Dover main line in order to compete better with the LCDR. The cut-off route from St Johns to Tonbridge was authorised on 30 June 1862 and opened to Chislehurst for passenger services on 1 July 1865, then on to Sevenoaks Tubs Hill on 2 March 1868, before finally reaching Tonbridge on 1 May 1868. A rail connection between the SER main line and the original station in the town opened on 1 August 1869. The two companies operating through Sevenoaks became the South Eastern & Chatham Railway Companies Joint Management Committee – better known as the South Eastern & Chatham Railway – on 1 January 1899 (with receipts split 59% to the SER and 41% to the LCDR). This organisation survived until the Grouping in 1923, although both companies retained their actual independence until the creation of the Southern Railway.

The station at Sevenoaks had two wooden buildings, as shown in this view, one on the Up side and one on the Down side. There were four through lines with two island platforms, two side platforms and two south-facing bay platforms, one on each side of the station. As can be seen, the outer through road in both the Up and Down directions had two platform faces, allowing passengers to access the trains on either side. Originally the station was not provided with a footbridge; the bridge illustrated in this 1920 view was added in the 1880s. The station

seen here survived unchanged for a further 15 years; it was in the mid-1930s that modifications were made as a result of the electrification of the ex-SECR lines. The completed work included the provision of new platform-level canopies, the conversion of the two bay platforms into sidings and the construction of a second footbridge. Electric services to Sevenoaks commenced via both the ex-LCDR and ex-SER routes on 6 January 1935. However, it was not until the British Railways era that electric services were extended further south.

The electrification of the main line south of Sevenoaks was approved in February 1956. Although main line electric services first operated through Sevenoaks on 12 June 1961, these ran to the timetable of the steam trains and it was not until 18 June 1962 that the full scheme was completed. The work at Sevenoaks included the lengthening of the platforms.

The station at Sevenoaks has had various suffixes in its time ('Tubs Hill', '& Rivermead' and 'Tubs Hill & Rivermead') but has been simply Sevenoaks since 5 June 1950. It has undergone a further modernisation since the arrival of the electric services. Although the 1935 platform canopies survive, during 1975 and 1976 the original station buildings on the Up and Down sides were demolished. The building on the Down side was replaced by a modern structure of brick and glass, while the site of the Up-side building is now additional station parking. The two footbridges – constructed in the 1880s and the mid-1930s – have both been replaced by a new footbridge to the south of the canopies. The station has also been reduced to four platforms – on the two island platforms, with the removal of the two side platforms visible in the 1920 view.

EPW001428

Shanklin
August 1928

Now once again a terminus, Shanklin station on the Isle of Wight is pictured here viewed from the south shortly after the station had been absorbed by the Southern Railway.

The line from Ryde to Ventnor was promoted by the Isle of Wight (Eastern Section) Railway. This railway was authorised on 23 July 1860 to construct the 18km line from Ryde (St Johns Road). Problems with fundraising and selecting an engineer meant that it was not until 20 March 1862 that John (later Sir John) Fowler (1817–98) was appointed the line's engineer. Following acceptance of a contractor's quote later that year, actual construction commenced early in 1863. The line opened from Ryde to Shanklin on 23 August 1864. By this date, however, following a further Act (of 28 July 1863), '(Eastern Section)' had been dropped from the company's name. Construction of the line south to Ventnor was delayed by the Earl of Yarborough, who forced the railway into a diversion through the 1.2km-long St Boniface Tunnel. The line from Shanklin to Ventnor opened on 10 September 1866. Although the line had been completed and inspected the previous month, the Board of Trade inspector, Col William Yolland (1818–85), found problems and would not sanction opening until these had been resolved.

Shanklin station was constructed for the opening of the line in 1864 and was extended in 1881 on the south-western side. The 1864 building included the stationmaster's house. As with the rest of the Isle of Wight Railway, Shanklin station passed to the control of the Southern Railway in 1923 and to British Railways (Southern Region) on 1 January 1948. The entire route from Ryde to Ventnor was listed in the *Reshaping* report of March 1963 for closure. However, permission was granted to close only the section from Shanklin to Ventnor. Services south of Shanklin ceased on 18 April 1966. Thus Shanklin station reverted to a terminus.

The next phase in the history of the line was electrification. Due to the loading gauge on the route, conventional rolling stock could not be utilised, with the result that it was decided to use modified second-hand stock acquired from London Underground. This required work installing the third rail and raising the track to ensure a level access from platform to carriage. As a result, the line was closed between 1 January and 19 March 1967 to permit the work to be completed. On privatisation in 1996, the line became a separate franchise – Island Line – but this was incorporated into an enlarged South Western franchise in 2007.

Today, the station uses the Down platform only; the subway linking this with the Up platform has been filled in, while the Up platform now forms a flower bed, with the buildings illustrated in the 1928 view now demolished. The main station building is Grade II listed and incorporates Isle of Wight Railway monogrammed brackets supporting the canopy to the rear of the building. South of the station, the bridge immediately adjacent to the platform ends has been demolished and the now closed line southwards to Ventnor has been incorporated into an entrance road to the Lower Hyde holiday park. The small goods yard, visible to the south of the station, closed on 6 December 1965. Beyond the park, the line can still be traced through to the outskirts of Wroxall.

EPW022917

Shrewsbury

August 1932

This complex triangular junction, with Severn Bridge Junction signal box at its centre, was recorded by the Aerofilms photographer in August 1932 at a time when the lines illustrated were still under joint ownership (although the Great Western Railway assumed sole control of the station that year). On the extreme right can be seen the train shed of Shrewsbury station, stretching over the bridge that carried the railway over the River Severn. Ironically, the London, Midland & Scottish Railway issued a publicity poster during the 1930s that portrayed Shrewsbury Castle, which is sited on a hilltop adjacent to the station, from across the river but, with a considerable amount of artistic licence, omitted the railway station and bridge from the view!

With three railways – the Shrewsbury & Chester, the Shrewsbury & Birmingham and the Shrewsbury & Hereford – all vying to serve the town, it was agreed that a joint station would be constructed rather than separate stations for each of the individual companies. The first meeting of the joint station committee took place in April 1847 and a site underneath the castle was selected. The Oswestry-based architect Thomas Mainwaring Penson (1818–64), who had designed the stations on the Shrewsbury & Chester line, was employed to design the station. The end result, which opened with the line to Chester on 12 October 1848, was designed in a neo-Tudor style and was constructed in Grinshill stone. The Shrewsbury & Birmingham (authorised by an Act of Parliament of 27 July 1846) opened from the town to Oakengates on 1 June 1849 and the Shrewsbury & Hereford (authorised on 3 August 1846) opened to passenger traffic on 6 December 1853.

The original station had two platforms under a wrought-iron train shed behind the two-storey building. The latter was extended to the west in 1854. The station as illustrated here, however, was the result of a major expansion project undertaken between 1899 and 1902. One of the original platforms was retained, but extended southwards over the river, while a new island platform with bays was added under a new train shed roof. The new station stretched over the River Severn on a widened viaduct. The main station building was also extended, this time by excavating beneath it and extending the existing cellars to provide a new entrance and a subway for access to the new island platform. This new work was designed by Robert Edward Johnston (c 1839–1913). As part of the widening of the viaduct across the river, the existing Severn Bridge Junction box, which had stood over the lines on the viaduct, was relocated. The original train shed roof at the northern end of the station was removed in 1924 and replaced by platform canopies.

The new signal box for Severn Bridge Junction was completed in 1903, being based on an existing London & North Western Railway design from 1876, and included a 180-lever frame. As befitted its ownership, equipment supplied by both the GWR and LNWR was incorporated.

Severn Bridge Junction still remains and is now Grade II listed; it is the largest surviving mechanical signal box in the world. There has been some – inevitable – track rationalisation, with the junction simplified and the two southernmost bay platforms now eliminated. The major change is to the station (also now Grade II listed): the train shed erected as part of the expansion between 1899 and 1902 was removed by the end of 1964 and replaced by platform canopies. However, the viaduct across the Severn, which has recently undergone a major refurbishment, retains the supports for the lost roof. In addition to Sutton Bridge Junction and Abbey Foregate boxes – neither of which is listed – there is also the Grade II listed Crewe Junction box situated immediately to the north of the station. This too dates to 1903 and includes a 120-lever frame.

EPW040078

Sowerby Bridge
September 1931

The original station serving Sowerby Bridge was located about 605m west of the later station, illustrated here, and opened with the section of the Manchester & Leeds Railway from Hebden Bridge to Normanton on 5 October 1840. This line, which had been authorised by an Act of Parliament of 4 July 1836, was engineered by George Stephenson (1781–1848) and Thomas Longridge Gooch (1808–82), and was renamed the Lancashire & Yorkshire Railway on 9 July 1847 after it had absorbed a number of other early railway companies. The importance of Sowerby Bridge grew on 1 January 1852 when the line from Milner Royd Junction to Halifax, authorised by an Act of Parliament of 18 August 1846, was completed. This permitted direct services from Manchester to Halifax and Bradford and, in 1854 (using running powers over the Great Northern Railway), to Leeds via Halifax.

The original station at Sowerby Bridge was a two-storey building constructed in stone in a neo-Perpendicular style with small crenellated square towers. This station was, however, replaced by a newer station. The impetus for the construction of this was the decision of the L&YR to construct, to main line standards, a branch to Rishworth. This was authorised by two Acts of Parliament – of 5 July 1865 and 20 June 1870 – and was part of a plan, never completed, to construct a cut-off route through Rishworth to Littleborough (*see* p 133) that would have reduced the Calder Valley main line by some 8km. To cater for the new line, the new Sowerby Bridge station opened on 1 September 1876 and the original station was demolished shortly after, to be replaced by a goods shed (visible in this view between the 1876 station and the mouth of Sowerby Bridge Tunnel, slightly to the east of the engine shed and on the south side of the line). Despite problems in its construction that almost led the railway to abandon work, the branch line opened to passenger services

as far as Rishworth on 5 August 1878, and through to Ripponden on 1 March 1881.

The new station, viewed here from the south-east, was built by the contractors Dransfield, Thomson & Holme, with its main building set at right angles to the existing main line. Behind this stone building was a concourse area that led, to the left, to the platforms; in front of the concourse was an open area – as illustrated in this 1931 view. The design of the station assumed that two platforms would be built on the Ripponden line; these were never constructed, leaving the station with the slightly strange arrangement portrayed. Initially, services on the Ripponden branch used the southernmost platform but the opening of Halifax Corporation's tram route from Sowerby Bridge to Triangle on 10 February 1905 resulted in the railway being at a competitive disadvantage and a basic platform, constructed in cinders and sleepers (visible to the south of the concourse and linked to it by a footpath), was added in 1907 when the branch service was taken over by steam railmotors. Although the branch was constructed with double track, for much of its impecunious existence only one was used for traffic, with the second effectively used as a long siding.

The introduction of railmotors was not a permanent panacea for the losses incurred on the branch service and the economic downturn in the late 1920s compounded the problem. As a result passenger services on the branch line ceased on 8 July 1929, although freight traffic to Ripponden continued until 1 September 1958. Sowerby Bridge station remained open to serve the main line.

The main station building at Sowerby Bridge was seriously damaged by fire in 1978 and subsequently the bulk of the structure was demolished by British Rail two years later. However, a fragment of the building – to the

west of the main block – survives and this has recently undergone refurbishment for use as a refreshment room. Also still remaining are the coal drops visible to the west of the station; these were constructed in the mid-1870s and are now Grade II listed. The final freight facilities were withdrawn from Sowerby Bridge in July 1984 and the once extensive goods yard is now the site of a supermarket. The station, reduced now to two platforms, has modern canopies – erected in 1981 – on both platforms.

EPW036872

Stamford

12 July 1947

The opposition of Brownlow Cecil (1785–1867), the 2nd Marquess of Exeter, of Burghley House, resulted in the Great Northern Railway taking a route from Peterborough northwards to the east of Stamford. Cecil was soon, however, to regret this decision and he backed the Stamford & Essendine Railway, which was authorised by an Act of Parliament of 15 August 1853 to construct a 6km branch from Essendine, on the GNR main line, to Stamford. The line opened on 1 November 1856 and Stamford was provided with a stone-built station on the site of the temporary station constructed for the earlier Peterborough & Syston Railway. This was designed by William Hurst in Tudor style and is visible, with its train shed and associated goods shed, in this view of Stamford looking towards the east in 1947.

The Stamford & Essendine Railway was operated from the outset by the GNR but the smaller railway undertook its own operation for a brief time between 1 January 1865 and 1 February 1872. During this period the London & North Western Railway branch from Wansford, which had been authorised on 25 July 1864, opened on 9 August 1867. The GNR resumed operation of the line to Essendine in February 1872 and, from 1 January 1893, the line was leased in perpetuity to the GNR. This action was confirmed in an agreement of 15 December 1893 and ratified by an Act of Parliament of 3 July 1894. Despite the lease, the Stamford & Essendine retained its notional independence through to the Grouping in 1923.

The ex-LNWR branch to Wansford lost its passenger services on 1 July 1929 and freight traffic seems to have ended a couple of years later, although there is photographic evidence that the line remained intact into the following decade. The ex-GNR station at Stamford became known as Stamford East from 25 September 1950, following the nationalisation of the railways two years earlier. It lost its passenger services on 4 March 1957, when they were diverted into the ex-Midland Railway station in the town via a connection between the ex-GNR and ex-MR routes, located slightly to the east of this view. Freight traffic continued to serve the goods yard at Stamford East until facilities were withdrawn on 4 March 1963. At this date the line from the Stamford Junction into Stamford East closed completely. Passenger services from Essendine to the surviving station in Stamford continued through until 15 June 1959.

Today the station building survives, listed Grade II, as two private houses, Welland Lodge and South View, while the goods shed, also listed as Grade II, has been converted into residential accommodation as part of the Welland Mews development. The station's train shed, which survived post-closure as part of a haulage business, has now been demolished.

Also visible in this view is the ex-MR line from Peterborough to Oakham. This line was promoted by George Hudson (1800–71) as the Syston & Peterborough Railway as part of his ambitious plans to gain access to East Anglia for the Midland Railway. Authorised by an Act of Parliament of 30 June 1845, it opened from Syston to Melton Mowbray (see p 143) on 1 September 1846 and from Peterborough to Stamford on 2 October of the same year (serving a temporary station that later became the site of the GNR station). The missing link, from Stamford to Melton Mowbray, opened to freight traffic on 20 March 1848 and to passenger services on 1 May 1848. This line remains operational, providing a link between Peterborough and Leicester.

EAW008126

Stockbridge
July 1930

Stockbridge station in Hampshire was one of the intermediate stations opened by the Andover & Redbridge Railway between Andover Junction, on the main line between Salisbury and Basingstoke, and the line from Southampton to Brockenhurst.

The Andover & Redbridge Railway was authorised by an Act of Parliament of 12 July 1858 to construct a broad gauge line along the route of the Andover Canal. This was not the first attempt to replace the existing canal with a railway; proposals had been made during the 'Railway Mania' of the mid-1840s for such a conversion, but these had come to nought as a result of the railway politics of the day. The Andover Canal had originally been proposed in 1770, but it was not until 1794 that the 35km-long waterway opened. The Andover & Redbridge Railway was backed by the Great Western Railway, which saw the line as a means of extending its influence into territory then dominated by the London & South Western Railway. However, the new company failed financially, with both the GWR and the LSWR seeking to gain control. In the event, it was agreed in 1863 that the latter would assume control – a decision confirmed by an Act of Parliament that backdated the transfer to 14 November 1862. Following completion of the now standard gauge line, plus an authorised extension at the northern end of the line to join the LSWR main line at Andover, the route opened throughout on 6 March 1865. In all, there were eight intermediate stations along the route: Andover Town, Clatford, Fullerton (which was to become the junction for the line to Hurstbourne), Stockbridge, Horsebridge, Mottisfont, Romsey (which was a pre-existing station on the line from Eastleigh to Salisbury) and Nursling. Nicknamed the 'Sprat & Winkle Line', the route was upgraded in the mid-1880s by the removal of certain severe curves, and proved an important link in the movement of troops in both World Wars. However, the section from Romsey to Andover Junction was slated for closure in the *Reshaping* report of 1963 and passenger services over this section were withdrawn on 7 September 1964, at which time the line between Andover Town and Kimbridge Junction at Romsey was closed completely as freight traffic ceased over the section. The stub at the northern end – from Andover Town to Andover Junction – survived until 18 September 1967. To the south, the section from Romsey to Redbridge survived, although Nursling station closed.

This view of Stockbridge, taken looking towards the north, shows to good effect the layout of the station and its associated goods yard. Among the rolling stock visible in the latter are a number of horseboxes – distinguishable by the roof vent over the grooms' compartment. The area around Stockbridge was the location for a number of stables and horsebox traffic was important. Although this traffic disappeared in the 1970s, British Railways constructed no fewer than 115 new horseboxes as late as 1957 and 1958. The layout of the station is a good example of the use of trailing – rather than facing – points to gain entry to the goods yard. This was a consequence of early railway experience, where trains had suffered derailment as a result of splitting the facing point. Following closure, the station at Stockbridge was demolished. Today there is little indication that there was ever a station, goods yard or even a road overbridge at this site as the location has been redeveloped to form a roundabout on the A30. Elsewhere, sections of the trackbed of the closed section of line form part of the long-distance Test Way footpath.

EPW033731

Stone
May 1929

Stone station in Staffordshire, seen here viewed from the west, is the junction on the West Coast Main Line south of Stoke-on-Trent where the line towards Stafford via Norton Bridge diverges from the route to Colwich Junction.

Promoted by the Potteries Railway – one of the three initial constituents of the North Staffordshire Railway – the line from Norton Bridge to Stoke was authorised on 26 June 1846. Other sections of the railway authorised on the same day were the lines from Stoke to Macclesfield, to Crewe, to Newcastle and to Silverdale, along with the line from Stone to Colwich. The first section of the new railway to open was that from Norton Bridge to Stoke on 17 April 1848. With the opening of the line, a station was provided at Stone. This was near the Newcastle Road bridge but closed the following year when, with the opening of the Stone-to-Colwich Junction section, the station illustrated in this 1929 view opened on 1 May 1849. The station building, which has been Grade II listed since 1972, was designed in a neo-Elizabethan style by Sir Henry Arthur Hunt (1810–89), who was also responsible for Stoke-on-Trent station and the associated Winton Square. Hunt had a wide-ranging career: he worked with Sir Charles Barry (1794–1860) on the rebuilding of the Houses of Parliament and was also employed by the London, Brighton & South Coast and Eastern Counties railways, among others. He was knighted for his work in 1876.

The station continued as a junction until, in 1947, the platforms on the main line south to Colwich were closed and subsequently demolished. The next major development saw the main Colwich Junction-to-Stoke and Norton Bridge-to-Stone sections converted to 25kV; new electric services over the routes were introduced on 5 December 1966. Apart from the passenger station, this view also records the goods shed on the east side of the line; freight facilities were provided at Stone until 7 August 1967. The goods shed still survives, and is now integrated into a tyre repair shop. The sidings illustrated on the Down side have also disappeared; these have been replaced by an industrial estate along Whitebridge Way. The station building was refurbished in 2003 by Stone Town Council for use by the local community.

From 2004 until December 2008 Stone station was devoid of stopping trains, with passengers to and from the station conveyed by bus. This was a consequence of upgrading work on the lines from Norton Bridge and Colwich to Cheadle Hulme, which resulted in the temporary withdrawal of the stopping service from Stafford to Stoke. However, this service was not reinstated following completion of the work and, when passenger trains were once again timetabled to stop at the station, Stone became a stop on the stopping service from London Euston to Crewe.

EPW026983

Stratford-upon-Avon Old Town

28 May 1947

The Stratford-upon-Avon & Midland Junction Railway operated a straggling network of cross-country lines that provided a link across the south Midlands from Northampton via Towcester and Stratford-upon-Avon to the Midland Railway line from Birmingham to Evesham.

The line east from Stratford was promoted by the East & West Junction Railway. This was authorised by an Act of Parliament of 23 June 1864 to construct a 53km line from just west of Towcester (where an end-on junction was to be made with the already authorised Northampton & Banbury Railway) to Stratford, where it would connect into the Great Western Railway. Although construction work started on 3 August 1864, lack of finance meant that building work was protracted and it was not until 1 July 1873 that the line was open throughout. Initially the new railway's services terminated at the existing GWR station, although an independent station – illustrated in this 1947 view from the south – was built and opened with the line. This was used as an intermediate station for trains heading to and from the GWR station. The company's parlous financial position continued after opening, with an Official Receiver being appointed on 29 January 1875. Passenger services were suspended over the route between 1 August 1877 and 2 March 1885, although the new service from Broom Junction to Old Town commenced on 2 June 1879.

West of Stratford, the line was constructed by the Evesham, Redditch & Stratford-upon-Avon Junction Railway. This 12.5km line was authorised on 5 August 1873 and opened on 2 June 1879. Operated by the East & West Junction Railway from opening, it too was weak financially and was taken over by the Official Receiver on 2 January 1886.

These two railways, along with the Stratford-upon-Avon, Towcester & Midland Junction Railway, formed the S&MJR on 1 January 1909, following an Act of Parliament of 1 August 1908. The railway expanded, following an Act of 29 April 1910, through the purchase of the Northampton & Banbury Junction Railway on 1 July 1910. The S&MJR retained its independence until the Grouping, when it became part of the London, Midland & Scottish Railway.

Although passenger traffic was relatively limited, the line was a useful route for freight – particularly for ironstone traffic – and was heavily used during World War II, resulting in the completion of a new east-to-south curve at Broom Junction on the ex-Midland Railway's Birmingham-to-Evesham line. Passenger services west of Stratford were temporarily withdrawn shortly after the date of this photograph, on 16 June 1947; the closure became permanent on 23 May 1949. The remaining passenger services over the ex-S&MJR line – from Stratford to Blisworth – were withdrawn on 7 April 1952. Freight traffic, however, remained and a new east-to-south curve at Stratford opened on 13 June 1960 in order to route ironstone from Banbury via a second new spur at Kineton over the S&MJR to the ex-GWR route from Stratford south to Cheltenham. This permitted the final closure of the section west to Broom from Stratford. This traffic did not last long and the surviving line from Stratford to Fenny Compton (where a Ministry of Defence depot was sited) closed on 5 July 1965.

Following withdrawal of passenger services from the station in 1952, the freight yard remained operational until general freight facilities were withdrawn on 11 November 1963. Limited private siding traffic continued for a period thereafter. The engine shed, which is visible to the south of the station along with two Class 4F 0-6-0s, dated originally to 1873 and was extended in 1908; the structure as seen in this view was the result of a rebuilding in 1934. The shed closed on 22 July 1957 and was subsequently demolished. Today nothing remains of the S&MJR presence in the town: the trackbed of the railway – along with that of the now closed ex-GWR line towards Honeybourne – has been incorporated into the A4390 Seven Meadows Road. However, the piers of the railway bridge across the River Avon, as shown in the 1947 view, were utilised in the construction of the replacement road bridge.

EAW006659

Sunningdale
September 1933

Located on the Surrey/Berkshire border, Sunningdale is an intermediate station on the former London & South Western Railway line from Waterloo to Reading. This view is of the station from the south-west, with the main A30 road from London heading across the level crossing at the station's eastern end.

The line through Sunningdale was promoted by the Staines, Wokingham & Woking Railway. This company was authorised on 8 July 1853 to construct a line linking the existing branch from Richmond to Windsor via Staines to the Reading-to-Farnborough line at Wokingham, along with a branch via Chertsey and Addlestone to meet the main line at Weybridge. The route opened from Staines to Ascot on 4 June 1856 – when the station at Sunningdale opened – and then on to Wokingham on 9 July 1856. The line was operated from its opening by the LSWR and the larger company took a lease on the line following an Act of Parliament of 28 August 1858. The Staines, Wokingham & Woking was formally absorbed by the LSWR on 1 July 1878. Visible in the photograph adjacent to the level crossing is Sunningdale signal box. This was an LSWR Type 2 box and was constructed at about the same time as the line was absorbed by the LSWR. The station was known as Sunningdale when it first opened, then had the suffix '& Bagshot' between 1 January 1863 and 1 March 1874 and the suffix '& Windlesham' between 1 March 1893 and December 1920.

Today, the scene is radically different. The A30 has been widened into a dual carriageway at the level crossing, with the railway platforms cut back at the London end to accommodate the wider road. This has resulted in the replacement of the footbridge by one located mid-platform. To cope with the longer trains now operated on the route, the platforms have been extended at the Reading end. Goods facilities were withdrawn from Sunningdale on 6 January 1969 and the goods shed was subsequently demolished; the site of the goods yard is now occupied by a supermarket and the station car park. The signal box was reduced to a gate box on 8 September 1974 with the opening of the power box at Feltham. With the modernisation of the crossing, the box was finally closed on 5 September 1975 and demolished.

The station buildings as illustrated in the 1933 view have been demolished and replaced. Those on the Down platform were constructed using the CLASP method. This type of relatively cheap construction, originally designed for school buildings, was adopted on a number of stations on, predominantly, Southern and Western regions between 1965 and 1977. CLASP was a type of prefabricated single-storey building with a flat roof; other examples on the Waterloo-to-Reading line included Virginia Water and Wokingham. Prone to rot, a number of these – but not Sunningdale – have been rebuilt.

EPW042992

Tattenham Corner
October 1928

There are few more important horse races in the Flat calendar than the Derby held annually at Epsom on the first Saturday in June. Vast numbers make their way to the racecourse to experience the classic race and, over the years, public transport for the event has been essential for its smooth running. The first railway to try to capitalise on the traffic that the racecourse might generate was the London, Brighton & South Coast Railway, which opened its short branch from Sutton to Epsom Downs station on 22 May 1865.

The line to Tattenham Corner was promoted by the independent Chipstead Railway. This was authorised by an Act of Parliament of 27 July 1893 but was a source of considerable friction between the LBSCR, which with justification saw it as a threat to its commercial interests, and the South Eastern Railway. The railway was promoted by Cosmo Bonsor (1848–1929), who was MP for Wimbledon between 1885 and 1900 as well as being chairman of the South Eastern Railway from 1897 until the creation of the joint committee with the London, Chatham & Dover two years later. The Act permitted construction of a branch from a junction on the Purley-to-Caterham line to Kingswood, a distance of some 11km. The single-track route opened on 2 November 1897. By this date a 2km line through to Tattenham Corner – the Epsom Downs Extension Railway of 1894, privately promoted by Bonsor – had been authorised. This opened in two stages: to Tadworth on 1 July 1900 and to Tattenham Corner itself on 4 June 1901. This was, appropriately, that year's Derby Day. The SER was authorised in 1898 to provide £200,000 towards the extension, formally taking it over on 13 July 1899. Although the extension was constructed as single track, work on converting the entire branch to double track was completed on 2 July 1900. The Chipstead Railway's

engineer was Sir John Wolfe-Barry (1836–1918), one of the most eminent of the late Victorian engineers.

The station was eventually provided with seven platforms, as well as extensive sidings to the south (and out of view in this photograph, taken from the north-west). The fact that it was closer to the racecourse meant that traffic on race days to Epsom Downs was reduced; even the Royal Train was diverted from 1925. The station closed in September 1914, as a result of cutbacks during World War I, and was used only for occasional race specials following reopening in 1920; Tadworth was the usual branch terminus. However, following electrification of the line, full services were restored through to Tattenham Corner on 25 March 1928, the year this photograph was taken.

Today, Tattenham Corner survives but its facilities have been much reduced. There are now only three platforms and the station accommodation has been reduced to a basic shelter. The once extensive sidings have been eliminated, with much of the land to the east, west and south of the station now developed for housing. The road parallel to the railway on the eastern side is named in memory of Emily Davison, the Suffragette who was killed by the king's horse, Anmer, during the Derby on 8 June 1913.

EPW025149

Tavistock (South)
September 1928

The South Devon & Tavistock Railway was incorporated on 24 July 1854. The company was authorised to construct a 21km broad gauge line from Plymouth to Tavistock, which was formally opened on 21 June 1859; public services commenced the following day. The goods yard at Tavistock opened on 1 February 1860. At this stage the station was a terminus; it did not become a through station until the completion of the Launceston & South Devon Railway. This was authorised by an Act of Parliament of 30 June 1862 to construct a 30.5km-long line linking Tavistock with Launceston. The broad gauge line opened officially on 1 June 1865, with public services commencing the following month. Both lines were operated from opening by the South Devon Railway. The Plymouth-to-Tavistock line was amalgamated with the South Devon following an Act of Parliament of 5 July 1865; the Tavistock-to-Launceston line merged with the South Devon following an Act of 24 June 1869.

When originally completed in 1865 the station at Tavistock had an overall train shed and station building. In addition, there was a small engine shed at the south end of the station but this closed with the completion of the extension to Launceston. The original wooden station building was destroyed by fire in 1887. The route became mixed gauge to permit the standard gauge trains of the Devon & Cornwall Railway to operate over the line. The powers for this were obtained in 1866 but it was not until 17 May 1876 that the first London & South Western Railway services operated through the station to Plymouth. The LSWR continued to use the line until the completion of its own route through Tavistock with the opening of the Plymouth, Devonport & South Western

Railway on 2 June 1890. By this date the South Devon had been incorporated within the Great Western Railway. The next significant change came at nationalisation: in order to avoid confusion, the ex-GWR station received the suffix 'South' on 26 September 1949.

As the finances of the railway industry deteriorated in the 1950s, two competing – and parallel – routes through to Plymouth were deemed one too many and, as the ex-LSWR route was part of a main line, it was the ex-GWR route that closed. Passenger services were withdrawn on 29 December 1962; however, appalling wintry weather meant that the last train did not actually operate and other services were abandoned earlier. The line south from Tavistock to Marsh Mills closed completely on the same day. The surviving freight traffic to the goods yard was served by the line north to Lydford until these, too, ceased with the closure of the yard at Tavistock South on 7 September 1964.

The view, taken looking towards the south, shows the train shed and goods shed. The main station buildings at Tavistock South were on the southbound platform, with the footbridge at the north. The signal box was located on the southbound platform immediately to the south of the train shed roof. Since the line's closure, virtually every trace that a railway existed south of the River Tavy in the town has disappeared. The station site has been redeveloped, with the Tavy Health Centre occupying part of it. The former LSWR station – Tavistock North – has fared better: Grade II listed, its buildings have been carefully restored for other uses.

EPW023606

Totnes
August 1937

Initially known as the Plymouth, Devonport & Exeter Railway, but authorised as the South Devon Railway following its Act of Parliament of 4 July 1844, the broad gauge line between Exeter and Plymouth was engineered by Isambard Kingdom Brunel (1806–59). Although Brunel was open-minded about the type of traction to be employed, the gradients of the route and doubts about the efficacy of contemporary steam locomotives ultimately led him to decide to adopt the atmospheric system. However, when the first section of line – from Exeter to Teignmouth – opened on 30 May 1846, the atmospheric system had not been completed and conventional locomotives were initially introduced. This was still the case when the line opened to Newton Abbot on 30 December 1846 and, effectively, when services were extended to Totnes – known as 'Totness' until around 1870 – on 20 July 1847. While the atmospheric system did operate briefly between Exeter and Teignmouth, it never reached Totnes, although an engine house was constructed for its use.

Totnes remained a terminus until 5 May 1848, when the line through to Plymouth (see p 43) opened to passenger traffic. The original station had canopies that extended over the platform loop lines; this effectively resulted in two parallel but unlinked train sheds. The Ashburton branch (see p 51), the junction for which was slightly to the east of this view of the station, taken from the south-east, opened on 1 May 1872. A second branch, the freight-only link to the quay, opened on 10 November 1873. This headed southwards from a point slightly to the east of the goods shed. Both of these lines were constructed to the broad gauge. The South Devon Railway was absorbed by the Great Western Railway on 1 February 1876 and the broad gauge through the station was finally abolished over 21–22 May 1892.

The view taken in 1937 illustrates the station after considerable work had been undertaken during the interwar years. This included the extension of the platform loop lines to the west and the remodelling of the junction for the Ashburton branch. The Down platform was extended in 1933 when the Down-side sidings were also modified. The signal box, which had originally stood towards the western end of the Down platform, was replaced by a new GWR Type 7 box on 7 January 1923. This contained a 74-lever frame and took over the work of the ground frame that had controlled access to the quay line and, in 1933, control of the junction to the Ashburton branch following the closure of Ashburton Junction box. After World War II, the Down platform loop was further extended.

After nationalisation, passenger services over the Ashburton branch were withdrawn on 3 November 1958; the branch closed completely on 10 September 1962. Subsequently preserved, the line now operates from a second station – Riverside – in Totnes as far as Buckfastleigh, although preserved services did operate into the main Totnes station between 5 April 1985 and 2 September 1987.

The main station buildings, on the Down platform, were destroyed by fire on 14 April 1962. These were replaced by a supposedly temporary structure. The line serving the quay remained open until 4 December 1967. The goods shed, visible at the bottom of the photograph, was demolished in 1965, but limited freight traffic – generated by a milk plant that had taken over the former atmospheric engine house at the east end of the Up platform – continued until 1980.

Today, the temporary structure established after the fire in 1962 has been replaced by a new main station building; this opened on 21 October 1983. The wooden station buildings on the Up platform, with narrowed canopy, remain, although the 1887 footbridge illustrated in the photograph is no more. This was destroyed in an engineering accident on 18 October 1987 and subsequently replaced. The signal box still survives; reduced in status to a fringe box on 17 December 1973 and finally decommissioned on 9 November 1987, it is now Grade II listed and is currently in use as a café. Another surviving structure is the former engine house, constructed by the South Devon Railway but never used for its original purpose; this is now listed Grade II.

EPW054792

Warminster
August 1937

Backed by the Great Western Railway, the Wiltshire, Somerset & Weymouth Railway was authorised by an Act of Parliament of 30 June 1845 to construct a broad gauge line from Chippenham to Weymouth, with a number of associated branches. The railway's engineer was Isambard Kingdom Brunel (1806–59) but it struggled financially and was able to open only its first section – from Thingley Junction to Westbury – on 5 September 1848. Little further was achieved until the GWR took over the company. The transfer of ownership took place on 14 March 1850 (confirmed by an Act of Parliament of 3 July 1851). The GWR took on the partly completed works and opened the section south from Westbury to Warminster on 9 September 1851. The town was the terminus of a 7.5km branch until the opening of the 31.25km single-line section to Salisbury on 30 June 1856. Conversion of the line from broad to standard gauge took place in June 1874 and the line was subsequently doubled.

When completed, Warminster station had a wooden train shed similar to that which survives at Frome; however, this was removed in about 1930 and replaced by the platform canopies visible in this 1937 view, taken from the south-east.

Today, Warminster station remains open, served by services between Westbury and Salisbury. The main – wooden – station building remains, along with its two platform canopies, as rebuilt in the early 1930s, although the footbridge has been replaced and the signal box closed. Freight facilities were withdrawn from the station, except for private siding traffic (although this too subsequently ceased), on 2 April 1973. The site of the goods yard has been converted to a retail park, while the sidings to the north of the station have been replaced by a car park.

EPW054762

Watford (Met)
August 1927

Viewed from the south-west when barely two years old, Watford's Metropolitan Railway station was the result of a project, begun before World War I, to provide a link from the existing Metropolitan & Great Central Joint line at Rickmansworth to Watford town centre. There was, however, opposition to the railway as the proposals involved the line running through Cassiobury Park on an embankment. As a result of the opposition, the Act of Parliament of 7 August 1912 that authorised the railway curtailed the branch south of the park.

Although land was purchased for the construction of the 4km line, the outbreak of World War I in August 1914 delayed construction until 1922. It was not until 2 November 1925 that passenger services commenced from the station illustrated here – electric on the Metropolitan-to-Baker Street line and steam on the London & North Eastern Railway line to Marylebone (the LNER was successor to the GCR after 1923). The railways made one further attempt to extend the line northwards in 1927, with property being acquired on Watford High Street as the site of a possible station. However, the cost of tunnelling under Cassiobury Park proved prohibitive and the project did not progress. The steam-operated service to Marylebone was an early casualty, being withdrawn shortly after the General Strike of 1926. One of the consequences of the failure to breach Cassiobury Park was that the station was ill-placed to compete with the existing station (Watford Junction) on the main line into Euston (*see* p 25).

The station building at Watford, along with that at Croxley (the only intermediate station on the branch), was designed by Charles Walter Clark (1883–1972), who was the Metropolitan Railway's architect from 1911 until the railway was absorbed into the London Passenger Transport Board in 1933. The station he designed for Watford, which is now Grade II listed, was completed in brick with a steeply tiled roof. It was in a domestic style to complement the tone set in the houses constructed as a result of the burgeoning property boom in the Metroland era.

Today, the station at Watford continues to handle Metropolitan line services; the small goods yard visible in the photograph has, however, disappeared. Freight facilities from the station were withdrawn on 14 November 1966. There are long-term plans for the revival of the moribund ex-LNWR branch to Croxley Green and its connection to the line between Watford (Met) and Rickmansworth. This would result in the diversion of Metropolitan line trains to Watford Junction and the possible closure of the short section of line from the new junction to the station illustrated here. Inevitably the possible closure has resulted in opposition from those likely to be inconvenienced by the change and the retention of the short section with some restricted shuttle service is a further possibility. At present, however, all is on hold as there is some doubt over the project's funding.

EPW019235

Whitley Bay
18 October 1927

Although Whitley had been served by two earlier stations, the opening of the North Eastern Railway's coastal route from Tynemouth to Monkseaton on 3 July 1882 resulted in the closure of the original alignment, inherited from the Blyth & Tyne Railway, situated inland from the later route. For the new line, the NER's then chief architect, William Bell (1844–1919), designed a third station, to be called Whitley; it acquired the suffix 'Bay' in 1899.

The major impetus to the growth in traffic along the route came with NER's Tyneside electrification programme. The coastal route through Tynemouth and Whitley Bay was converted in a number of stages, with electric services commencing between Monkseaton and Tynemouth on 21 June 1904. Such was the success of the new services – in terms of commuter traffic, day trippers and holidaymakers – that the relatively new station at Whitley Bay was no longer adequate and a new station, slightly relocated, was constructed to cater for the booming traffic. The new station, again designed by Bell (he retired in 1914), opened on 9 October 1910. The building featured a highly decorated clock tower, clearly visible in this view, as well as an overall train shed spanning platforms and lines, along with a substantial station building in brick. The station and train shed have been listed Grade II since 1986.

The original electric services over the line were withdrawn in 1967, with the last rush-hour services via Whitley Bay operating on 17 June 1967. The replacement DMUs had a life of just over a decade until the development of the Tyne & Wear Metro. Re-electrification of the line resulted in services from Whitley Bay to Newcastle via Monkseaton being suspended on 23 January 1978, with those via Tynemouth following on 10 September 1979. The line reopened with the introduction of Metro services on 11 August 1980.

In the 90 years since the photograph was taken (viewed from the west), the station building has survived. The train shed, however, has been significantly reduced in length – it now has seven bays as opposed to the 13 visible in 1927, having been cut back at both ends. A replacement footbridge has been installed at the Monkseaton end.

EPW019767

Wilmslow
June 1932

Wilmslow in Cheshire is now one of the more important intermediate stations on the line between Crewe and Manchester and is also the point at which the alternative line to Manchester, via Styal, branches off from the main line. The route through Wilmslow was proposed by the Manchester & Birmingham Railway, which was authorised by an Act of Parliament of 30 June 1837 to connect these two important manufacturing centres. However, only the section from Manchester to Crewe was completed. Following completion of the 22-arch viaduct at Stockport, services were extended through to Crewe on 10 August 1842. The Manchester & Birmingham had a relatively short independent existence; it merged with the Grand Junction and London & Birmingham railways to form the London & North Western Railway on 16 July 1846.

By the end of the 19th century the existing main line south of Manchester was no longer adequate, with the result that the LNWR promoted the construction of a second route from Slade Green Junction, near Longsight, through to Wilmslow. This line opened on 1 May 1909 and resulted in the construction of the second viaduct to the north of Wilmslow station and the remodelling of the station itself to four platforms, those on the east dealing with main line traffic and those on the west with that for the Styal line.

Since the photograph was taken in 1932 (viewed from the south-west), both the main line and the Styal branch have been electrified. Electric services over both routes were formally launched by the then Minister of Transport, Ernest Marples MP, on 12 September 1960, although full services were not introduced until June 1961. As part of the work, the ex-LNWR signal box, visible to the south of the station, was replaced by a new box designed by the London Midland Region's architect William Robert Headley. This box survived an attack by the IRA on 26 March 1997. It was demolished in April 2006, as a result of the upgrade of the West Coast Main Line.

Today, the street-level buildings remain intact from the 1932 view, as do the platform buildings that serve the Styal line and the Down main; those on the Up main have, however, been replaced. To the east of the station, the A34 dual carriageway now cuts its way north–south parallel to the railway, and the area immediately to the east of the station has been redeveloped.

EPW038616

Worcester Shrub Hill
17 September 1971

When the Birmingham & Gloucester Railway opened in 1840, the line bypassed Worcester, passing to the east of the city. It was the development of the Oxford, Worcester & Wolverhampton Railway that resulted in the construction of Shrub Hill station. The OWWR was authorised by an Act of Parliament of 4 August 1845 to construct its 142.5km route. This was planned to pass over the Birmingham & Gloucester line at Abbot's Wood and the Midland Railway, which had leased the Birmingham & Gloucester on 1 July 1845 and formally taken it over on 3 August 1846, proposed the construction of a link to connect with the OWWR route and thus serve Worcester. It was the MR line from Abbotswood Junction that opened first, to a temporary station at Tallow Hill, Shrub Hill, on 5 October 1850. The first section of the OWWR – from Evesham to Stourbridge – opened officially on 1 May 1852. The OWWR also constructed a link from Droitwich Spa to Stoke Works, on the ex-Birmingham & Gloucester line. This opened in mid-February 1852 and thus permitted through services from Birmingham Curzon Street to reach Worcester from the north; prior to that date, these services had operated over the link from Abbotswood Junction. Until his resignation on 17 March 1852, the OWWR's engineer had been Isambard Kingdom Brunel (1806–59).

This view from the north-west shows to good effect the main station building at Shrub Hill. It was constructed in 1865 largely in brick, with stone detailing and a slate roof, and has been modified and extended over the years. The structure is attributed to Edward Wilson (1820–77), who was appointed locomotive and permanent way engineer of the OWWR in 1858 and was subsequently involved in the construction of Liverpool Street station in London, having set himself up in private practice in 1864.

The station at Shrub Hill had a curved roof constructed of wrought-iron lattice girders with ridge-and-furrow glazing, although it was removed in the mid-1930s. The main station building has been Grade II listed since 1971; one feature, however, is Grade II* listed. This is the iron-framed waiting room situated towards the southern end of the eastern platform, which was originally one of two; the waiting room on the western platform has been demolished. The construction date of this waiting room is uncertain, but it was probably built in the late 1860s. The cast iron for the frame was supplied by the locally based Vulcan Ironworks (which was later known as McKenzie & Holland, one of the country's leading signalling engineering companies), which operated from the south side of Shrub Hill Works. The waiting room's highly decorative tiling was supplied by the noted manufacturer Maw & Co, of Broseley in Shropshire. For a number of years this structure was considered to be at risk, but a major project, completed in 2015, saw it restored to its original condition.

Worcester, at the time of writing, remains controlled by semaphore signalling. Shrub Hill station is controlled by Shrub Hill box, located slightly to the south of the station (and thus out of view in this image). This structure contains an 84-lever frame and dates to 1935. Although Network Rail has plans to eliminate all manual signal boxes eventually, the box at Shrub Hill is scheduled to survive for some years, and some mechanical equipment was replaced in 2016.

EAW215580

Ashford Wagon Works
15 July 1947

The railway first arrived in Ashford, in Kent, courtesy of the South Eastern Railway (authorised as the London, Deptford & Dover Railway by an Act of Parliament of 21 June 1836), on 1 December 1842, with the opening of the line from Headcorn. Ashford was the terminus of the company's line until 18 December 1843, when the line through to Folkestone opened.

The importance of the town to the SER grew in 1847 when the company purchased a 75-hectare site on the south side of the main line towards Folkestone, in order to construct a new locomotive works (not shown in this photograph) in place of the earlier workshops at New Cross. Alongside the new workshops, the railway also constructed housing for its workers in a district that became known as Alfred (or later New) Town. This district also included a number of public buildings, designed by the SER's architect Samuel Beazley (1786–1851) and his successor William Tress.

The carriage and wagon works – which are illustrated here viewed from the south-east – were constructed on a separate site in 1850. The works – known as Kimberley – included in 1947 extensive timber drying sheds, on the extreme south-west side, still showing evidence of the wartime camouflage paint scheme in this photograph. The main workshop area was to the north with, from west to east, the wagon building and repairing shop (with sawmill at the northern end), the carriage and wagon wheel shop and the wagon lifting and repairing shops.

The locomotive works was rebuilt and enlarged during the first decade of the 20th century, following the closure of the London, Chatham & Dover Railway's works at Longhedge, with all the successor South Eastern & Chatham Railway's locomotive work now concentrated at Ashford. It closed in July 1962. The carriages work undertaken at Ashford was transferred to Lancing (*see* p 203) in the 1920s. However, the wagon works remained operational until its final closure in late 1981, with the loss of almost 1,000 jobs.

Today, there is nothing left of the former wagon works; the site was redeveloped after closure and is now occupied by a Richard Rogers-designed retail centre and supermarket. The Ashford-to-Hastings railway line remains, although it was threatened with closure in the 1963 *Reshaping* report. It is the only passenger line in Kent that is operated by diesel traction. On the western side of the former works runs the A2042, a dual carriageway constructed to provide a link between Ashford and the M20. Ashford station, visible in the distance, was substantially rebuilt in the early 1960s as part of the Kent Coast electrification scheme and underwent a further modernisation in the early 1990s as a result of the opening of the Channel Tunnel. The completion of HS1, from the Channel Tunnel to St Pancras, which opened on 1 November 2007, has further altered the local railway scene.

Of the former locomotive works there are, however, some structures that survive at the northern end of Newtown Road. These include a red-brick clock tower, gatehouse, kiln and engine shed (latterly used as a paint shop and now occupied by Network Rail), which are Grade II listed. After closure, the bulk of the locomotive works was converted into an industrial estate and the main buildings subdivided. Part of the site has now been cleared, with residential development planned, and the remaining structures are now in a near-derelict condition. Of Alfred Town (which was also expanded after the transfer of work from Longhedge in 1900), a number of the public buildings survive, although the housing has been replaced.

EAW008274

Lancing Carriage Works
26 November 1927

The London Brighton & South Coast Railway initially established its workshops at Brighton. However, by the early 20th century the existing facilities were proving inadequate, so the railway decided to construct a second workshop to handle carriage and wagon work. In 1910 the company acquired 270,000m^2 at Lancing for this purpose. Construction was completed in 1912 and the following year the then chief mechanical engineer of the railway, Lawson Butzkopfski Billinton (1882–1954), proposed the closure of the existing Brighton Works and the transfer of all locomotive work to the new site. In the event, World War I prevented this move being completed and the plan was not resurrected after the end of the war. The carriage works was located west of Lancing station and to the south of the line from Brighton to Worthing. The facility was served by a short branch that headed south from the main line and this view records the works from the south-west, with the main line visible in the distance.

The date of the photograph is significant: following the Grouping in 1923, the newly created Southern Railway decided to close the former South Eastern & Chatham Railway carriage works at Ashford (*see* p 201; the wagon works continued to operate at Ashford until 1981) and transfer the work to Lancing. As a result, some 500 workers were relocated from Kent to Sussex and the works was considerably expanded. By 1931 the works included large carriage and paint shops, with a traverser providing a link between the separate shops that dealt with normal and Pullman rolling stock.

With nationalisation, Lancing's importance continued and, in 1954, proposals were made to increase the workload through the works to include the maintenance of EMU stock. However, with the gradual reduction in the size of the railway network and the reduced need for carriage maintenance, British Railways decided to rationalise its workshops. Of the two carriage works then serving the Southern Region – Eastleigh and Lancing – it was announced on 19 September 1962, as part of a statement covering all BR workshops, that the former would be retained and the latter closed. At the time, Lancing employed 1,670 people; in all, the announcement led to the loss of some 18,000 jobs out of the 56,000 then employed by BR's workshops throughout the UK. Work was progressively transferred away from Lancing over the next three years and Lancing Works closed completely on 25 June 1965. Following closure, the site was acquired by West Sussex County Council and has been redeveloped as an industrial estate named after Winston Churchill. The main sheds, albeit in a much modified form, still exist in a variety of commercial uses.

EPW020178

Oswestry
14 August 1954

Situated close to the Welsh border, Oswestry was the headquarters of the Cambrian Railways and site of the company's workshops. This view, taken from the north-east, shows the former Cambrian line from Whitchurch, via Ellesmere, approaching Oswestry past the works, with the former Great Western Railway line from Gobowen coming in from the north. Beyond the station, the Cambrian line extends southwards towards Welshpool.

The first railway to reach Oswestry was the Shrewsbury & Chester Railway's branch from Gobowen. This had been authorised by an Act of Parliament of 27 July 1846 and opened on 23 December 1848. The Shrewsbury & Chester became part of the Great Western Railway on 1 September 1854. Following the opening of the Oswestry & Newtown Railway in 1860 (*see* below), the GWR obtained running powers into the former's station but an independent GWR station in the town survived until after the GWR and Cambrian merged, finally closing on 7 July 1924. At the date of this photograph, the former GWR station site was still in use as a goods yard; freight facilities survived until 6 December 1971.

The first phase of the future Cambrian presence in the town came with the opening of the Oswestry & Newtown Railway, to a station south of the existing GWR station, on 1 May 1860. The line had been authorised by an Act of Parliament of 26 June 1855 and was completed through to Newtown on 10 June 1861. The Oswestry & Newtown line was extended eastwards courtesy of the Oswestry, Ellesmere & Whitchurch Railway; this had been authorised on 1 August 1861. Although the eastern section of the route opened on 20 April 1863, it was not until 27 July 1864 that the section from Ellesmere to Oswestry opened. This, however, was two days after the two smaller companies had merged with two others to

form the Cambrian Railways. The Cambrian constructed a new station building to act as its headquarters and, following a further merger in 1865, decided to construct a new works in the town. This is seen in this view as the large building immediately south of the junction.

With a design by John Robinson (1823–1902), of the Manchester-based engineers Sharp, Stewart & Co, derived from the existing Shrewsbury & Hereford Railway's workshops at Coleham in Shrewsbury, the works was built in red brick and cost £28,000 to construct. Capable of handling locomotives, carriages and wagons, the works – along with the rest of the Cambrian Railways – became part of the GWR on 1 January 1922. The works survived until closure on 31 December 1966 and was listed as Grade II in 1986. The building remains and has been converted for a number of new uses (including a health centre, following renovation work to the southern part of the building). Its listing cites the rarity value of the building, noting that 'relatively few buildings of this type survive with associated contemporary buildings, and in a recognisable form.'

Oswestry is no longer on the railway map, although the ex-Cambrian station is home to a preservation group whose long-term aims include the restoration to service the moribund track of the line from Gobowen. Passenger services over the ex-Cambrian line from Whitchurch to Welshpool (Buttington Junction) ceased on 23 November 1964 and the line closed completely east of Oswestry on 18 January 1965. The ex-GWR branch to Gobowen lost its passenger services on 7 November 1966 but the line remained open for freight traffic, primarily stone from the quarry at Blodwell (accessed via the ex-Cambrian route southwards). This line was effectively closed in the late 1990s but has remained mothballed since then. Apart from the railway

works, a number of other railway structures in the town also survive; these include the ex-Cambrian railway station and the signal box, constructed in 1892, to its south, which are also both now listed Grade II.

EAW056424

Wolverhampton (Stafford Road) Works and Sheds
6 September 1946

The extensive facilities provided at Wolverhampton by the Great Western Railway shortly before nationalisation are clearly apparent in this view, taken from the east. Although the origins of Stafford Road dated back to the Shrewsbury & Birmingham Railway of 1849, much of the site visible in 1946 dated to major investment completed in 1932 following the Loans & Guarantees Act of 1929. This Act was passed to permit major investment as a means of alleviating unemployment and, following approval, work commenced at Stafford Road on 5 November 1929.

In the foreground can be seen the engine shed. The oldest structure here was the northernmost of the two long sheds that ran from east to west. This was originally a three-road shed opened by the GWR on 14 November 1854. It was extended to a four-road shed in 1865 and from 1869 until 1932 was used as the workshop's tender shop; it was reroofed as part of the 1932 programme of work. The next shed to be completed was the first of the two roundhouses. No 1 shed was the westernmost of the three blocks in the foreground; this opened in 1860 and was reroofed at a later date (probably as part of the 1932 programme). Between the original long shed and the first roundhouse, the second long – two-road – shed (No 4) opened in 1865; this was also reroofed in 1932. The second roundhouse, No 2 shed (visible here without a roof but with turntable extant), was completed in 1874 and again subsequently reroofed. By the date of this photograph it had largely fallen into disuse, although locomotives continued to be stabled on its roads until the shed's final closure. The third roundhouse, shed No 3, was completed in 1875. Again reroofed, probably as part of the 1932 programme, the building fell out of use and, as can be seen in this 1946 view, was already devoid of track. To the south of the three roundhouses can be seen the

final development of the shed complex; this was No 5 shed, which was completed in 1882. This ceased to accommodate locomotives in 1932, being used as a motor transport depot thereafter. The shed was finally closed by British Railways on 9 September 1963 and the site was eventually cleared.

The Shrewsbury & Birmingham Railway was authorised by an Act of Parliament of 3 August 1846 to construct a line between Wolverhampton and Shrewsbury. It opened from Shrewsbury to Oakengates on 1 June 1849 and on to Wolverhampton on 12 November the same year. The new railway established a small works and shed at Stafford Road, which passed to the GWR when the latter acquired the Shrewsbury & Birmingham on 1 September 1854, following an Act of Parliament of 7 August 1854. The original works was sited to the east of the running line, on the west side of Stafford Road, and can be seen clearly beyond the northernmost of the locomotive sheds. The works was considerably expanded by the GWR in 1855, when it became the railway's principal workshops for dealing with standard gauge locomotives. The first locomotives constructed at the workshops were completed in 1859 and by the time that such work ceased in 1908, 794 locomotives had been built. Thereafter, the works concentrated on locomotive maintenance.

As part of the 1932 programme, a new repair shop was constructed. This was 137m in length and 60m in width. This is the building visible with its three gables to the west of the Wolverhampton-to-Shrewsbury line in the photograph. The end for Stafford Road Works was foreshadowed by the Modernisation Plan of 1955 and, on 26 May 1959, British Railways announced that the workshops would be closed. This was partially reversed on 3 September 1960 with an announcement

that Stafford Road would be retained for diesel repair work but with a reduced workforce. However, as part of the Railway Workshops Reorganisation Plan, which was announced on 23 August 1962 and which led to a reduction of 18,000 in British Railways' UK workshops workforce, that reprieve was rescinded. On 21 August 1963 formal notice of closure was given. The last locomotive to be overhauled at Stafford Road was ex-GWR 2-8-0 No 2859 (which was subsequently preserved), with work completed on 11 February 1964. The works formally closed on 1 June the same year.

Today nothing survives to indicate the presence of either the locomotive sheds or the works. The site of the 1932 workshops is now occupied by the Dunstall Trading Estate, while the former shed site is now occupied by industrial units. Dunstall Park station, visible to the east of the original workshops, closed on 4 March 1968. The line from Wolverhampton to Shrewsbury remains and is now electrified as far as the carriage sidings at Oxley. The ex-GWR line towards Wolverhampton Low Level also remains, although it is now modified to curve northwards to provide a link into the West Coast Main Line at Bushbury Junction. The main line itself has closed, being replaced by the Midland Metro east of Priestfield station.

EAW002444

Arnside Viaduct
May 1929

Viewed from the south, a freight train has just crossed the Kent Viaduct at Arnside, travelling east towards Arnside station. Authorised by an Act of Parliament of 24 July 1851, the Ulverstone (sic) & Lancaster Railway constructed a 32km line linking the Furness Railway with the Lancaster & Carlisle Railway at Carnforth. Backed by the Furness, the single-track line, which was subsequently doubled, opened throughout on 10 August 1857 to freight traffic and to passenger services on 1 September that year. An Act of Parliament of 12 July 1858 empowered the Furness Railway to purchase the new line, which it had operated from opening, but this was not completed until 21 January 1862.

There were two significant engineering features on the new line: the viaducts that crossed the Leven and Kent estuaries. Both were relatively low-lying – that at Arnside is a maximum of 8m above sea level at low tide. They were designed by James (later Sir James) Brunlees (1816–92), who replaced two earlier engineers and who was appointed as a result of his success in dealing with a similar problem when engineering the Londonderry & Coleraine Railway in Ireland. The viaducts were built by W & J Galloway & Sons of Manchester (William Galloway, 1796–1893, and his brother John, 1804–94). The construction was challenging in that both viaducts crossed wide expanses of sand, which could be between 9m and 21m in depth. In seeking out the bedrock on which to locate the supporting iron columns, the contractors adopted the then novel method of using high-pressure water jets to clear the intervening sand.

The resulting viaduct at Arnside extends over the Kent estuary for a distance of 505m and includes 50 piers. Although 50 of the wrought-iron lattice spans were 9m in length, towards the eastern side of the viaduct, and clearly visible in this 1929 view, there was a single but longer 11m wrought-iron span. It was originally planned that this would open, to permit the passage of ships up and down the Kent estuary to Sandside. However, following agreement between the railway and the shippers, this was replaced by a fixed span, with the railway funding the provision of a new quay at Arnside – again visible in the view – and a new road. The viaduct was modified in 1915 when the original iron supporting columns were encased in stone in order to reduce corrosion.

The viaduct remains operational, handling all traffic to and from the Cumbrian coast southwards. The structure is currently unlisted. Out of shot to the east, Arnside signal box is, however, Grade II listed. This Furness Railway box, dating to 1897, was added to the list in November 2013. It is stone built, using limestone with red sandstone dressing, and is probably the work of the architectural practice of Edward Graham Paley (1823–95) and Hubert James Austin (1841–1915). It is regarded as a little-altered example of an FR Type 4 box.

EPW026572

Belmont Viaduct

15 April 1948

Viewed here from the south, Belmont Viaduct is a nine-arch structure that spans the River Wear to the north of Durham on the now closed line that once linked the direct line from Durham to Gateshead with the original main line to the north-east via Leamside.

Although there had been proposals to construct a line west from Leamside through Durham to Bishop Auckland in the 1840s – indeed powers for its construction had been granted by an Act of Parliament of 30 June 1848 – the fall from grace of George Hudson (1800–71) resulted in construction being delayed and it was not until 1 April 1857 that the line opened. The line and viaduct were designed by the North Eastern Railway's newly appointed chief engineer, Thomas Elliot Harrison (1808–88). Old mine workings caused problems during the construction of the viaduct and the ground had to be stabilised before work could be completed. The viaduct was constructed in stone with brick soffits. Each of its nine arches has a span of 18.25m and the structure stretches for 213.5m, with a maximum height of 39.5m.

Passenger services between Durham and Sunderland were scheduled for closure in the *Reshaping* report of March 1963 and were withdrawn on 4 May 1964. The section of line from Newton Hall to Leamside closed completely on 22 October 1964. Today the viaduct is Grade II listed. The bulk of the trackbed is traceable for virtually its entire line, although it has been severed slightly to the east of the viaduct by the upgraded A1(M). Belmont Viaduct is now owned by Durham County Council. There were plans to refurbish the structure as part of an ambitious proposal to improve facilities for walkers and cyclists but although funding was available, problems with land acquisition resulted in the project's failure.

EAW014529

Bollington Viaduct
July 1930

With the 23-arch viaduct stretching north to south, this view taken from the west shows the Cheshire town of Bollington, with the Waterhouse Cotton Mills in the foreground. The sizeable cotton industry was one factor in the development of the line through the town, as were the quarries and collieries.

The Macclesfield, Bollington & Marple Railway was backed by the North Staffordshire and the Manchester, Sheffield & Lincolnshire railways and authorised by an Act of Parliament of 14 July 1864. The primary factor behind its development was the desire of the NSR to gain an independent route into Manchester, thereby bypassing the London & North Western Railway (and its excessive charges). The line opened throughout for passenger services on 2 August 1869, with freight traffic following on 3 April 1871. The ownership of the new railway was vested – on 25 May 1871 – in the two larger companies and so, by the date of this photograph, had passed to the joint ownership of the London, Midland & Scottish Railway and the London & North Eastern Railway. The line was initially laid as a single track but was doubled in 1871, when second platforms were provided at the intermediate stations. In addition to through trains, there was a shuttle service from Bollington to Macclesfield for workers; this was served from 1921 by a petrol railcar operated by the Great Central Railway (as successor to the MS&LR) and from 1935 by a Sentinel-built steam railmotor. It was withdrawn in 1939.

Effectively a duplicate route, the line's position was closely examined in the 1963 *Reshaping* report and the entire 17km route was scheduled for closure. In the event, the short section at the northern end serving Rose Hill, Marple, was retained as it handled a considerable amount of commuter traffic to and from Manchester. The remainder of the route closed completely with the withdrawal of passenger services south of Rose Hill on 5 January 1970. Removal of the track was completed by the end of the following year.

The most impressive structure along the route was the viaduct at Bollington, which was situated to the north of the station. Constructed primarily in stone, on a slight curve, the viaduct has 23 arches, including two blanks, and is currently unlisted. It was threatened with demolition in the 1970s but was reprieved after a vociferous local campaign. More recently, it has undergone refurbishment and now forms part of the Middlewood Way. This footpath occupies much of the trackbed of the former railway, and was established in the early 1980s following purchase of the trackbed by Macclesfield Borough Council for £1 in 1981. The council wished to increase leisure facilities within the borough and the line of the closed railway was ideal for its purposes. Today the viaduct still stands proudly over the valley; it no longer looks out over cotton mills, however, as the Waterhouse Mills have been demolished and replaced by a housing estate. North of Bollington, it is possible to walk the entire route to Rose Hill; south of the town, however, the alignment of the railway has been incorporated into the route of the A523 into Macclesfield town centre.

EPW034223

Brackley Viaduct

21 June 1938

This view from the north-east records the substantial viaduct constructed to the east of Brackley to carry the Great Central main line from Rugby towards Aylesbury across the River Great Ouse. Brackley's first station (on the Banbury-to-Verney Junction line, which opened to passengers on 1 May 1850 and closed on 2 January 1961) can be seen in the background.

Authorised by an Act of Parliament of 29 June 1893, construction of the Great Central Railway's London Extension was split into two divisions: north, from Annesley to Rugby, and south, from Rugby to Quainton Road, where the GCR connected into the existing Metropolitan Railway. Brackley was part of the Southern Division, and a second station was built in the town for the line. The engineers for the Southern Division were Sir Douglas Fox (1840–1921) and his brother Francis Fox (1844–1927), who was also later to be knighted. The contractor for the work at Brackley was Walter Scott & Co of Newcastle and construction started in November 1894. Although locals had warned the contractors about the unstable nature of the land at the southern end of the proposed viaduct and extra work had been undertaken at this end to strengthen the foundations, it became obvious when the viaduct was nearly complete that cracks had started to appear and that remedial action was necessary. As a result, the southernmost two arches of the viaduct were replaced by two steel girder spans and by a strengthened second pier (this was effectively the combining of the second and third piers and the infilling of the original arch). This work can clearly be seen in the photograph. With work

completed, the viaduct extended over some 233m in length, with 19 brick-built spans each of just under 10.5m and the two girder spans (each of 11m). The maximum overall height of the viaduct was 19m.

Like the rest of the GCR, control passed to the London & North Eastern Railway at Grouping and to British Railways (Eastern Region) at nationalisation. Transferred to the London Midland Region, the ex-GCR main line north of Aylesbury was listed for closure in the *Reshaping* report of 1963 and through services north of Aylesbury ceased on 5 September 1966, when the line north of Calvert Junction to Rugby closed completely. The viaduct survived unused for a further decade. However, despite local opposition, it was demolished, for hard core used to construct roads in Milton Keynes, in 1978.

Today, although there are traces of Brackley Central station in the town, all that survives of the viaduct is the springing of the northernmost arch. Improvements to the main A43 to the east of Brackley have seen the elimination of some of the trackbed, as well as the small road underbridge visible to the north of the viaduct in the 1938 view. Brackley's population has grown considerably since the line's closure and Chiltern Railways, the current franchisee for services out of London Marylebone, has identified the ex-GCR route to Rugby and Leicester as a possibility for restoration in the long term.

EPW057718

Breydon Viaduct
May 1928

Viewed from the north-west, the five-span Breydon Viaduct was situated to the west of Great Yarmouth as part of the line constructed to link Yarmouth Beach station with Lowestoft.

Following an agreement made between the Great Eastern and Midland & Great Northern Joint railways on 18 March 1897, the Norfolk & Suffolk Joint Railway was created on 25 July 1898. The new company was to control two separate sections of line: from North Walsham to Cromer via Mundesley-on-Sea and from Great Yarmouth to Lowestoft. In order to connect to the new line from Lowestoft, the M&GNJR sponsored the construction of a 3.5km line – the Lowestoft Junction Railway – from Yarmouth Beach station to Gorleston North Junction. This was authorised by an Act of Parliament of 6 August 1897 and opened on 13 July 1903.

The Lowestoft Direct had to cross the River Yare and the Breydon Viaduct was the solution. The mechanical and structural design was completed by William E Newman, with Alexander Ross (1845–1923) acting as engineer-in-chief and William Marriott (1857–1943), of the M&GNJR, in overall control. As river traffic had to be accommodated, the second span from the south was designed to swing open – as evident in this view from 1928 – which allowed for two 18m passages for the river traffic. The bridge was largely constructed in steel, although the swing section sat on a cast-iron pivot and 5cm ball bearings. The resulting structure was so easy

to move that it could be handled by a single individual. In all, the bridge extended for 240m and was single track throughout. The remainder of the Lowestoft Junction railway was constructed to double track and entry to and exit from the viaduct was controlled by two signal boxes, one at either end of the structure.

As with the rest of the M&GNJR network, operation of the Lowestoft Junction Railway passed to the London & North Eastern Railway on 1 October 1936 and thus to British Railways (Eastern Region) at nationalisation. However, concerns that the viaduct required major repair work resulted in the withdrawal of passenger services over the line on 21 September 1953. It was not until 1962 that the viaduct was finally demolished. Even though it had been out of use for almost a decade, the condition of the structure at demolition was much better than anticipated, contrary to the concerns outlined prior to the structure's closure.

Following demolition, the pilings of the original viaduct survived for a quarter of a century, not being removed until the construction of the new road viaduct carrying the A12 Gorleston relief road in the late 1980s. The new road bridge, which still has to accommodate the river traffic, follows the alignment of the railway bridge, and the trackbeds north and south of the River Yare have also been incorporated into the modern road.

EPW021193

Calstock Viaduct
September 1928

Pictured from the south, Calstock Viaduct straddles the River Tamar to the north of the more famous Royal Albert Bridge to the west of Plymouth.

The branch line from Bere Alston to Callington was a relatively late addition to the railway network. Backed by the Plymouth, Devonport & South Western Junction Railway, which operated the line from opening until being formally absorbed into the London & South Western Railway in 1922, the Bere Alston & Calstock Railway was authorised under a Light Railway Order of 12 July 1900 to build a connection from the Plymouth-to-Tavistock main line at Bere Alston to connect with the existing East Cornwall Mineral Railway at Calstock. The latter was a 3ft 6in gauge mineral line that ran from quarries in the Gunnislake area to Calstock, where a cable-operated incline allowed access to a quay on the River Tamar. The East Cornwall opened on 8 May 1872. Although initially successful, its fortunes went into decline and the line was finally purchased by the Plymouth, Devonport & South Western Junction Railway on 4 January 1894 (following powers granted in an Act of Parliament of 19 July 1887). The original LRO permitted the construction of the line to 3ft 6in; this was amended by a second LRO on 12 October 1905 to standard gauge. The new powers also permitted the conversion of the East Cornwall line to standard gauge as well. The line opened throughout from Bere Alston to Callington on 2 March 1908; the cable-operated incline continued to operate until 1934.

The most spectacular engineering feature of the line is undoubtedly the single-track viaduct at Callington. The viaduct, which has twelve 12.25m spans plus a small arch in the Calstock abutment, stretches a distance of 240m, with a maximum height above the river level of 37m. It was designed by William Robert Galbraith (1829–1914) and Richard F Church, who set up in partnership in 1892; the former had been an engineer with the LSWR since 1862. The main contractor was Liskeard-based John Charles Lang. Although appearing to be constructed in stone, the viaduct, which is now Grade II* listed, was completed in concrete and is the largest concrete railway viaduct in the British Isles. The blocks of concrete were precast to 1.5m by 1.25m by 0.9m; in all some 11,148 were used to complete the work, with foundations stretching into the local sandstone to a maximum depth of 14.25m.

The line passed from the LSWR to the Southern Railway and then to British Railways in 1948. With the publication of the *Reshaping* report in March 1963, not only was the branch line from Bere Alston to Callington threatened with closure, so too was the main line from Plymouth (*see* p 43) through Bere Alston to Okehampton. Although permission to close the latter north of Bere Alston and the section of the branch west of Gunnislake to Callington was given, lack of suitable crossings of the Tamar, along with the poor quality of the local road network, meant that the line from Gunnislake to Bere Alston and on to Plymouth was reprieved. Services from Callington to Gunnislake ceased on 7 November 1966 and those on the main line on 6 May 1968. Today, Calstock viaduct is still providing an essential link for passenger services across the Tamar.

EPW023620

Cams Hill (Portchester Road) Viaduct, Fareham
August 1928

Situated between Fareham and Portchester, on the former London & South Western Railway line towards Portsmouth, the now Grade II listed Cams Hill Viaduct historically crossed the A27 Portchester Road and the Wallington River. The viaduct has 17 brick-built arches; of these 16 are just over 9m in span, with that over the A27, with a severe skew, being slightly longer at 11m.

Following the completion of its line to Southampton (*see* p 47), the LSWR was keen to reach Portsmouth, as was its rival, the London, Brighton & South Coast Railway (which had received powers in 1845 to extend westwards from Chichester). Fearing the competition, the two railways negotiated a deal – that the LSWR would extend eastwards from Fareham (*see* p 95) to Cosham, where a joint station would be opened, and that the line from there into Portsmouth would be joint. Following the line's construction, the Fareham-to-Cosham section opened on 1 September 1848, with LSWR through services to Portsmouth commencing exactly a month later.

To construct the line, the LSWR employed Joseph Locke (1805–60) and he undertook the design of the viaduct. The viaduct is constructed in red brick with a yellow-brick string course below the parapet. Since the viaduct's construction, the only significant change to the railway has been the electrification of the Fareham-to-Cosham line; third-rail services over this section were introduced in May 1990.

Since the photograph, taken from the south-east, the most significant change to the view has not been to the railway but to the local road network and to the estuary of the river. Immediately to the north of the viaduct, and running parallel to it, is the improved A27. The original course of the A27 through the skew bridge is now incorporated into a new roundabout, which has resulted in the road also now passing under one of the more eastern spans. Much of the marshy land around the viaduct has been drained and the Wallington River now occupies a much more well-defined channel. The new link road to the M27 heads to the north-east at the eastern end of the viaduct.

EPW023065

Charlton Viaduct
1924

Located north of Shepton Mallet, the 27-arch Charlton Viaduct was one of seven viaducts and five tunnels constructed for the Somerset & Dorset line as it traversed the Mendip Hills between Evercreech Junction and Bath. At 290m in length, it is the longest of the septet and is now Grade II* listed.

The Somerset & Dorset Railway was authorised by an Act of Parliament of 21 August 1871 to construct the 42km line north from Evercreech Junction, with work commencing the following year. Despite the number of significant engineering works required, the line opened throughout on 20 July 1874. The new line, however, strained the railway's finances and approaches were made to larger railways to take it over. Following agreement with the Midland Railway and the London & South Western Railway, and formalised by an Act of Parliament of 13 July 1876, the line was leased to the larger railways from 1 November 1875 and retitled the Somerset & Dorset Joint Railway.

This view records the viaduct from the south-west. The viaduct was built in stone and was single track. Each of the arches spans 8.5m, while the 30-chain radius of the structure required the use of strengthening buttresses on the outside of every third pier on the eastern side. The stresses of the structure are complex because the centre point of the viaduct is approached on a descending 1 in 55 gradient from both the north and south ends. Between 1888 and 1894 much of the Somerset & Dorset line was doubled and Charlton Viaduct was widened by 5m in 1892 on the western side. Although the outer facing of the new work was completed in stone, the voussoirs, soffits and pier insides were brick. The ninth and 18th piers are wider than the remaining 25 and, on the western side, have strengthening pilasters.

Charlton Viaduct remained operational until the closure of the Somerset & Dorset line on 7 March 1966. Today, the viaduct still dominates the valley. The trackbed to the north is largely extant and, beyond the crossing of the A37, forms part of the East Mendip Way footpath. South of the viaduct is, however, a different story as the route through Shepton Mallet has been largely obliterated and it is possible to retrace the trackbed only intermittently once it emerges to the south of the town.

EPW011757

Chester Burn Viaduct
June 1930

Situated slightly to the north of Chester-le-Street station in County Durham, Chester Burn Viaduct extends for a length of 230m and crosses the Chester Burn. It is formed of 11 semi-elliptical arches, each of 18m span, with a maximum height of 27m. Constructed in red brick with tapered piers, the structure was designed by Thomas Elliot Harrison (1808–88), who was appointed the North Eastern Railway's first chief engineer in 1854, a post he held until his death. The construction work was supervised by Benjamin Carr Lawton (1815–89) under Harrison's overall control.

Proposals for the construction of a direct line from Gateshead to Durham – the Team Valley line – had first been proposed in 1846 and the York, Newcastle & Berwick Railway had been authorised by an Act of Parliament of 1848 to construct the line. However, following the downfall of George Hudson (1800–71), the 'Railway King', in 1849, work on the project ceased and it was not until late 1861 that the NER sought to renew the powers for the line's construction.

This was granted the following year and the line opened throughout to freight traffic on 2 May 1868 and to passenger services on 1 December 1868.

The Team Valley line was part of a project by the NER to improve the East Coast Main Line. As a result, following the line's opening, the route carried many of the principal express passenger services, with the earlier, less direct, Leamside route becoming less significant.

The viaduct remains in use. Since the photograph was taken (from the south-east), the line has been electrified (with services being introduced in 1990 between York and Newcastle) and the structure slightly modified to include refuges and railings. The structure was Grade II listed in February 1987. To the south of the viaduct, public freight facilities were withdrawn from the goods yard on 4 October 1965 and surviving private siding traffic ceased slightly later.

EPW032776

Conisbrough Viaduct
June 1925

By the end of the 19th century a number of railways were promoted by industrialists concerned about the monopoly position held by some of the major railway companies. One of these was the Hull & Barnsley Railway, which was designed to provide competition to the port of Hull for the coal traffic from the West Riding of Yorkshire. Another was the Dearne Valley Railway; this line was backed by the owners of Carlton Main, Hickleton Main and Houghton Main collieries to provide a link from the Hull & Barnsley line near Hemsworth to the GN/GE Joint line to the north of Doncaster. The line, which was authorised by an Act of Parliament of 6 August 1897, opened to freight traffic on 17 May 1909 and to passenger traffic – Wakefield as far as Edlington only – on 3 June 1912. Although the Dearne Valley initially approached the Hull & Barnsley to operate the line, it was the Lancashire & Yorkshire Railway that was appointed. It was also the L&YR that undertook the extension of the line north from Hemsworth to Crofton.

In order to cross the River Don, the Dearne Valley constructed the spectacular Conisbrough Viaduct. The viaduct includes 21 brick-built spans (each of 16.75m), seven to the east of the river and 14 to the west, and a single iron girder span of 45.75m across the river itself. The viaduct extends for 465.5m, with a maximum height above the ground of 35.5m. It was constructed by the contractors Henry Lovat Ltd using some 15 million bricks, most of which were locally manufactured.

The work, undertaken during 1906 and 1907, involved the use of a Blondin cradle across the river for the movement of men and materials. The line as shown in this view from the south-west was single track initially, although weight of traffic eventually resulted in its being doubled. The L&YR was formally absorbed by the London & North Western Railway on 1 January 1922; the Dearne Valley was also taken over at the same time. Passenger services over the section of line to Edlington were withdrawn on 10 September 1951 and all traffic over the viaduct ceased on 11 July 1966. By this stage the railway had reverted to single track.

The viaduct, albeit unlisted (as indeed remains the case), was not, however, dismantled but remained in a disused condition under the care of British Railways and then BRB Residuary Ltd (the successor to the British Railways Board) until 2001. In that year agreement was reached to transfer ownership to Railway Paths Ltd. Following its conversion in 2010 by Sustrans, the viaduct now forms a connection through to the Trans Pennine Trail. The work undertaken by Sustrans, with the support of the Railway Heritage Trust, included the resurfacing of the trackbed, the waterproofing of the section over the lattice girder and the incorporation of steel fencing within the earlier railings; the latter had been installed at some point after the date of the photograph.

EPW012959

Harecastle Tunnels
21 May 1948

The tunnels at Harecastle, situated on the ex-North Staffordshire Railway from Stoke-on-Trent to Kidsgrove, opened with the line through to Crewe on 9 October 1848. The Act of Parliament permitting the construction of Potteries Railway – one of three that formed the NSR, the others being the Churnet Valley and the Harecastle & Sandbach – was passed on 26 June 1846. It allowed for the construction of the main line from Macclesfield to Colwich via Stoke, along with the branches to Crewe, Newcastle, Norton Bridge and Silverdale. There were three tunnels – North, Middle and South. In all, these three extended over a distance of almost 2km. This view, taken from the south, shows the southern portal of Harecastle South tunnel.

The three tunnels survived until the 1960s. With the electrification of the West Coast Main Line, the three were deemed unsuitable for conversion to 25kV. The easiest of the trio to deal with was the North Tunnel; at 120m in length and at a relatively shallow depth, it was decided that it could be opened out. However, the same was not practical for the other two. As a result, the decision was made to construct a 5km deviation line slightly to the west of the original route, along with a shorter – 200m – tunnel to replace the original tunnels. On 25 February 1966 engineers broke through the last few metres of rock in the new tunnel and full electric services, via the deviation route, through Stoke commenced on 5 December 1966. The track over the original alignment was disconnected and eventually lifted.

Both Middle and South tunnels remain, although the latter is prone to flooding. The north and south portals of Middle (now known as North) and the northern portal of South are now all Grade II listed. All three were constructed in engineering brick in a semi-elliptical arch form with a rusticated surround of hammer-dressed ashlar and framed by wide pilaster buttresses.

EAW016090

Hownes Gill Viaduct
9 May 1949

During the first half of the 19th century, the growing demand for coal and other raw materials to feed Britain's burgeoning economy resulted in the construction of a number of early mineral railways. One of these was the Stanhope & Tyne, built to transport coal and other minerals from the Stanhope area to docks on the River Tyne at South Shields. Authorised by a Deed of Settlement, rather than an Act of Parliament, and using way leaves, the line, which employed Robert Stephenson (1803–59) as consulting engineer, opened from Stanhope to Annfield Plain on 15 May 1834 and on to South Shields on 10 September 1834. The terrain that the railway crossed, particularly on the western section, was hilly and a number of valleys needed to be crossed – including that at Hownes Gill (this is the spelling under which the viaduct has been listed; alternative spellings include Hownsgill and Hown's Gill). In order to avoid the cost of constructing a viaduct, inclined planes were used here and at a number of other locations along the line. The railway was, however, not a success and, following a board meeting held on 29 December 1840, the assets of the northern section of the line were transferred to a new company – the Pontop & South Shields Railway – and the original company was dissolved.

The southern section did not pass to the new railway and was sold to the Derwent Iron Co in 1842; this company had established an ironworks in Consett. Needing raw materials, the company leased the line to the Stockton & Darlington Railway on 1 January 1845. The line was sold to the Wear Valley Railway on 22 July 1847; this company was itself leased by the Stockton & Darlington in September of the same year (and formally absorbed on 23 July 1858).

One of the operating constraints over this section of the former Stanhope & Tyne was the presence of the inclined planes at Hownes Gill. Although the Stockton & Darlington had improved the efficiency of their operation, they were still inadequate for the growing traffic and the railway therefore decided to replace them with a viaduct. The railway commissioned Thomas (later Sir Thomas) Bouch (1822–80), who is better known as the designer of the ill-fated first Tay Bridge, to design the bridge, with Stephenson again acting as consultant. John Anderson won the contract to construct the single-track viaduct, which was completed in 1858. The structure, which comprises 12 arches (each with a 15m span), extended over 210m and, at its maximum, was 46m above ground level. Built using some 3 million white firebricks, manufactured in nearby Crook, along with sandstone dressings and iron railings, the design incorporated buttressed piers and inverted arches under the five central arches in order to spread the weight.

Although passenger services over the viaduct ceased on 23 May 1955, the line over the viaduct (viewed here from the northwest) survived for a further quarter of a century. The steelworks at Consett, the principal source of traffic for the line in its later years, closed in 1980 and the line from Consett to Blackgill coal yard closed on 15 March 1983, with the remainder of the route east of Consett closing in March 1985. Following the removal of the track in 1985, the viaduct, which is now Grade II* listed, passed to the Northern Viaduct Trust. It now forms part of the Sustrans long-distance Sea-to-Sea route, linking the Cumbrian coast to the North Sea.

EAW022989

Lockwood Viaduct

13 July 1937

Authorised by an Act of Parliament of 30 June 1845, the 21km Huddersfield & Sheffield Junction Railway was designed to shorten the distance between Huddersfield and Sheffield by constructing a link from the former to the Manchester, Sheffield & Lincolnshire Railway at Penistone. The line opened throughout on 1 July 1850 and was operated by the MS&LR initially. However, the Huddersfield & Sheffield had been absorbed by the Manchester & Leeds Railway on 27 July 1846 and, from 1 July 1870, services over the line were operated by the Lancashire & Yorkshire Railway as successor to the Manchester & Leeds.

The construction of the line required a number of significant engineering works, including Paddock Viaduct, Thurstonland Tunnel, Cumberworth Tunnel, Denby Dale Viaduct and Penistone Viaduct. The longest viaduct on the line was that at Lockwood, which crosses the valley of the River Holme. It is slightly to the south of Lockwood station, and is seen here viewed from the north-east. The viaduct was designed by John (later Sir John) Hawkshaw (1811–91) and was built in sandstone quarried from the route of the line to the south. The viaduct includes 32 arches of 9.1m span plus two skew arches, one at either end: 21.3m at the north and 12.8m at the south. At the southern end, a plaque records those involved: alongside Hawkshaw, there was John Fraser (1819– 81) as resident engineer, the contractors were Miller, Blackie & Shortridge and the inspector of works was William Bain.

Lockwood station opened with the line. As can be seen in this view, the station had a sizeable goods yard, with, by this date, much of its traffic being to and from the adjacent factories of David Brown. This was – and remains – a major engineering company in Huddersfield. Although famous as a manufacturer of tractors, one of the company's key products was gears.

Although threatened with closure in the *Reshaping* report of March 1963, the Huddersfield-to-Penistone line remains operational, although services are now routed to Sheffield via Penistone and Barnsley rather than direct from Penistone to Sheffield. The line through Lockwood station and over the now Grade II listed viaduct has been singled; this work was undertaken in 1989. While both platforms still remain, only the northbound one is in use. The platform possesses a basic modern shelter alongside a fragmentary remnant of the 19th-century station; this is the covered exit staircase, constructed in sandstone and wood, down to the road level. The main station building (on the southbound platform), the goods shed and the David Brown factory immediately to the north of the goods yard have been demolished. Although David Brown still manufactures gears in the factory north-west of the station with the 'V'-shaped end, all raw materials and finished products now arrive or leave the factory by road. Freight facilities were withdrawn from Lockwood station on 5 August 1968.

EPW054262

Ouse Valley Viaduct, Balcombe
29 April 1949

The London & Brighton Railway was authorised by an Act of Parliament of 15 July 1837 to construct a railway line linking the planned London & Croydon Railway at Selhurst to Brighton, along with branches to Lewes and Shoreham. Part of the line incorporated the route of the Croydon, Merstham & Godstone Iron Railway (an extension of the Surrey Iron Railway), which had opened on 24 July 1805. The London & Brighton's Act required it to acquire the earlier railway, which closed in 1838.

The new railway appointed John Urpeth Rastrick (1780–1856), who had been involved with John Rennie (1794–1874) in drawing up the plans for the line, as consulting engineer for the project. Work started on the construction of the line at Merstham on 4 February 1839. The first section of the railway to open was that from Brighton to Shoreham, on 12 May 1840. The line from Norwood Junction to Haywards Heath opened on 12 July 1841, with the line through to Brighton opening on 21 September 1841. Following acquisition of the Brighton & Chichester and the Brighton, Lewes & Hastings railways and the merger with the London & Croydon, authorised by an Act of Parliament of 27 July 1846 (which had also authorised the purchase of the Brighton, Lewes & Hastings Railway), the railway was renamed the London, Brighton & South Coast Railway.

In constructing the line, Rastrick faced a number of challenges; one of these was the crossing of the valley formed by the River Ouse between Balcombe and Haywards Heath. Here Rastrick oversaw the construction of a 450m, 37-arch viaduct with a maximum height over the valley of 29.25m. The viaduct was constructed largely in red brick; these were manufactured in the Netherlands and shipped across the Channel before being brought up the then navigable River Ouse almost to Haywards Heath. In all, some 11 million bricks were used; the number would have been considerably greater were it

not for Rastrick's design, which incorporated in each of the supporting piers a jack arch with a semicircular soffit. Working alongside Rastrick was the London & Brighton's architect, David Mocatta (1806–82), whose adoption of an Italianate style for the railway was reflected in the eight ornamental stone pavilions constructed at the north and south ends of the viaduct, as well as the stone balustrading that ran the full length of the structure.

This view, taken looking towards the north, shows a southbound service comprised of a four-car EMU. The London-to-Brighton main line was the first in the UK to be converted to electric traction; under the LBSCR, work started before World War I on the conversion of the suburban section of the line to overhead power and, before the Grouping of the railways in 1923, the company had plans to extend this through to Brighton. However, the Southern Railway favoured the third-rail electrification adopted by the London & South Western Railway, with the result that the earlier Brighton overhead scheme, which covered the line as far south as Coulsdon North, was converted to third-rail during 1928 and 1929. Third-rail electrification reached Three Bridges, to the north of the viaduct, in July and Brighton itself on 1 January 1933.

Today, the viaduct, which is now Grade II* listed, remains an essential part of the main line linking Brighton with London. In the late 1990s work was undertaken on its restoration. This was supported by grants from English Heritage and the Railway Heritage Trust and included the importation of matching Caen stone from France to restore the pavilions and balustrade work. The restoration project was completed in 1999.

EAW022733

Phear Park Viaduct
September 1928

One of the late additions to the railway network of south Devon was the extension of the Budleigh Salterton Railway line from Budleigh Salterton (*see* p 77) through to Exmouth. The original line from Sidmouth through to Budleigh Salterton opened on 15 May 1897. From the outset the line was operated by the London & South Western Railway (which formally absorbed the smaller railway in 1912 following an Act of Parliament of 18 August 1911). It was the LSWR that undertook the construction of the 7.25km link from Budleigh Salterton through to a junction with the existing branch line to Exmouth, just north of the station. The line opened on 1 June 1903.

The most significant engineering work on the branch was the brick-built Phear Park Viaduct between Exmouth and Salterton, seen in this view taken from the south-west. This 24-span viaduct – 23 arches and a single girder span over Withycombe Road – was built for double track, although it was only ever occupied by a single track. The line descended from Littleham station to the east on a steep gradient over the curved viaduct. Once open, the line was used by the Exmouth portion of the 'Atlantic Coast Express' and other through services to and from London, as well as local trains.

The line from Budleigh Salterton to Exmouth, along with the rest of the LSWR, passed to the Southern Railway in 1923 and to British Railways (Southern Region) at nationalisation. However, by the 1950s the economics of many routes in predominantly holiday areas were in decline and the ex-LSWR routes in south Devon were no exception. Despite rationalisation in 1960, the line was scheduled for closure in the *Reshaping* report and passenger services over the route were withdrawn on 6 March 1967. With freight traffic being withdrawn from the stations along the route on 27 January 1964, all traffic between Exmouth and Tipton St John's ceased and the track was lifted shortly after closure.

Today little remains to remind locals and tourists that a railway once linked Exmouth and Budleigh Salterton. The trackbed from the junction with the surviving Exmouth branch has been incorporated into the new A376. The viaduct itself has been demolished, with work on its clearance being completed in the mid-1980s. The land where the viaduct once stood has been redeveloped primarily for residential properties. East of the viaduct, however, through Phear Park towards Bradham Lane, the trackbed is now in use as a cycleway and footpath and a road overbridge still exists. The section of trackbed between Littleham station and Bear Lane, on the outskirts of Budleigh Salterton, also survives as a cycleway.

EPW023658

Runcorn (Queen Ethelfreda) Bridge
22 July 1947

Photographed from the south-east, this view across the Manchester Ship Canal in the foreground and the River Mersey beyond shows two masterpieces of Victorian engineering: the railway viaduct carrying the West Coast Main Line towards Liverpool and the transporter bridge.

The transporter bridge, promoted by the Widnes & Runcorn Bridge Co, was the first to be built in Britain. Designed by John Webster (1845–1914), construction commenced in December 1901 and the structure was opened formally by Sir John Brunner, standing in for an indisposed King Edward VII, on 29 May 1905. The two towers were 55m in height and 300m apart. The bridge continued in use until 22 July 1961, when it was replaced by the current road bridge. Although the bridge itself was subsequently demolished, the power house on the north side of the river in Widnes still survives and is now Grade II* listed.

The railway line through the Runcorn Gap was initially promoted by the Grand Junction Railway. This railway had been authorised by an Act of Parliament of 6 May 1833 to build the main line from Birmingham to Warrington to connect to the Liverpool & Manchester via the Warrington & Newton Railway. The line through Runcorn was authorised later – in 1846 – but would be engineered by the London & North Western Railway; the Grand Junction's merger with the London & Birmingham and Liverpool & Manchester railways to form the new railway was authorised by an Act of Parliament of 16 July 1846. The 1846 Act permitting the bridge's construction had allowed for a seven-year period for the work to be completed; however, this was not fulfilled and it was not until 1861 that the LNWR obtained further powers to build the line through

Runcorn. The stone and wrought-iron railway bridge was designed by the LNWR's chief engineer, William Baker (1817–78), with construction commencing in 1863. The main contractor was Brassey & Ogilvie, with the wrought iron – more than 4,000 tons in all (each of the six girders included 700 tons) – being supplied by Cochrane Grove & Co of Middlesbrough. The bridge formally opened to transport on 10 October 1868, although traffic did not actually commence until the following year, with freight trains first operating on 1 February 1869 and passenger services on 1 April of that year.

The bridge was approached by stone viaducts on both sides of the river: effectively 65 arches north of the river (49 known as Ditton Viaduct, plus 16 separated by a short embankment) and 33 from the south. The viaduct itself, which is now Grade II* listed, includes three pairs of wrought-iron spans, each of 93m in length, supported by sandstone abutments with a clearance of 23m above the high-water mark.

Runcorn Bridge – also known as Britannia Bridge or Queen Ethelfreda Viaduct (after a Saxon queen who set up a fortified settlement on the south bank of the river in AD 915) – still forms an essential part of the West Coast Main Line. The major change since this view was taken, just after World War II, is the electrification of the line through to Liverpool Lime Street. Work on the conversion of the Crewe-to-Liverpool line was completed in late 1961 and electric services were introduced on 1 January 1962. The most significant change in the view is the replacement of the transporter bridge with the new road bridge completed in 1961.

EAW008431

St Pinnock Viaduct
27 April 1948

The Cornwall Railway, backed ultimately by the Bristol & Exeter, Great Western and South Devon railways, was designed eventually to provide a link from Falmouth to the existing terminus of the South Devon at Plymouth (*see* p 43). Part of the impetus for the line's promotion was the fear that Southampton (*see* p 47) would supplant Falmouth as one of the key ports for dealing with the packet trade to and from the growing empire, particularly after the opening of the London & Southampton Railway.

Earlier – more ambitious – plans for an independent route to London were jettisoned, particularly after the government announcement on 29 May 1842 that the bulk of the packet trade was to be transferred to Southampton. At a stroke, the proposed railway had lost some 75 per cent of its anticipated revenue and its plans had to be revised as a result. Consequently, discussions were held with the GWR that led to the decision to construct an extension from the South Devon Railway at Plymouth. Following the rejection by Parliament of the railway's proposals in 1845, Isambard Kingdom Brunel (1806–59) was brought in to produce a new design and he employed William Johnson to resurvey the route. With their work completed, a new bill was submitted on 30 November 1845. The Cornwall Railway was authorised by an Act of Parliament of 3 August 1846. The broad gauge and largely single-track line opened from Plymouth to Truro officially on 2 May 1859; the Falmouth branch followed on 24 August 1863. The line was leased to its backers – the Bristol & Exeter, Great Western and South Devon railways – from opening and solely by the GWR after 1 January 1877. The Cornwall Railway maintained its independence until an Act of Parliament of 24 June 1889 formally dissolved it.

In designing the route of the railway, Brunel faced challenges from the topography of the county, with its numerous river valleys that run north to south. As a result, he was forced to design and construct more than 40 viaducts along the route. The potential cost of constructing these structures in masonry was prohibitive, so Brunel proposed building the piers in stone but with timber decking and bracing. While this reduced the cost of construction, the cost of future maintenance was greater. The result was that the timber viaducts were, progressively, from 1875 onwards either replaced by wholly new constructions or their timberwork was replaced by masonry.

One of the viaducts built was that at St Pinnock, near Trago Mills, as seen in this 1948 view from the south as a 'Castle' Class 4-6-0 heads eastbound. This was one of three Class B viaducts built – the others were at Largin and Ponsanooth – where additional bracing to support the timber decking was employed. At 46m, the viaduct at St Pinnock was the tallest on the line. The viaduct is 193m long and is supported by nine piers. St Pinnock viaduct was rebuilt in 1882 under the supervision of Peter John Margary (1820–96), who had been appointed chief engineer of the Cornwall Railway in 1868 and resident engineer of the GWR's Western Division in 1876. The work included the raising of the masonry piers and replacement of the wooden decking with iron decking.

Today the viaduct at St Pinnock remains in use. Listed Grade II in 1985, the only significant change since the 1948 view was taken is that the line over the viaduct reverted to single track on 24 May 1964 in order to reduce the load on the structure.

EAW014990

Sandsend Viaduct
September 1929

An Act of Parliament of 16 July 1866 authorised the Whitby, Redcar & Middlesbrough Union Railway to construct a link from Whitby northwards to connect to the existing Cleveland Railway at Loftus. Problems in raising finance meant that it was not until 3 May 1871 that the contract for the work was signed, with construction finally commencing three weeks later. The initial contractor was John Dickson, but work ceased the following year and Dickson went bankrupt. The North Eastern Railway took over the assets of the moribund railway on 1 July 1875 (confirmed by an Act of Parliament of 19 July 1875) in order to get work restarted. Employing the Edinburgh-based engineer John Waddell (1828–1888), the NER expected work to be completed by the summer of 1881. However, it was not until 3 December 1883 that passenger services commenced. This was partly because Waddell found that the initial work had been poor, but also due to a partial collapse of the incomplete line north of Sandsend into the sea. (Coastal erosion along this stretch of the North Riding coast was a major problem for the line and resulted in Waddell taking the line further inland north of Sandsend, through Sandsend and Kettlewell tunnels, rather than the original cliff-top alignment.)

The line had five viaducts, constructed in tubular steel: at Upgang, Newholm Bank, East Row, Sandsend and Staithes. The shortest of the quintet was the 10-span, part-stone structure at Sandsend, seen in this view taken from the east; this was almost 82m in length, with a maximum height of just over 19m. Sandsend station was immediately to the north of the viaduct.

The line, as with the remainder of the NER, passed to the London & North Eastern Railway in 1923 and to British Railways (North Eastern Region) in 1948. By the 1950s, however, although traffic in the summer months might be substantial, the increasing costs of maintenance, particularly of the steel viaducts, meant that the route's future was brought into question. In September 1957 BR announced plans to close the section of route from Whitby West Cliff through to Loftus in order to save the cost of repairing the viaducts; the line closed completely on 5 May 1958. The track was removed during 1959 and the five viaducts demolished for scrap the following year.

Today, the station at Sandsend, brick built with a slate roof, remains in private ownership as a house. It is still possible to see evidence of the viaduct on either side of the valley and north of Sandsend much of the trackbed has been incorporated into the long-distance Cleveland Way footpath. Coastal erosion of this stretch, however, remains a major issue. Part of the line – from Skinningrove to Boulby, south of Loftus – reopened on 1 April 1974 to serve a potash mine and remains operational.

EPW029145

Severn Railway Bridge
September 1929

Straddling the River Severn from Sharpness in the south-east to Lydney in the north-west, the Severn Railway Bridge was designed primarily as a means of moving coal from the Forest of Dean mines to the docks at Sharpness for onward shipping. Although the bridge was useful as a diversionary route when the later Severn Tunnel was undergoing work, it was too lightly constructed to handle the heaviest trains. The bridge consisted of 21 bowstring girder spans across the river itself. A swing bridge at the southern end, clearly visible in this 1929 view taken from the south-east, crossed the Gloucester & Sharpness Canal. This later structure was the only part of the bridge constructed to accommodate double track. In all, the bridge was 1,269m in length with a clearance of 21m.

Construction of the bridge was authorised by an Act of Parliament of 18 July 1872, which empowered the Severn Bridge Railway to construct the viaduct and to build railways to link with the Great Western Railway at Lydney and to the proposed Midland Railway branch to Sharpness. The bridge was designed by George Baker Keeling (c 1814–1894) and his son, George William Keeling (1839–1913), with George Wells Owen in charge of the engineering, and George Earle as manager. The main contractor was Hamilton's Windsor Ironworks Co Ltd, based in Garston, Liverpool. In all, the bridge consumed 6,800 tons of iron, while the stonework was built of locally quarried limestone. Work started on 3 July 1875. Following problems in driving the piles, particularly on the southern side, it was not until 17 October 1879 that the bridge formally opened. By this date, however, the Severn Bridge Railway's independent existence had effectively ceased; a new holding company – the Severn & Wye & Severn Bridge Railway – was authorised on 21 July 1879. This was controlled by the Severn & Wye and Severn Bridge railways, which formally merged in 1885. The new company, however, struggled financially and, following authorisation by an Act of Parliament of 17 August 1894 (which predated the acquisition to 1 July 1894), the railway and bridge passed to the joint ownership of the GWR and the MR. Ironically, it was the opening of the former's Severn Tunnel in 1886 that had resulted in the deterioration of the Severn & Wye's finances.

Recognising that the bridge was a potentially useful diversionary route, work started in the late 1950s on its strengthening. However, this effort was in vain as, on 25 October 1960, in fog, two barges – the *Arkendale H* and the *Wastdale H* – overshot Sharpness Docks and, carried by the strong tide, collided with one of the bridge columns. This collapsed, resulting in two of the spans dropping into the river. Following survey work undertaken in December 1961, British Railways planned to restore the structure. However, two further incidents – one when a tanker hit Pier 20 and another when a contractor's crane hit the same pier – added to the cost of reconstruction and the decision was taken in 1965 that the bridge should be demolished. Demolition work started in August 1967 but, just as construction had proved more problematic than anticipated, the bridge's removal was also more complex. It was not until 1970 that work was completed. Although all of the ironwork has been removed, evidence of the stonework can still be seen, most notably that which supported the swing bridge over the canal.

EPW029340

Tees Viaduct, Barnard Castle
October 1927

Backed by the Stockton & Darlington Railway, the South Durham & Lancashire Union Railway was an ambitious scheme to connect north-east England with Cumberland. The route was designed primarily for the movement of coke from the Durham coalfield to the ironworks in the north-west and the shipment of purer iron ore to the Durham and Teesside ironworks to supplement the phosphorus-rich iron ore found in the north-east. The route was surveyed by Thomas Bouch (1822–80) and the line was authorised by an Act of Parliament of 13 July 1857. The Act empowered the railway to construct a line from West Auckland to join the Lancaster & Carlisle Railway at Tebay via Barnard Castle. From Barnard Castle the pre-existing Darlington & Barnard Castle Railway (which opened on 8 July 1856) would provide a link through to the Stockton & Darlington line. The first sod was cut by the Duke of Cleveland on 25 August 1857, although the work was primarily undertaken after the letting of contracts in 1859 and 1860. In addition to six contracts for the construction of the line, there were also separate contracts for three of the iron viaducts along the route – at Barnard Castle, Deepdale and Belah. The first of these is pictured from the south shortly after the line had become part of the London & North Eastern Railway in 1923. The line opened throughout for mineral traffic on 4 July 1861, with the formal opening to passenger services on 7 August that year. The line was operated from opening by the Stockton & Darlington. Following an Act of Parliament of 30 June 1862, it was formally absorbed by the larger railway on 1 January 1863. The Stockton & Darlington was itself absorbed by the North Eastern Railway on 13 July 1863.

The route was engineered by Thomas Bouch and he also designed the four wrought-iron viaducts along the line. The longest of the quartet was that at Belah, at 317m in length; the viaduct across the River Tees at Barnard Castle was 223m in length, with a maximum height above ground level of 40m. At this time Bouch was one of the most successful of the Victorian engineers; his career would reach its apogee two decades later with the construction of the first Tay Bridge, work for which he was knighted. However, the collapse of the Tay Bridge in December 1879 ruined his reputation, and he died less than a year later, in October 1880.

Bouch's viaducts on the Stainmore line proved more long-lasting. However, by the mid-20th century, as traditional industries declined, so too did traffic across Stainmore. Passenger traffic on the section from Kirkby Stephen (East) to Tebay ceased on 1 October 1952 (although use by seasonal trains continued until 2 September 1961). Trans-Pennine passenger traffic west of Barnard Castle was concentrated on the later line from Kirkby Stephen (East) to Penrith, until this too ceased (on 22 January 1962). With the transfer of freight traffic to the direct line between Newcastle and Carlisle in July 1960, the section of line between Merrygill Quarry, slightly to the east of Kirkby Stephen, and Barnard Castle closed completely with the withdrawal of passenger services. Following closure, the wrought-iron viaducts were dismantled: Deepdale in 1963, Gaunless in 1964 and Belah in 1965. The last of the quartet to survive was that at Barnard Castle, which was taken down in 1971. Today, all that remains of the viaduct are the stone abutments on either side of the River Tees. The trackbed of the line still extends on both sides of the river; that on the east to the outskirts of a much-expanded Barnard Castle, and that on the west for some distance, up to the point where it has been incorporated into the A66 Bowes bypass.

EPW019870

Truro Viaduct

24 June 1938

Viewed from the south-east, Truro (or Moresk) Viaduct is situated to the east of Truro station on the former Great Western Railway main line towards Plymouth (*see* p 43). The railway from Plymouth to Truro and then on to Falmouth was promoted by the Cornwall Railway, which was financially backed by the Bristol & Exeter, Great Western and South Devon railways. Authorised by an Act of Parliament of 3 August 1846, following earlier failures, and designed by Isambard Kingdom Brunel (1806–59), work on the line's construction was delayed by difficulties raising finance after the collapse in confidence following the 'Railway Mania'. It was not until 1854 that substantial work on the route commenced.

On Brunel's recommendation and in order to save money, the broad gauge line included 42 timber viaducts of varying lengths; these saw masonry piers supporting timber fans and decking. While Brunel was aware that the use of timber would mean greater maintenance costs in the future, the savings during construction were substantial. One of these timber viaducts was constructed at Truro; this used 20 piers and extended a distance of 405m, with a maximum height above ground level of 28m. Following completion of the Royal Albert Bridge over the Tamar at Plymouth, the line from Truro to Plymouth was officially opened by Prince Albert on 2 May 1859, with public services commencing two days later. The Cornwall Railway was worked by the GWR from

1 January 1877 but was not formally absorbed by the larger company until it was dissolved following an Act of Parliament of 24 June 1889.

The Cornwall Railway began the process of converting the timber viaducts to stone in 1875. When built, the Cornwall Railway was single track throughout; this was a severe constraint to traffic and, combined with the need to introduce standard gauge track, the GWR was keen to see the replacement viaducts constructed to accommodate double standard gauge track. This led to a dispute with the Cornwall Railway in 1884, with the latter refusing to fund the widened viaducts on the basis that its operational lease with the GWR stipulated broad. This was not finally resolved until 1889 and the demise of the Cornwall Railway as an independent railway. Following the final demise of the broad gauge in May 1892, the Truro-to-Plymouth line was progressively doubled and work on the replacement of the surviving timber viaducts recommenced. The replacement stone and brick viaduct at Truro opened on 14 February 1904.

Today, the unlisted Truro Viaduct remains operational. Immediately to its south can be seen traces of 14 of the stone piers erected to construct the original Brunel-designed viaduct opened in 1859.

EPW021658

Welwyn Viaduct
28 June 1939

Situated on the ex-Great Northern Railway main line, Welwyn – or Digswell – Viaduct, is located between Welwyn South Tunnel (the entrance of which is visible at the northern end of the viaduct) and Welwyn Garden City station. This 1939 view is taken from the west.

The GNR was authorised on 26 June 1846 to construct a line from London to York via Grantham, Retford and Doncaster, along with a loop from Bawtry to Peterborough via Lincoln and Boston – in all a distance of some 460km. The first sections to open were those from Peterborough to Lincoln (on 17 October 1848) and from Retford to Doncaster (on 4 September 1849). The section from Peterborough south to the GNR's original London terminus – via Digswell – opened for freight traffic on 15 July 1852 and to passenger traffic on 1 August that year.

Now Grade II* listed, the viaduct at Digswell across the Mimram valley was designed by William Cubitt (1785–1861) and his son Joseph (1811–72) and was engineered by Thomas Brassey (1805–70). It was constructed between 1848 and 1850 and cost £69,397. The viaduct is 475m in length and comprises 40 arches of 9m span and, at its greatest, is 30m from trackbed to ground level. It is built from brick; in all some 13 million bricks were used and these were fired from clay quarried locally. Queen Victoria officially opened the viaduct on 6 August 1850 (she knighted William Cubitt the following year). The opening was not, however, straightforward as the queen was afraid of the viaduct's height and refused to cross it by train. A coach transported her from one side of the viaduct to the other at ground level, allowing her to regain the train once it had crossed the viaduct.

Between the viaduct and the southern portal of Welwyn South Tunnel is Welwyn North station; this too was built by Cubitt and constructed in local brick. It was known as Welwyn until 20 September 1926, when it acquired the suffix 'North' in order to differentiate it from the newly opened Welwyn Garden City located to the south. An earlier station – Welwyn Garden City Halt – had opened on 1 September 1920 on the ex-GNR branch to Luton but this closed with the opening of the main line station. Welwyn North had a goods yard but this closed on 26 November 1967 and the site is now used as a station car park. The main station buildings are a rare survival of one of Cubitt's lineside stations and are now Grade II listed.

The viaduct remains an essential part of the infrastructure associated with the East Coast Main Line. Since the photograph was taken in 1939, there has been considerable residential development both north and south of the viaduct. More significant for the railway, the line was electrified. This resulted in the erection of 25kV overhead masts over the viaduct, with services commencing on 8 November 1976. The section from Welwyn Garden City over the viaduct and through Welwyn North and the two tunnels is the only two-track section of the East Coast Main Line south of Stevenage. As such it is a potential pinch point on the network, but quadrupling the line – as has happened elsewhere – is not practical.

EPW062060

West Vale Viaduct
September 1931

The 2.4km branch from North Dean to Stainland ('& Holywell Green' from 15 March 1892) was promoted by the Lancashire & Yorkshire Railway and originally authorised by an Act of Parliament of 5 July 1865. However, delays meant that a further Act, of 16 July 1874, was required before work on its construction commenced. The line, double track throughout, opened to passenger traffic on 1 January 1875 and to freight on 29 September the same year. When the line opened, there was one intermediate station – West Vale – which is pictured in this view taken from the west; a second station – Rochdale Road Halt –followed on 1 March 1907.

The short line had two viaducts, including that straddling the Black Brook valley between Greetland and West Vale. The 13-arch West Vale viaduct was designed by Sturges Meek (1816–88), the L&YR's engineer-in-chief between 1853 and 1885, and was constructed in sandstone. The 13 spans are each of 11.75m and the viaduct stands a maximum of 21.25m above ground level.

As with a number of other short branches constructed in predominantly industrial areas, the Stainland branch suffered financially with the development of improved local public transport. Halifax Corporation electric trams commenced operation of the West Vale route on 2 August 1905. One consequence of this was the introduction of steam railmotor services in 1907, contemporaneously with the opening of Rochdale Road Halt. While the railmotors may have been a temporary solution, the extension of the tram route to Holywell Green (which opened on 31 March 1921) further undermined the viability of the L&YR branch. The introduction of bus services six years later and the worsening economic condition sealed the fate of the passenger service. The London, Midland & Scottish Railway withdrew passenger services from Greetland to Stainland on 23 September 1929. Freight traffic lasted for a further three decades, finally being withdrawn on 14 September 1959.

This view has a particular resonance for the author as the viaduct straddles the Onecliffe Mills complex in West Vale; indeed there were way leaves between the railway company and the mills' owners. The mills had been owned, until shortly prior to the date of the photograph, by the author's grandfather and great-uncle for some 40 years and his father had grown up in the house across the road from West Vale station. Unusually for the West Riding of Yorkshire, Onecliffe Mills handled cotton, including cotton waste, rather than the wool for which the region was better known. Another member of the family acted as a salesman, using West Vale station for his travels until it closed: first class when travelling for the company but third class when it was personal!

West Vale Viaduct remains and is now listed Grade II. It recently underwent a refurbishment under the ownership of Sustrans, who wanted to incorporate it into the national cycle network. However, opposition meant that it did not become part of the national network, although the trackbed north of the viaduct and south as far as the former level crossing adjacent to West Vale station is in use as a footpath and the viaduct was opened for use by cyclists in 2014. West Vale station has been demolished and the area reused for housing. The once extensive Onecliffe Mills complex has also disappeared, with the exception of a two-storey stone-built block that once served as offices. Following final closure of the mills, the site was cleared in the early 1980s and has been redeveloped with newer industrial units.

EPW036863

Wharncliffe Viaduct
April 1931

Wharncliffe Viaduct is named in honour of James Stuart-Wortley-Mackenzie, the first Lord Wharncliffe (1776–1845), who was chairman of the parliamentary committee that oversaw the bill permitting the construction of the Great Western Railway and whose coat of arms adorns the central pier on the south side. The viaduct is situated between Hanwell and Southall. It was listed Grade I on 8 November 1949 and was thus one of the earliest railway structures to be recognised following the legal introduction of the listing procedure two years earlier.

The GWR was authorised by an Act of Parliament of 31 August 1835 and this viaduct was one of the earliest structures that Isambard Kingdom Brunel (1806–59) designed for the new railway. The contract for the viaduct – the first for the entire railway – was let in November 1835, with Thomas Grissell (1801–74) and Samuel Morton Peto (1809–89) appointed contractors. Construction started almost immediately, with the foundation works being undertaken by William Brother and his son Rowland (1812–83). Another engineer employed was Charles Richardson (1814–96), who later played a significant role in the construction of the Severn Tunnel. Work on the viaduct was completed in 1837 at a cost of £40,000 and the first trains to operate over it ran on 3 May 1838.

The viaduct was constructed in engineering brick with sandstone detailing and extended over some 270m, with eight semi-elliptical arches each spanning some 21m. Designed to accommodate two broad gauge tracks, the viaduct crosses the Brent Valley with a maximum height of almost 20m. It is approached by two high embankments; when initially constructed, these caused problems as a result of settlement. The success of the GWR meant that the double track became insufficient. This, combined with the Gauge Act of 1846 that favoured George Stephenson's 4ft 8½in gauge over Brunel's broad gauge, meant that the decision was taken to widen the viaduct to accommodate a single additional line. This work was completed in 1877 to the design of William George Owen (1810–85), chief engineer of the GWR from 1868 until his death, who replicated Brunel's original design by adding additional piers to the north of the existing viaduct and widening the whole structure to 17m. With the final abolition of the broad gauge in 1892 it was possible to instal four standard gauge lines across the viaduct.

The view illustrated in this 1931 photograph, taken from the south, records one of the GWR's numerous 4-6-0 locomotives heading west with a Down service. Today, the viaduct remains in use, an essential part of the main line from Paddington westwards. The only significant change to the viaduct since it was widened in the 1870s has seen the introduction of masts for the electrification of the line out of Paddington. This was initially undertaken during the 1990s as part of the Heathrow Express project to provide a link to the airport. The new line left the GWR main line at Heathrow Airport Junction, just to the west of Hayes & Harlington station, and the first services were introduced to a temporary station at the junction in January 1998, with the full service commencing on 23 June 1998. At the time of writing, work is in progress to extend the electrification of the GWR main line to South Wales and to Bristol.

EPW035002

Woodhead Tunnel
16 May 1952

Aside from work in expanding the London Underground tube network and the construction of the Channel Tunnel, the most significant railway tunnel constructed in Britain during the 20th century was the new Woodhead Tunnel between Sheffield and Manchester. This view, taken from the north-west, records work in progress at the eastern end of the tunnel, with the original Dunford Bridge station to the east of the construction work.

One of a number of trans-Pennine lines, the route through Woodhead was originally promoted by the Sheffield, Ashton-under-Lyne & Manchester Railway, which was authorised by an Act of Parliament of 5 May 1837. The line's original engineer was Charles Blacker Vignoles (1793–1875), with Thomas Brassey (1805–70) as contractor. Work started on construction to the west of Woodhead on 1 October 1838 but Vignoles soon resigned following differences with the board and was replaced as consulting engineer by Joseph Locke (1805–60), who had already had some limited role in the line's planning. The line from Manchester to the western side of the tunnel opened on 8 August 1844 and from the first station at Dunford Bridge to Sheffield on 14 July 1845. The first – single-track – Woodhead Tunnel opened on 23 December 1845. At the time, the completed tunnel, stretching almost 5km, was the longest in the UK. This single bore soon became inadequate and, in 1846, the decision was taken to construct a second bore. This opened on 2 February 1852. By this date, however, the Sheffield, Ashton-under-Lyne & Manchester Railway had merged with three other lines to form the Manchester, Sheffield & Lincolnshire Railway (later the Great Central Railway).

As a result of the heavy coal trains, particularly over the Penistone-to-Wath section via Worsborough, electrification of the route was first considered by the GCR prior to Grouping. However, it was not until 1936 that the London & North Eastern Railway drew up definitive plans for a 1,500V scheme, with a limited amount of work being undertaken prior to the outbreak of World War II. After the war, the project was revived by the newly nationalised British Railways. This time, however, the scheme included the construction of a new twin-bore Woodhead Tunnel as the condition of the original bores precluded electrification. The work entailed the construction of a temporary encampment – clearly visible in this 1952 view – reminiscent of the navvy settlements of 19th-century projects (albeit better equipped).

Completion was delayed slightly due to a collapse during work on the new tunnel, but new electric services commenced operation on 30 May 1954. At the same time, Dunford Bridge station was relocated slightly to serve the new lines, with the original tunnels closed and abandoned.

Although through passenger services over the Woodhead route were not scheduled for closure under the *Reshaping* report of 1963, they were withdrawn on 5 January 1970. The line was used regularly as a diversionary route thereafter, largely to permit the concentration of freight traffic over the route. However, the decline in coal traffic resulted in the decision to close the line between Penistone and Hadfield and all traffic ceased on 17 July 1981.

Today, following the lifting of track in 1986, nothing now remains of either of the two stations at Dunford Bridge, although the trackbed to Dunford Bridge now forms part of the Trans Pennine Trail. In 1963 the National Grid took over the 1852 bore to accommodate the 400kV electricity link. In 2008, despite fierce opposition, the National Grid commenced work in transferring the electricity link from the 1852 tunnel to the modern one. The 1845 bore has suffered a partial collapse and, following completion of the National Grid's work, both of the Victorian tunnels are now fully sealed.

EAW043358

Holbeck (NER) Shed
19 September 1946

This view, taken from the west shortly after the end of World War II, shows to good effect the once extensive locomotive sheds owned by the North Eastern Railway, to the south-west of Leeds Central station. Also visible in the view are the ex-GNR Holbeck High Level and ex-Midland Railway Holbeck Low Level stations (to the right of the roundhouses in this photograph). The more famous ex-MR Holbeck shed was further to the south, alongside the line to Woodlesford, and is not visible in this view.

The first sheds constructed here were the westernmost of the two roundhouses and, probably, the semi-roundhouse to its north. The former was completed by the Leeds & Thirsk Railway, which opened into Leeds on 9 July 1849, and was designed by John Bourne (1811–74) and Thomas Grainger (1794–1852). There is some doubt as to the date of the semi-roundhouse; it appears on a map of 1850 – albeit without track – but some authorities quote it as having been designed by Thomas Prosser (1817–88), the first architect permanently employed by the NER, and completed in 1864. The two buildings are in a markedly different style – although both in red brick – and this would suggest perhaps the later date is more likely. The building is certainly more utilitarian than that completed in 1849. The building between the semi-roundhouse and the canal is a rail-served workshop. This also dates to 1849 and was the work of Bourne and Grainger, and probably acted as the railway's carriage and wagon works. The original roundhouse had 20 roads, with a 42ft 6in (13m) turntable. There was a further element to the original facility provided by the Leeds & Thirsk: a two-road shed located at the south-east corner of the original roundhouse and parallel to the main line. This building was, however, relatively short-lived and had been demolished by 1908.

The Leeds & Thirsk became the Leeds Northern Railway on 3 July 1851. This company itself soon disappeared. Following an Act of Parliament of 31 July 1854, it became a constituent part of the North Eastern Railway. It was under the NER that the final phase of the development of Holbeck shed occurred: the construction of the second – eastern – roundhouse, which opened in 1873. This was the only one of the trio to be fully enclosed, having a slated, multi-pitched roof with a central structure over the turntable itself.

The enlarged Holbeck shed closed in 1904, with the transfer of the NER's locomotives to the newer shed at Neville Hill and the surviving buildings sold for commercial use. However, it was not until the 1970s that the 1873-built roundhouse was demolished, while the surviving roundhouse and semi-roundhouse are now both Grade II listed and survive in commercial use. Another survivor is the rail-connected workshop shown on the 1850 map. All three are built in brick and slated; the complete roundhouse also has rusticated stone detailing around the locomotive entrances on the north and east sides.

EAW002638

Hull (Botanic Gardens)
1 May 1981

By the date of this photograph, which records the depot from the north-west, Botanic Gardens was the last remaining of a number of locomotive sheds and depots that had once served the city of Hull. Situated on the former North Eastern Railway line from Hull to Scarborough via Bridlington and Filey, the original shed at Botanic Gardens opened in 1901 to replace the NER's existing facilities at Paragon station (*see* p 15); these were transferred in order to permit an expansion of the passenger station.

When completed, the Botanic Gardens shed comprised two roundhouses; the facilities included a ramped coaling stage and water tank. The shed survived in a largely unchanged form for more than 50 years. However, following the Modernisation Plan of 1955, the North Eastern Region developed proposals for the introduction of diesel traction over its network. Among the routes that were already operated by DMUs by the start of 1956, or were scheduled to receive DMUs during that year, were the lines from Hull to Brough, Scarborough, Hornsea and Withernsea, while a number of other routes were scheduled to be operated by DMUs during 1957 (Brough to Leeds, to Selby via Goole and to Doncaster, and from Beverley to York). This meant that by the end of 1957 the majority of local services running into Hull Paragon were scheduled to be DMU operated. In order to accommodate the new units that had been,

and were to be, introduced for these services, British Railways decided to modernise a number of the existing sheds. In Hull two sheds were modernised – Botanic Gardens and Dairycoates (the latter situated in a triangle to the west of Paragon station). Modernisation work on the two sheds took place during the late 1950s. At Botanic Gardens, the work included the removal of the turntables and stalls and the conversion of the structure to accommodate five through roads. As part of the work, a new concrete-and-glass roof was constructed. The work was completed in 1959 and the depot officially closed to steam on 13 June of that year.

With the rationalisation of local passenger services – the Hornsea and Withernsea branches both closed on 19 October 1964 and Beverley to York followed on 29 November 1965 – and with the demise of steam, by the end of the 1960s there was an over-provision of depot facilities in the Hull area. As a result, Hull Dairycoates lost its steam allocation on 24 June 1967 and closed completely on 21 June 1970. This left Botanic Gardens to continue to maintain and house its allocation of DMUs; some of the first-generation DMUs that were still in service in 1981 can be seen in this view. Today, Botanic Gardens is still an operational depot.

EAC410772

Leicester (LMS) Shed
27 May 1948

Located to the north of Leicester station on the Midland main line, the shed illustrated here was virtually brand new when recorded by the Aerofilms photographer shortly after nationalisation. Towards the end of World War II, the London, Midland & Scottish Railway started to redevelop the existing locomotive sheds at Leicester and replace them with this single polygonal roundhouse constructed in concrete. The new shed, seen here from the north-east, opened in 1945.

The origins of the locomotive shed at Leicester dated back to the Midland Counties Railway. This was authorised by an Act of Parliament of 21 June 1836 to construct a line from Derby to Rugby via Leicester, along with branches to Nottingham and Pinxton. The Derby-to-Nottingham section opened on 4 June 1839, the section from Trent to Leicester on 5 May 1840 and the section to Rugby on 30 June of the same year. The first locomotive shed at Leicester was a small brick-built roundhouse constructed immediately to the east of the line north of the station. This structure was subsequently modified to allow the widening of the main line. A second roundhouse opened further to the east in 1865 and the final development of the original shed took place in 1893, when a three-road structure was erected immediately to the south of the existing

two roundhouses. These were the buildings demolished as part of the LMS's rebuilding. The new shed housed steam until 13 June 1965 and was then used as a diesel maintenance depot until final demolition in 1970.

In the background can be seen Leicester London Road station. The original Leicester station was opened by the Midland Counties. It acquired the suffix 'Campbell Street' on 1 June 1867 and was known as London Road from 12 June 1892 until after the closure of Leicester Central (*see* p 129) on 5 May 1969. The station illustrated is the result of major rebuilding completed between 1892 and 1894 to the design of Charles Trubshaw (1840–1917), who was the Midland Railway's Northern District architect from 1874 to 1884 when, following the death of John Holloway Sanders (1825–84), he became chief architect. He held this position until he retired in 1905. The platform-level buildings and canopies were all removed during the reconstruction of the station in 1982. However, the impressive street-level building on London Road, constructed in brick with sandstone and terracotta detailing plus original decorative tilework, remains. Now Grade II listed, this building has recently undergone considerable restoration work.

EAW016187

Toton Shed
27 May 1948

Viewed from the north-east, this photograph shows work in progress at Toton shed in reroofing the second-oldest of the three roundhouses.

There had been an earlier shed constructed for the Midland Railway close to Stapleford & Sandiacre station, on the Derbyshire/Nottinghamshire border, prior to the construction of the shed illustrated here. The original shed existed from 1857 to 1870, when it was replaced by the first of the three roundhouses at Toton. This brick-built structure was completed in 1870 and is partially visible in this 1948 view to the north of No 2 shed (the shed which is being reroofed in this photograph). No 2 shed was added three years later and was again constructed in brick. Both these sheds – Nos 1 and 2 – were reroofed shortly after the control of the shed passed to British Railways (London Midland Region) at nationalisation. The third roundhouse, No 3 shed, was immediately to the south of No 2 shed and was completed in 1901. Again built in brick, this is the structure visible in this view with the three gable ends.

The internal straight track adjacent to the eastern wall of Nos 2 and 3 shed was provided to accommodate the Beyer Peacock 2-6-6-2 Garratt locomotives that the London, Midland & Scottish Railway acquired in order to avoid the necessity of double-heading the coal trains between Toton and Brent Junction. Examples of the type can be seen both on the internal line as well as on the adjacent sidings outside (LMS No 7974). The LMS acquired the first three examples in 1927,

with a further 30 following in 1930; numbered 7967 to 7999 by the LMS, these became BR Nos 47967 to 47999 after 1948. Withdrawal of the type began in 1955 and all bar one example had been withdrawn by the end of 1957. The last survivor, No 47994, was taken out of service in April 1958.

Alongside the Beyer Garratt outside the shed, it is possible to identify a number of locomotives within No 2 shed itself. These include a number of LMS Class 8F 2-8-0s; among those identifiable are No 48618 (now bearing its new BR number) and Nos 8182 and 8204 (which still retain their LMS numbers). Also in the shed is evidence of the new order in the guise of a diesel shunter.

Toton shed closed to steam in December 1965 and the original three roundhouses were demolished to permit the construction of a new diesel depot. This depot, home now to a significant part of the DB Schenker fleet of diesel locomotives, remains active as a traction maintenance depot, although the coal traffic, which was core to the development of the shed and its associated marshalling yard, is now much diminished. Part of the Toton site is now identified by the HS2 project as the location of the East Midlands station that is designed to serve Derby and Nottingham and will be accessed via a link road off the main A52 Brian Clough Way between the two cities.

EAW016189

Wimbledon
July 1924

Following its decision to start to electrify some of its suburban services out of London Waterloo in December 1912, in July 1913 the London & South Western Railway purchased land at Wimbledon both for the construction of a new power station to generate the necessary electricity and also for the siting of a new depot to accommodate the rolling stock required for the new services.

The facilities that the LSWR provided on this site are viewed here looking towards the north shortly after the Southern Railway took over. The Durnsford Road power station, which drew water from the adjacent River Wandle for cooling, had 16 boilers (supplied by Babcock & Wilcox) that worked with five Dick Kerr-produced 5,000kV turbo-generators to generate three-phase electricity at 11kV. This was distributed from Durnsford Road via lineside cabling to substations at Barnes, Clapham Junction, Hampton Court Junction, Isleworth, Kingston, Raynes Park, Sunbury, Twickenham and Waterloo, for conversion into the 600V DC required for traction purposes. Visible in the photograph is the 168m viaduct that allowed the coal used in the power station to be stored in the 10,000-ton bunker. In later years the power station was supplied by coal that was worked on a nightly basis from Feltham; for internal work, the power station employed its own departmental Bo-Bo electric locomotive, No 74S, which was built by the LSWR initially for the Waterloo & City line prior to transfer to Durnsford Road in 1915. This locomotive was withdrawn for scrap in July 1965. In order to cope with the increased power requirements as a result of further expansion of the electrified network, the generating capacity at Durnsford Road was increased in 1935.

The initial rolling stock comprised 84 three-car units, which were all allocated to the new depot and repair shed established at Wimbledon. The first electric services

to be operated were those from Waterloo to Wimbledon via East Putney. These commenced on 25 October 1915 and were followed on 30 January 1916 by the services from Clapham Junction to Kingston, Shepperton and Twickenham. The next route to be converted was the Hounslow loop, from Barnes to Twickenham, where services were introduced on 12 March 1916, followed on 18 June 1916 by the Hampton Court branch. The final expansion of the LSWR electrified network occurred on 20 November 1916 when services were introduced to Claygate. Plans for this line to be extended through to Guildford were thwarted by World War I. It was only after the creation of the SR that the electrification of the former LSWR suburban network recommenced, with the conversion of a number of routes, including that from Claygate to Guildford on 12 July 1925. The most significant change to the local railway infrastructure completed between then and the outbreak of World War II was the opening of the Durnsford Road flyover on 17 May 1936. This diverted the Up slow line over the Up and Down main lines.

During World War II the power station was damaged during a raid in October 1940 that resulted in its chimney being rebuilt. After nationalisation, the power station survived for a further two decades, until final closure came in 1965. Thereafter the power required was sourced from the National Grid. Both the power station and the original LSWR depot at Wimbledon have been demolished, with the new facility comprising two large depots parallel to the ex-LSWR main line located to the east and west of Durnsford Road.

EPW010963

Bishopsgate
1 October 1947

The origins of the once extensive goods depot at Bishopsgate – seen here from the west with the ex-North London Railway line from Dalston Junction to Broad Street in the foreground – date back to the arrival of the Eastern Counties Railway.

The railway was authorised by an Act of Parliament of 4 July 1836 to construct a line between London and Great Yarmouth. The 5ft 0in gauge line, engineered by John Braithwaite (1797–1870) and Charles Blacker Vignoles (1793–1875), opened from Mile End to Romford on 20 June 1839, while the line to Bishopsgate – known as Shoreditch until 27 July 1846 – opened on 1 July 1840. The line was converted to standard gauge during 1843 and 1844. The Eastern Counties, which never reached the North Sea, became part of the Great Eastern Railway in 1862. Alongside Bishopsgate, the GER also used Fenchurch Street as a terminus, but lack of capacity resulted in the decision to construct a new terminus – Liverpool Street. Following that station's opening, Bishopsgate effectively closed as a passenger station on 1 November 1875, although some limited use continued until 1879.

Between 1878 and 1880 the original Bishopsgate station was substantially rebuilt to serve as a major goods depot. The new work was designed by the GER's engineer Alfred Andrew Langley (c 1840–1904). It is in this guise, with later modifications, that the Aerofilms photographer recorded the goods station in 1947, shortly before nationalisation. The goods station was on three levels; two were rail served with turntables and hoists, while the upper level was a warehouse. The two rail-served levels both had road access. There was no direct connection between the lower rail level and the main line; all rail traffic to and from the yard gained access via the upper rail level.

On 5 December 1964 Bishopsgate suffered a catastrophic fire, which destroyed the bulk of the upper structure. Following the fire, the remains of the warehouse were demolished, leaving the upper rail levels exposed. Although Bishopsgate closed from the date of the fire, the neighbouring yard (Spitalfields), which was slightly to the east, survived; this closed on 6 November 1967. For almost four decades the site at Bishopsgate lay largely derelict. However, plans for the extension of the East London line and the reopening of the ex-North London line (which had closed on 30 June 1986) towards Dalston Junction saw much of the site cleared during 2003 and 2004, despite considerable opposition.

Today, the extended East London line bisects the northern part of the former goods yard and a bridge across Shoreditch High Street provides a connection through to the route of the North London to Dalston. A new passenger station, Shoreditch High Street, has been constructed on the site of the former goods depot; it opened on 27 April 2010. Although much of the site was cleared, two important historical elements remain. These are the surviving 260m-long section of the original Braithwaite viaduct of 1840 (which was the primary concern of the majority of the objectors to the site's redevelopment), which is Grade II listed, and the forecourt wall with decorative iron gateway, also now Grade II listed.

EAW011380

Carne Point

24 June 1928

One of the most significant freight flows that emanated from Cornwall was china clay, which was quarried from the area to the north and west of St Austell. While much of this traffic was moved by rail to the Potteries and to other users domestically, a considerable quantity was taken by rail to ports for export. One of the most important of the facilities handling the transfer of china clay from rail to ship was – and remains – Carne Point, on the branch from Lostwithiel to Fowey. It is seen in this view taken looking towards the west, upstream along the River Fowey.

The broad gauge line from Lostwithiel to Fowey was authorised as the Lostwithiel & Fowey Railway by an Act of Parliament of 30 June 1862. The line, which was for freight traffic only, opened on 1 June 1869. However, its monopoly on the china-clay traffic to the Fowey estuary was short-lived: the Cornwall Minerals Railway (authorised by an Act of Parliament of 21 July 1873 to take or construct a number of lines serving the china-clay area and to construct new wharfs in Fowey itself) opened its line from Par to Fowey to freight traffic on 1 June 1874. Passenger services were introduced over the line from Par on 20 June 1876. The Lostwithiel & Fowey responded to the new competition by reducing its rates; disastrously so, as the railway's finances deteriorated and the line was forced to close on 1 January 1880.

Following an Act of Parliament of 27 June 1892, the Cornwall Minerals Railway, which had been operated by the Great Western Railway from 1 October 1877, acquired the moribund line from Lostwithiel. After being converted to standard gauge, the line reopened on 16 September 1895. On the same date, a connection opened between Carne Point and Fowey station and, for the first time, a passenger service was introduced between Lostwithiel and Fowey. The Cornwall Minerals Railway was formally absorbed by the GWR following an Act of Parliament of 7 August 1896.

At the date that this photograph was taken, timetabled passenger services were still operating over the original Cornwall Minerals Railway route to St Blazey. These ceased on 8 June 1929, although workmen's services continued until 31 December 1934. Passenger services continued to operate from Lostwithiel to Fowey, albeit suspended for a period during World War I and on three occasions during World War II. They were listed for closure in the *Reshaping* report of 1963, and were withdrawn on 4 January 1965. At this date the entire route, from Lostwithiel to St Blazey, remained open for freight traffic. However, following an agreement between British Rail and English China Clays of 1 July 1968, the line from St Blazey to Carne Point closed on 4 August 1968. This was to permit English China Clays to convert the railway into a road to provide vehicular access to Carne Point (which was more suitable for larger vessels than the tidal harbour at Par).

Carne Point is still a major facility for the export of china clay and remains linked to the railway network via Lostwithiel. It has been significantly upgraded since the view taken in 1928. The former trackbed through to St Blazey has been converted into a road, and the station at Fowey has been demolished. More recently, there have been proposals for the re-extension of the line back towards the town of Fowey and the reintroduction of passenger services.

EPW021671

Halifax North Bridge
21 February 1950

Halifax, like a number of other mill towns in the West Riding, experienced significant population and industrial growth during the mid-19th century and became a target for a number of railway companies. The town had been served by the Lancashire & Yorkshire Railway since the opening of the Manchester & Leeds Railway branch on 1 July 1844. The Great Northern Railway, having exercised running powers to gain access to the town since 1854, sought its own independent route. The result was the creation of the 'Queensbury Triangle' routes to the west of Bradford, which eventually linked Bradford, Halifax and Keighley. One link in this line was the Halifax & Ovenden Junction Railway. Originally authorised by an Act of Parliament of 30 June 1864 and backed financially by both the GNR and the L&YR, work was slow and it was not until 1 August 1870, when the line was vested in its two main backers as a joint railway (the Halifax & Ovenden Joint Committee), that serious progress was made. Following a further delay after a landslip in Halifax, the 4.5km line opened to freight traffic from the L&YR station to Halifax North Bridge on 17 August 1874 and to Holmfield on 1 September 1874. Passenger services over the entire line commenced on 1 December 1879 (when the line from Queensbury opened).

This view, taken from the west shortly after nationalisation, shows the extensive goods yard at North Bridge in the foreground, with the viaduct connecting North Bridge with the ex-L&YR station heading off in the background to the south. To the south-east of the railway line is the small power station built to serve Halifax, with its cooling towers. The power station originally dated to 1894, when it was constructed by the Halifax Corporation Electricity Department. It was upgraded in the 1930s, with the first of the concrete cooling towers erected in 1937. The power station remained active until 1970 and was demolished four years later.

By the date of the photograph, the rise of the bus and the private motor car had started to affect the economics of lines such as those linking Halifax with Bradford and Keighley. Heavily engineered with steep gradients and some significant tunnels and viaducts, the lines also suffered from the fact that a number of stations were some distance from the settlements they purported to serve. Passenger services over the routes were withdrawn on 23 May 1955, although freight services continued for a period until they were slowly withdrawn. The line from North Bridge to Holmfield closed completely on 27 June 1960 (when general freight facilities were also withdrawn from North Bridge). Coal traffic, however, continued to serve North Bridge until the final freight facilities were withdrawn on 1 April 1974.

Today, there is very little to remind people that there was once a railway through this part of Halifax. Although traces of the trackbed can be identified to the west of the site of North Bridge station, the valley itself has been straddled by the A58 road bridge built to divert traffic away from the original North Bridge. The closed railway station has been demolished and replaced by a leisure centre. The goods shed and yard have been replaced by a car park, while the site of the power station has also been redeveloped. Even the viaduct has been demolished; it was removed in the early 1980s, although much of its former route remains derelict. One constant feature of the scene is the circular tank visible at the northern end of the viaduct, which remains almost 70 years on.

EAW028061

Harwich

4 June 1952

Britain's railway companies were among the most significant developers of ports and harbours from the mid-19th century onwards. In the 20th century, among the most significant were the docks constructed by the Great Central Railway at Immingham, while as late as the mid-1930s, the London & North Eastern Railway created an enlarged Parkeston Quay on the Harwich branch to serve its North Sea steamer services. At both Dover and Harwich there were also train ferry terminals, and it is the latter which is viewed here from the north, with the then relatively new train ferry – the *Suffolk Ferry* – at the berth.

Train ferries had operated from Richborough to Calais and Dover and from Southampton to Dieppe during World War I to move military equipment across to the front. With the cessation of hostilities, the Great Eastern Railway acquired the equipment from Richborough in order to establish a link across to Zeebrugge in Belgium. The new service, operated by Great Eastern Train Ferries Ltd, commenced on 24 April 1924. The original operator was acquired by the LNER in 1932. Prior to World War II, the service was operated by three ferries but two of these were lost due to enemy action and the *Suffolk Ferry*, built by John Brown & Co Ltd at Clydebank, entered service in August 1947. The ferry, which was capable of carrying 35 freight wagons, as well as 12 passengers, passed to the British Transport Commission on 1 January 1948. It remained in service until September 1980, by which time the ferry was owned by Sealink UK Ltd, and was scrapped in Belgium the following April. The train ferry service from Harwich survived until it was withdrawn on 29 January 1987, leaving Dover to operate the final train ferry services. These were withdrawn following the opening of the Channel Tunnel in 1994. Also visible in this view is the earlier Continental Pier. This dated to 1866 and was used by GER passenger ships until

the opening of the first Parkeston Quay – named after the then chairman of the railway Charles Henry Parkes (1816–95) – in 1883.

The promotion of the railway to Harwich came courtesy of the Eastern Union Railway, which had originally been authorised by an Act of Parliament of 19 July 1844 to construct a line between Colchester and Ipswich. Three years later, on 22 July 1847, the railway obtained powers to construct the branch to Harwich but financial problems and opposition from the Eastern Counties Railway resulted in construction being delayed. With powers renewed in 1850, construction commenced in 1853 and the line from Manningtree opened throughout on 15 August 1854.

Today the train ferry berth is still extant and is now Grade II listed, but is in a derelict condition. Double track remains on the fixed link to the quay and on the ramp but the connection through to Harwich Town station has largely disappeared. There remains, however, a single track crossing the A120 with, on the southern side, a surviving level crossing gate. To the north, a modern office block now obstructs the trackbed through to the harbour. The passenger station is now reduced to a single platform, although the single-storey brick and slate station building remains. Another survival is the former goods shed; this structure, which lost its freight facilities on 4 October 1965, is now home to the Harwich Mayflower Heritage Centre. One other significant railway structure also survives and is now Grade II listed; this is the former railway hotel – the Great Eastern – which can be seen facing towards the east on the quayside. The four-storey structure, designed by Thomas Allom (1804–72), was constructed in a neo-Italianate style in yellow brick with stone dressing.

EAW043676

Horrocksford
26 July 1938

Situated slightly to the north of Clitheroe in Lancashire is the cement works at Horrocksford. Cement has provided a considerable amount of freight traffic for the railway industry, with coal being moved in and cement being taken out from a significant number of works nationwide. Although the number of cement producers has diminished over the past 40 years, several are still major customers of the railway industry.

The line between Blackburn and Long Preston, as well as the 1.5km branch to serve the existing lime works at Horrocksford, was authorised by an Act of Parliament of 27 July 1846. Work started on its construction when Lord Ribblesdale cut the first sod on 30 December 1846 in Clitheroe. The Blackburn, Clitheroe & North West Junction Railway opened from Blackburn to Chatburn, slightly to the north of Clitheroe, on 22 June 1850; the Horrocksford branch opened on the same day.
By that date, however, the railway had already merged with the Blackburn, Darwen & Bolton Railway – on 9 July 1847 – to form the Bolton, Blackburn, Clitheroe & West Yorkshire Railway. This became the much simpler Blackburn Railway on 24 July 1851. From 1 January 1858 the Blackburn Railway was taken over jointly by the East Lancashire and Lancashire & Yorkshire railways (an acquisition ratified by an Act of Parliament of 12 July 1858). The Lancashire & Yorkshire Railway absorbed the East Lancashire Railway on 13 May 1859. The northern part of the line, in abeyance since the opening to Chatburn in 1850, was again authorised by a new Act of Parliament of 24 July 1871. The line opened from Chatburn to Gisburn on 2 June 1879 and on to Hellifield on 1 June 1880. Regular passenger services over the Blackburn-to-Hellifield section ceased on 10 September 1962, with the exception of one Manchester-to-Glasgow service that used the line until 15 September 1964. Retained for freight traffic, regular services to Clitheroe were reintroduced on 29 May 1994 and a limited service also now operates through to Hellifield on Sundays.

This view of the cement works in 1938, taken from the north-east, shows the connection to the main line at Horrocksford Junction heading to the south. Heading to the west of the works is the connection through to the limestone quarry. Among the facilities at the cement works are slurry blending silos, a kiln house, limestone store and cement silos.

Now owned by Hanson Cement, the Ribblesdale cement works is still operational and has expanded considerably in the 80 years since the photograph was taken. The view to the east and south of the works shows vividly the massive impact of extractive industries on the landscape. For a period, the branch line was mothballed but freight traffic from the cement works restarted on 29 March 2008. The line that once served the limestone quarry has, however, disappeared, with its route now occupied by part of the expanded cement works.
The junction with the Clitheroe-to-Blackburn line is still controlled by the – unlisted – ex-L&YR Horrocksford Junction signal box. This is a standard Saxby & Farmer design supplied to the L&YR in 1873; the eight-lever frame was a replacement provided by the London, Midland & Scottish Railway in 1928.

EPW058438

Long Marston
29 January 1953

Britain's armed forces have long been a major user of the railways for the movement of people and equipment. The two World Wars of the 20th century imposed a considerable strain on the resources of the country. The railway network was an essential facet of Britain's total war effort and the railway's ability to handle the vastly increased military traffic was one factor in enabling the country to emerge victorious. A number of lines – such as the Shropshire & Montgomery – passed into military control, while around the country new military depots, bases and Royal Ordnance factories were established or enlarged. One of the new depots constructed during World War II was that at Long Marston, in Warwickshire, which was served by the Great Western Railway main line from Cheltenham to Stratford. This view, taken from the west, shows the extensive facilities at Long Marston shortly after the depot had undergone an enlargement.

The site of the future depot at Long Marston was acquired by the Ministry of Defence in 1940, shortly after the department itself was established, and became the No 1 Engineering Stores Depot. It was renamed the Central Engineer Park in the late 1960s. The depot's principal purpose was to accommodate and repair the engineering equipment used by the Royal Engineers. As can be seen in this view, an extensive network of railway lines – some 72km at its peak – served the depot, with the main line forming a loop that connected at both ends into exchange sidings that were located on the east side of the Stratford-to-Cheltenham main line just to the south of Long Marston station. To operate the system, the MoD employed a fleet of locomotives, initially steam, then diesel.

Although the ex-GWR main line from Stratford to Cheltenham closed in 1977, the section from Honeybourne to Long Marston was retained for freight traffic to and from the depot. In the 1960s part of the site was leased to a scrap merchant, Bird's Commercial Motors of Stratford, which undertook the scrapping of redundant railway equipment at the site using the line both to bring in the condemned stock and to remove the scrap for reprocessing. Over the years, reflecting the overall decline in the size of Britain's military, traffic to and from the MoD depot declined and the site was finally sold off to the property developer St Modwen in November 2004. Many of the buildings illustrated in this 1953 view, in particular the four large sheds on the southern side, remain and have found new commercial uses. The site is still rail connected and one source of traffic is new cars for distribution. Elsewhere, some of the sidings are used for the secure storage of redundant rolling stock – including ex-London Underground units and some of the trams supplied to both Manchester Metrolink and Midland Metro. The long-term future of the site is, however, likely to be in the form of a residential redevelopment.

EAW048191

Matlock
July 1930

Quarried stone was, and remains, one of the most significant sources of freight traffic and Station/Cawdor Quarry was, until its closure, a major contributor to freight traffic from Matlock. This view from the east shows the northern extremity of the platforms at Matlock station, with its goods yard located to the east of the main line, with the River Derwent running parallel to the railway. There were two adjacent quarries to the north-west of the station – Station and Cawdor – and as extraction of stone proceeded, the two quarries effectively merged into a single working and were operated as such by 1931. The view shows to good effect the extensive sidings, with loaded limestone ready for despatch.

The railway first arrived in Matlock, courtesy of the Manchester, Buxton, Matlock & Midland Junction Railway, in 1849. This ambitious line, which was surveyed by George Stephenson (1781–1848), was authorised by an Act of Parliament of 16 July 1846. The first section – the 18.5km from Ambergate to Rowsley – opened on 4 June 1849 but lack of finance resulted in work ceasing, despite the backing of the then Duke of Devonshire. It was the duke's backing that resulted in Joseph (later Sir Joseph) Paxton (1803–65), who was head gardener at nearby Chatsworth House and was to find fame as designer of the Crystal Palace, designing the station buildings at Matlock. These were completed in 1850 and are still extant, being Grade II listed. It was not until 25 May 1860 that the Midland Railway, which formally absorbed the earlier company on 1 July 1871 (following an Act of Parliament of 20 June 1870), was authorised to construct the line north from Rowsley to Buxton. This opened on 30 May 1863 and resulted in Matlock now being served by express trains once the MR gained access to Manchester.

As part of the MR, the line through Matlock passed to the London, Midland & Scottish Railway in 1923 and to British Railways (London Midland Region) at nationalisation. In the *Reshaping* report of March 1963, the ex-MR main line from Derby to Manchester was listed as a route on which the passenger services were to be modified. This was, in theory, simply the closure of most of the intermediate stations – but not Bakewell and Matlock – with express services being retained. However, in the event, permission to close the route was sought; the section south from Matlock was, however, retained. All traffic – passenger and freight – was withdrawn from the section from Matlock to Peak Forest Junction, near Buxton, on 1 July 1968, with the exception of a short section immediately to the north of Matlock, which was retained for a period to continue handling stone from Cawdor Quarry. The quarry itself closed in the early 1990s, although rail traffic from it had ceased earlier.

Today, the site of the quarry now accommodates a supermarket, which opened in 2007, and the once extensive sidings, goods yard and shed have been replaced by a car park. Running on the south bank of the River Derwent is the new A6 Derwent Way. There is still, however, a railway presence: Matlock station is still served by passenger services to and from Derby, while the line northwards now forms part of the preserved Peak Rail route to Rowsley. Initially, Peak Rail served its own terminus in Matlock – Matlock Riverside – to the north of the original station, but since July 2011 it has been operating into the original station. Matlock Riverside has, however, been retained for occasional use.

EPW033981

Peterborough

23 February 1974

One of the consequences of World War I was the realisation that, despite its empire, Britain was very vulnerable to unrestricted submarine warfare. Although Germany and its allies had eventually been defeated, the success of the German submarines in sinking the merchant vessels supplying Britain with food and raw materials had led to serious concerns in government and, after the war, to the development of a strategy to improve the nation's resilience. This strategy included the establishment of the Forestry Commission in 1919 and the determination to boost the domestic production of sugar through the processing of sugar beet. Historically, most sugar was imported as processed cane from the West Indies, although limited sugar beet production had developed domestically in the decade prior to the war.

After the war, sugar production expanded rapidly (particularly after a government White Paper of 1927), with new processing plants being constructed in many rural areas. To process the beet, coal was required and so the new factories were rail served and brought new traffic to the lines that were served. The production industry was nationalised on 12 June 1936 when the 13 existing companies, with their 18 plants, were merged into the British Sugar Corporation. This view records the factory constructed in Peterborough by the Central Sugar Co Ltd on Oundle Road; this first started to process sugar beet on 4 October 1926. The factory was rail served by both the London, Midland & Scottish Railway – off the Wansford-to-Peterborough East line – and the London & North Eastern Railway – with a connection to the ex-GNR sidings at Old Fletton. In addition, there was an extensive internal network; by the date of this photograph, taken from the north-west, steam had been largely replaced by diesel, although some steam was retained for emergency use, and the sidings were also occupied by locomotives owned by the Peterborough Railway Society (this formed the basis of the preserved Nene Valley Railway). Following the closure of the line from Peterborough East to Wansford, all traffic to the sugar factory was routed via the ex-LNER link.

Following Britain's entry into the EEC and the introduction of the Common Agricultural Policy, sugar beet production in Britain declined and, with it, the number of processing factories. Four factories – Ely, Felsted, Nottingham and Selby – closed in 1981 shortly before the British Sugar Corporation was fully privatised. Further factory closures followed: Spalding in 1989, Brigg and Peterborough in 1991, King's Lynn in 1994, Bardney and Ipswich in 2001, Kidderminster in 2002 and Allscott and York in 2007. Currently there are four sugar beet factories in England – at Bury St Edmunds, Cantley, Newark and Wissington – although none have been rail served for many years.

In 2005, prior to the redevelopment of the site for housing, the Museum of London Archaeology unit undertook an investigation of the now demolished factory, although little of interest was discovered. The site of the factory is now a housing estate. The ex-LMS line past the site now forms the preserved Nene Valley Railway, which is connected to the East Coast Main Line via the link line to Fletton Junction that once carried traffic to and from the sugar factory. This section of line is now also owned by the Nene Valley Railway.

EAC273399

Tewkesbury
September 1928

When the Birmingham & Gloucester Railway, as surveyed by Captain William Scarth Moorsom (1804–63), was proposed initially, it bypassed both Worcester and Tewkesbury. These omissions were carried through to the company's initial authorisation by an Act of Parliament of 22 April 1836. However, local pressure resulted in a further Act, of 15 May 1837, authorising the construction of short branches to Worcester and Tewkesbury. Moorsom's plans were scrutinised by Joseph Locke (1805–60) before construction commenced. He gave the scheme, including the notorious incline at Lickey, his approval and work began. The first section of the main line, from Cheltenham to Bromsgrove, opened on 24 June 1840; the branch to Tewkesbury followed on 21 July 1840. Although the branch service was initially horse operated, the station constructed was substantial and included a roof extending some 50m in length. Beyond the station, the line continued through to serve a quay on the River Avon. The Bristol & Gloucester Railway was leased to the Midland Railway from 1 July 1845 and was formally absorbed by the bigger company on 3 August 1846.

The original station survived until the completion of the Tewkesbury & Malvern Railway. This had been authorised by an Act of Parliament of 25 May 1860 to construct a line north from Tewkesbury via Upton-on-Severn to connect with the Great Western Railway at Great Malvern. In 1862, the railway required further funding, with the Midland Railway becoming a shareholder. The line opened from Great Malvern to Upton on 1 July 1862 and on to Tewkesbury on 16 May 1864. A new station serving Tewkesbury opened; this is visible slightly to the north in this view of the original station site, taken from the west, in 1928. With the opening of the new station, the original station survived and remained the town's goods yard. The new railway

was not, however, a financial success; ongoing problems resulted in the appointment of an Official Receiver in 1866 and, in 1867, the MR (which had been operating the line since it opened) tried to take over the lease. While this was unsuccessful, a decade later, following an Act of Parliament of 11 August 1876, the MR formally acquired the smaller company on 1 January 1877. After the MR's takeover, the once single-track route was converted to double track.

The line passed from the MR to the London, Midland & Scottish Railway at Grouping and to British Railways (London Midland Region) at nationalisation. However, both passenger and freight services over the section between Upton and Great Malvern were withdrawn on 1 December 1952. The short section from the engine shed located immediately to the west of the malthouse (the large building prominent in the foreground) to the quay closed on 1 February 1957. Passenger services from Ashchurch, on the main line, to Upton were withdrawn on 14 August 1961, although freight traffic continued through to Upton until 1 July 1963. The section from Ashchurch to Tewkesbury remained open to serve the goods yard until freight facilities were withdrawn on 2 November 1964.

Today, relatively little remains to indicate that the railway once served Tewkesbury. It is possible to trace the trackbed of the line east from the goods yard through the junction with the Tewkesbury & Malvern Railway route into the outskirts of Ashchurch, as well as the line of the route to Malvern as it skirts around the town's northern edge. All physical traces of the station and the goods shed have, however, been eliminated.

EPW023942

Vane Tempest Colliery
August 1934

Situated on the Durham coast near Seaham, Vane Tempest Colliery was developed by Londonderry Collieries Ltd from the early 1920s. The company decided to open the colliery in January 1923 and work started on the sinking of the first shaft in December the same year. Two shafts – Vane and Tempest – were completed and the colliery opened in 1926; the shafts extended to a depth of almost 650m. The colliery was served by a short 0.75km branch from Hall Dene Junction that ran east from the ex-North Eastern Railway line from Hartlepool to Sunderland. As with the rest of the coal industry, the pit was nationalised, following the Coal Industry Nationalisation Act of 1946, on 1 January 1947. At its peak, in the early 1950s, the pit employed almost 2,000 people above and below ground. On 11 July 1983 working of the colliery was combined with neighbouring Seaham – located to the west – but the last working shift was on 23 October 1992 and the pit closed on 5 June 1993.

This view from the south shows to good effect the pit eight years after its opening. Among the facilities visible is the small engine shed; the colliery employed a number of industrial locomotives during its life. At nationalisation, there were two based at Vane Tempest: the Andrew Barclay-built 0-4-0ST *Castlereagh*, which was new in 1926, and the Robert Stephenson-built 0-6-0ST *Vane Tempest*, new in 1935. Over the 70-year life of the pit, the facilities were extended and the land to the west used for the depositing of spoil. The railway continued to serve the colliery through to its closure.

Today, the site has been cleared and redeveloped. The B1287 road bisects the site and much of the surrounding land to the west, where the spoil heap once stood, has been used for housing. Part of the trackbed of the former branch from Hall Dene Junction has been converted into a footpath but the westernmost section is still readily identifiable as a disused railway line.

EPW045918

Warboys
26 June 1953

Brickworks were once a common feature of the landscape and often provided a valuable source of traffic for the railway industry. The brickworks at Warboys, on the Somersham-to-Ramsey East line, dated to the last decade of the 19th century. The site was acquired by Alfred Fuller in 1891 with the first bricks manufactured two years later. Although the date of the construction of the siding is uncertain, it probably dates to the plant's early years and it was certainly in existence by 1901. Ownership of the brickworks passed to the Warboys Brick Co in 1920 and to Forder & Sons three years later; this company also had a site on the Bedford-to-Bletchley line. The London Brick Co was also involved in the Warboys factory from the late 1920s.

The Ramsey & Somersham Railway was authorised by an Act of Parliament of 2 June 1865, but it was not until 16 September 1889 that the 11km branch, with its one intermediate station at Warboys, opened. It was the second branch to serve Ramsey, following on from the one that opened on 1 August 1863 from Holme on the Great Northern Railway main line. Although there were proposals to connect the two lines in Ramsey, these were never completed. Operated by the Great Eastern Railway from opening, the branch passed to the control of the Great Northern & Great Eastern Joint Railway from 1 January 1897. The branch's terminus, known as Ramsey High Street when originally opened, became Ramsey East on 1 July 1923.

Following the Grouping, both branch lines to Ramsey fell under the control of the London & North Eastern Railway. However, the line to Ramsey East lost its passenger services on 22 September 1930.

Although some traffic to the brickworks at Warboys was taken over by road vehicles during the interwar years, shipment of the finished bricks out by rail continued. The brickworks was hit during a Luftwaffe raid in 1941 and production was suspended between 1942 and 1946.

In this 1953 view, taken from the north, the station buildings and platforms can still be seen, although it was almost 25 years since regular passenger services had called at the station; occasional excursion traffic had run after timetabled services ceased.

The plant was modernised during the mid-1950s, but the use of rail declined. Freight services north of Warboys ceased on 17 September 1956. The Somersham-to-Warboys section closed completely on 13 July 1964. The brickworks, by now owned by the Hanson Trust (as successors to the London Brick Co), closed in August 1983; the relatively small size of the plant had made it uneconomic.

As with many other industrial sites, the brickworks at Warboys also employed a small internal railway. The most significant part of this was the almost 1km of 1ft 11½in gauge line that linked the factory to the clay quarry. Evidence of this line can be seen running north from the factory on the west of the line. This survived until the factory's closure and was lifted in 1985. The salvaged track was acquired by the Lynton & Barnstaple project.

Today, very little remains to indicate that there was either a railway or a brickworks at Warboys. The buildings were demolished in the early 1980s, following the closure of the brickworks. From 1996 the quarry was used as landfill and a reclamation business now occupies part of the site. The cutting that the railway occupied has been largely infilled, although the road overbridge carrying Fenside Road remains. The two Hoffmann kilns, with their distinctive tall chimneys, were both demolished in 1966, having been replaced by a long oil-fired kiln a decade earlier.

EAW050177

Although the Eastern Counties Railway was initially promoted to construct a line from London to Great Yarmouth, on 1 January 1844 it leased the Northern & Eastern Railway's short route from Stratford to Broxbourne and, on 4 June 1844, was authorised by an Act of Parliament to construct a line northwards to Cambridge and Brandon. This route, which linked to the Norfolk Railway's route into Norwich, opened on 29 July 1845.

The 12.5km line from March to Wisbech was backed by the Eastern Counties and authorised by the Wisbech, St Ives & Cambridge Junction Railway Act of 7 August 1846. The line was constructed quickly and opened from March to Wisbech on 3 March 1847 and from March to St Ives on 1 February 1848. The line had been formally absorbed by the Eastern Counties prior to opening and a wooden station served the route in the town. Named 'Wisbeach', this was located on the site of the future Wisbech East goods yard shown in this view from the south in late 1934. A second railway serving the town – the East Anglian Railways' branch from Magdalen Road – opened from the east on 1 March 1848 to a second station (again called 'Wisbeach'), the site of the future Wisbech North, and a connection between the railways was completed. Both of these stations continued in operation until, following the financial collapse of the East Anglian Railways in 1851, the Eastern Counties took over the line's operation in early 1852; thereafter the original Eastern Counties site was used solely for freight traffic. Both the Eastern Counties and East Anglian railways became constituents of the Great Eastern when that company was established on 7 August 1862.

The change of the station name's spelling to Wisbech took place on 4 May 1877 and the station, with its associated goods yard, became Wisbech East on 27 September 1948 in order to distinguish it from the ex-Midland & Great Northern Joint Railway station in the town, which became Wisbech North on the same date.

Passenger services, while not listed for closure in the *Reshaping* report of 1963, were withdrawn between March and Magdalen Road on 9 September 1968, at which point the line between Wisbech Goods Junction and Magdalen Road closed completely. Freight traffic over the line from March to Wisbech East goods yard continued. In the later years the traffic was exclusively from a pet-food factory, but this ceased in the summer of 2000 and the sidings were lifted three years later.

Today, the site of the goods yard is now dominated by the pet-food factory and its associated car park. The site was sold to the manufacturer in 1995 to enable it to expand its production. South of the site, to Weasenham Lane, the trackbed is still identifiable. South of Weasenham Lane, where one level crossing gate stands as a memorial to the railway presence in the town, the track remains, albeit heavily overgrown (and tarmacked over at the various level crossings), through to March. There is strong local pressure for the line to be reopened to passenger services and, with housing development planned for the Wisbech area as part of the local council's '2020 Vision' project, this is looking an increasingly likely possibility.

EPW046289

The name Darlington resonates through much of
Britain's railway history: the Stockton & Darlington
Railway, North Road station, Bank Top station, the
North Eastern Railway's primary locomotive workshops,
the home of Robert Stephenson & Hawthorns and
the Faverdale wagon works were all part of the town's
railway fabric. The presence of the railway also required
the construction of significant quantities of housing
for the staff and administrative offices to provide the
backroom support for the company.

The NER's chief architect, William Bell (1844–1919),
designed the new Stooperdale offices for the railway's
Mechanical Engineer's Department. These were
completed in 1912 and were built in a Baroque Revival
style around a ferro-concrete framing clad in Normanton
brick and terracotta, and with a Welsh slate roof.

The offices (viewed here from the south-east) are still
extant and were listed Grade II in 2001. They are now
occupied by Railway Pensions Management Ltd, which
manages the pension funds for a number of railway-
oriented businesses, including British Transport Police.

EPW019858

Morecambe

20 August 1934

During the interwar years, the London, Midland & Scottish Railway constructed or rebuilt a number of hotels; these included the Queens Hotel in Leeds and the completion of the Gleneagles Hotel adjacent to the famous golf course. Notable among these was the new hotel constructed in Morecambe to replace the existing – but ageing – North Western (or Midland from 1871) Hotel in the town.

Designed by Oliver Hill (1887–1968), the new hotel was constructed on land acquired by the LMS from the local corporation. The curve of the design followed the lines of the new sea walls and promenade, then recently completed. The building opened in July 1933 and so was barely a year old when recorded by the Aerofilms' photographer during the summer of 1934, viewed from the west. The hotel, which was constructed from reinforced concrete with rendered brick in an art deco style, incorporated some 40 bedrooms with a central circular tower that contained the main entrance and staircase, along with a circular café at the northern end. The building also featured murals by Eric Gill (1882–1940) in some of the public rooms.

The hotel had a relatively short peacetime career; following the outbreak of World War II, the building was requisitioned by the military and was used as a hospital for the duration of the hostilities. With peace restored, the hotel – along with other railway hotels – was nationalised on 1 January 1948, being transferred to the British Transport Commission's Hotel Executive on 1 July 1948. Public ownership did not last long, however, as the hotel was sold in 1952. The Grade II* listed hotel, which was unused for a number of years, was subject to a major restoration and refurbishment programme between 2006 and 2008. The design work for the project was undertaken by the design consultants Union North on behalf of the hotel's owners, Urban Splash.

The hotel was constructed across the road from the ex-Midland Railway Morecambe Promenade station. This had opened on 24 March 1907 to replace the existing – and inadequate – station on Northumberland Street. The station was designed by Thomas Wheatley in a neo-Gothic style. Carrying the suffix 'Promenade' from 2 June 1934 until 6 May 1968, the station closed on 7 February 1994 when a new station, sited slightly further inland, opened. Following closure, the platform area, sidings and approach lines were removed to facilitate redevelopment, although the main station building, constructed in stone with a slate roof, remains in commercial use, having been carefully restored during the late 1990s.

EPR000309

Bridgnorth
10 May 1972/17 June 1992

Authorised by an Act of Parliament of 20 August 1853 to construct a 63km line from Hartlebury to Shrewsbury through Bewdley and Bridgnorth, the Severn Valley Railway opened, after some delays during construction, on 1 February 1862. The line was leased from the outset by the West Midland Railway, following an Act of Parliament of 14 June 1860. This company had already been leased to the Great Western Railway – from 30 May 1861 – before being formally absorbed by the larger railway on 1 August 1863 following an Act of Parliament of 13 July 1863. It was the GWR that constructed the 5km link from Bewdley to Kidderminster, which opened on 1 June 1878.

The Severn Valley line from Hartlebury to Shrewsbury, with the exception of the Bewdley-to-Kidderminster section, was one of those lines already under consideration for closure when the *Reshaping* report was published in March 1963. Passenger services were withdrawn on 9 September 1963 between Bewdley and Shrewsbury; the Hartlebury-to-Bewdley section lost its passenger services on 5 January 1970. The same day witnessed the cessation of passenger services between Bewdley and Kidderminster, although this service had not originally been identified for closure in 1963. Through freight services north of Alveley, where there was a colliery that continued to be rail served, ceased on 30 November 1963 and freight facilities were officially withdrawn from Bridgnorth on 2 December 1963.

In 1965, faced with the progressive demolition of the line south towards Bridgnorth, preservationists determined to try to save the southern section. Following purchase of the section between Bridgnorth

and Alveley and the granting of a Light Railway Order, passenger services were reintroduced between Hampton Loade and Bridgnorth on 23 May 1970. The first of these two images (*left*) illustrates the station from the north-west. It shows to good effect the sandstone station building. Now Grade II listed, this structure remains, although the preservation society is, at the time of writing, constructing a new, brick block to its south in order to improve facilities. Also still remaining is the footbridge; the brick base to the signal box is also original, although the upper timber section is reused from another ex-GWR box (Pensnett South). With the end of coal traffic from Alveley Colliery in 1973, the Severn Valley Railway's services were later extended southwards to Bewdley and eventually to Kidderminster.

The second view, taken from the south, records the ongoing development of the railway's facilities at Bridgnorth; the main workshops have been established there and these, combined with the main operational depot for the railway's steam locomotives, now dominate the site of the former goods yard. The success of the Severn Valley, one of the country's leading preserved railways, demonstrates the paradox of preservation: success inevitably leads to the loss, sometimes, of the original atmosphere of the line. With stations such as Arley and Highley, which have maintained their traditional character well, the Severn Valley has been more successful than some other preserved lines in retaining its historical ambience.

EAW229387/EAC614713

Haworth
5 May 1992 (both)

The original Keighley & Worth Valley Railway, backed by the Midland Railway, was authorised by an Act of Parliament of 30 June 1862 to construct a 7.6km branch from Keighley south through the mill town of Haworth, famous now as the home of the Brontë family, to Oxenhope. Work started on the line's construction on 9 February 1864 and the line opened throughout for passenger services on 15 April 1867 and to freight on 1 July 1867. The line was operated from opening by the MR and was leased by the larger company on 11 August 1876, prior to formally absorbing it on 1 July 1881. As such the line passed to the London, Midland & Scottish Railway in 1923 and to British Railways (London Midland Region) at nationalisation. Passenger services ceased over the branch on 1 January 1962, with freight traffic withdrawn on 18 June 1962. The last train to operate over the route in BR ownership was a special from Bradford to Oxenhope and return on 23 June 1962. There the story might have ended – as with so many other lines, closure might have resulted in the track being lifted and the structures gradually being demolished.

In the case of the Keighley & Worth Valley, however, preservation beckoned. At Keighley, the Worth Valley platforms had once been shared with the services over the Queensbury Triangle routes to Bradford and Halifax. It was the fate of these lines, closed to passenger services in 1955 and to freight in a piecemeal fashion thereafter, that inspired a group of locals, including the future MP the late Bob Cryer, to try to save the line for the future. Although narrow gauge preservation had already been established for a decade, standard gauge was relatively recent. The Middleton Railway, a preserved industrial line in Leeds, was the first standard gauge line to be preserved in part, reopening in 1959, but the preservation of ex-BR standard gauge lines was in its formative years. However, the preservationists were successful and, now owned by the new Keighley & Worth Valley, passenger services were restored on 29 June 1968. Two years later, the railway achieved enduring fame as the setting for the classic film *The Railway Children*, directed by Lionel Jefferies and involving a number of the railway's volunteers.

These two views show the railway's station (*left*) and goods shed at Haworth (*inset*) taken from the east. The original stone station at Haworth dates to 1867. Given the original company's backing by the MR, it was probably designed by the MR's chief architect, John Holloway Sanders (1825–84). This structure is now Grade II listed. The sizeable goods shed, not currently listed, and yard demonstrate how much freight traffic a relatively small mill community could generate in an era before the lorry. The yard was used by the preservation society for the storage of locomotives and rolling stock and remains the railway's primary base for operating the line and locomotive maintenance.

EAC608562/EAC608563

Bibliography

Awdry, C 1990 *Encyclopaedia of British Railway Companies.* Sparkford: Patrick Stephens Ltd

Beck, K M 1983 *The West Midland Lines of the GWR.* Shepperton: Ian Allan Ltd

Biddle, G 1973 *Victorian Stations.* Newton Abbot: David & Charles

Biddle, G 2011 *Britain's Historic Railway Buildings: A Gazetteer of Structures and Sites.* Shepperton: Ian Allan Publishing

Binney, M and Pearce, D (eds) 1979 *Railway Architecture.* London: Orbis Publishing Ltd

Brindle, S 2013 *Paddington Station: Its History and Architecture.* Swindon: English Heritage

British Railways Board 1963 *The Reshaping of British Railways.* London: HMSO

Carter, O 1990 *An Illustrated History of British Railway Hotels 1838–1983.* St Michael's, Cumbria: Silver Link Publishing

Christiansen, R 1995 *Regional Rail Centres: North West.* Shepperton: Ian Allan Publishing

Clark, R H 1976 *An Historical Survey of Selected Great Western Stations: Layouts and Illustrations.* Oxford: Oxford Publishing Co

Clark, R H 1979 *An Historical Survey of Selected Great Western Stations: Layouts and Illustrations – Volume 2.* Oxford: Oxford Publishing Co

Clark, R H 1981 *An Historical Survey of Selected Great Western Stations: Layouts and Illustrations – Volume 3.* Oxford: Oxford Publishing Co

Clinker, C R 1978 *Clinker's Register of Closed Passenger Stations and Goods Depots in England, Scotland and Wales 1830–1977.* Bristol: Avon Anglia

Collins, P 1990 *Rail Centres: Wolverhampton.* Shepperton: Ian Allan Ltd

Collins, P 1992 *Britain's Rail Super Centres: Birmingham.* Shepperton: Ian Allan Ltd

Daniels, G and Dench, L A 1973 *Passengers No More,* 2 edn. Shepperton: Ian Allan Ltd

Dow, G 1959 *Great Central Volume 1: The Progenitors 1813–1863.* London: Locomotive Publishing Co

Dow, G 1962 *Great Central Volume 2: The Dominion of Watkin 1864–1899.* London: Locomotive Publishing Co

Dow, G 1965 *Great Central Volume 3: Fay Set the Pace 1900–1922.* London: Ian Allan Ltd

Fawcett, B 2001 *A History of North Eastern Railway Architecture: Volume 1 – The Pioneers.* Manchester: North Eastern Railway Association

Fawcett, B 2003 *A History of North Eastern Railway Architecture: Volume 2 – A Mature Art.* Manchester: North Eastern Railway Association

Fawcett, B 2005 *A History of North Eastern Railway Architecture: Volume 3 – Bell and Beyond.* Manchester: North Eastern Railway Association

Gillham, J C 1988 *The Age of the Electric Train.* Shepperton: Ian Allan Ltd

Griffiths, R and Smith, P 1999 *The Directory of British Engine Sheds and Principal Servicing Points: 1: Southern England, the Midlands, East Anglia and Wales.* Shepperton: OPC

Griffiths, R and Smith, P 2000 *The Directory of British Engine Sheds and Principal Servicing Points: 2: North Midlands, Northern England and Scotland.* Shepperton: OPC

Heath, A 2013 *David Brown Tractors.* Manchester: Crecy Publishing

Hoole, K 1985 *North-Eastern Branch Line Termini.* Oxford: OPC

Hurst, G 1992 *Register of Closed Railways 1948–1991.* Worksop: Milepost Publications

Kay, P 1997 *Signalling Atlas and Signal Box Directory: Great Britain and Ireland.* Teignmouth: Peter Kay

Kellett, John R 1969 *Railways and Victorian Cities.* London: Routledge & Kegan Paul

Lane, B C (ed) 1987 *Branchlines of the L&YR No 5: The Meltham Branch.* Keighley: Lancashire & Yorkshire Railway Society

Larkin, E 1992 *An Illustrated History of British Railways' Workshops: Locomotive, Carriage and Wagon Building and Maintenance, from 1825 to the Present Day.* Oxford: OPC

Lester, C R 2001 *The Stoke to Market Drayton Line and Associated Canals and Mineral Branches.* Usk: The Oakwood Press

Lingard, R 1973 *The Woodstock Branch.* Oxford: Oxford Publishing Co

MacDermot, E T 1927 *History of the Great Western Railway: Volume 1 1833–1863 (Part 1).* London: Great Western Railway

Maggs, C G 1985 *Rail Centres: Exeter.* Shepperton: Ian Allan Ltd

Marshall, J 1969 *The Lancashire & Yorkshire Railway – Volume 1.* Newton Abbot: David & Charles

Marshall, J 1970 *The Lancashire & Yorkshire Railway – Volume 2.* Newton Abbot: David & Charles

Marshall, J 1972 *The Lancashire & Yorkshire Railway – Volume 3.* Newton Abbot: David & Charles

Marshall, J 1978 *A Biographical Dictionary of Railway Engineers.* Newton Abbot: David & Charles

Morriss, R K 1986 *Rail Centres: Shrewsbury.* Shepperton: Ian Allan Ltd

Pevsner, N et al 1951 onwards 'Buildings of England' series. London: Penguin and Yale University Press

Potts, C R 1985 *An Historical Survey of Selected Great Western Stations: Layouts and Illustrations – Volume 4.* Oxford: Oxford Publishing Co

Pryer, G A and Bowring, G J 1980 *An Historical Survey of Selected Southern Stations Track Layouts and Illustrations.* Oxford: OPC

Abstract

Quick, M 2009 *Railway Passenger Stations in Great Britain: A Chronology.* Oxford: Railway & Canal Historical Society

Radford, B 1986 *Rail Centres: Derby.* Shepperton: Ian Allan Ltd

Robinson, P 1986 *Rail Centres: Carlisle.* Shepperton: Ian Allan Ltd

Simmons, Jack 1986 *The Railway in Town and Country 1830-1914.* Newton Abbot: David & Charles

Simpson, B 1978 *The Banbury to Verney Junction Branch.* Oxford: Oxford Publishing Co

Smith, P and Smith, S 2014 *British Rail Departmental Locomotives 1948–1968.* Hersham: Ian Allan Publishing

Thomas, D StJ et al 1960 onwards 'A Regional History of the Railways of Great Britain'. Newton Abbot: David & Charles

Vanns, M A 1998 *Severn Valley Railway: A View from the Past.* Hersham: Ian Allan Publishing

Vanns, M A 2013 *abc Signalboxes (2nd Edition).* Hersham: Ian Allan Publishing Ltd

Waller, P 2013 *Rail Atlas: The Beeching Era.* Hersham: Ian Allan Publishing Ltd

Waller, P 2017 *England's Maritime Heritage from the Air.* Swindon: Historic England

Williams, K and Reynolds, D 1977 *The Kingsbridge Branch.* Oxford: Oxford Publishing Co

Magazines

Backtrack
Railway Magazine
Railway World
Steam Days
Trains Illustrated/Modern Railways
Tramway Review

BR	British Rail(ways)
BTC	British Transport Commission
CLC	Cheshire Lines Committee
DMU	Diesel multiple-unit
EEC	European Economic Community
EMU	Electric multiple-unit
GCR	Great Central Railway
GER	Great Eastern Railway
GNR	Great Northern Railway
GWR	Great Western Railway
HS1	High Speed 1 (Folkestone to London)
HS2	High Speed 2 (London to Birmingham, Manchester and Leeds)
HST	High Speed Train (or InterCity 125)
L&YR	Lancashire & Yorkshire Railway
LBSCR	London, Brighton & South Coast Railway
LCDR	London, Chatham & Dover Railway
LMS	London, Midland & Scottish Railway
LNER	London & North Eastern Railway
LNWR	London & North Western Railway
LPTB	London Passenger Transport Board

LSWR	London & South Western Railway
MoD	Ministry of Defence
MR	Midland Railway
M&GNJR	Midland & Great Northern Joint Railway
MS&LR	Manchester, Sheffield & Lincolnshire Railway
MSJ&AR	Manchester, South Junction & Altrincham Railway
NER	North Eastern Railway
NSR	North Staffordshire Railway
OWWR	Oxford, Worcester & Wolverhampton Railway
RCAHMS	Royal Commission on the Ancient and Historical Monuments of Scotland
RCAHMW	Royal Commission on the Ancient and Historical Monuments of Wales
RTC	Railway Technical Centre
S&MJR	Stratford-upon-Avon & Midland Junction Railway
SECR	South Eastern & Chatham Railway
SER	South Eastern Railway
SLS	Stephenson Locomotive Society
SR	Southern Railway

Location index